T0276403

Praise for *Sexed*

'I loved reading this vital account of the defence of sex-based rights in Britain, contextualized within the rich history of women's political activism. It's good to remind ourselves that women have, for centuries, grappled with the intersections of feminism, socialism and anti-racism and that, rather than being a barrier to progress, they are a driver; and that there is a long history of men failing to support women's equality and liberation.'

Karen Ingala Smith, author of *Defending Women's Spaces*

'This is a brilliant and unmissable history of British feminism. Susanna Rustin traces the common causes and splits from Wollstonecraft to Mumsnet. Her book is vital to understanding why the 2020s have brought a resurgence of grassroots feminism that many would not have predicted.'

Sonia Sodha, the *Observer*

'*Sexed* takes us through the history of British feminism, describing the battles that women have fought and won across the centuries, including less familiar examples, such as Elizabeth Fry's achievement of having women prisoners housed separately from men. For a generation of women fighting to reclaim our rights anew, there is much inspiration to be found in this history.'

Alice Sullivan, Professor of Sociology,
University College London

'Susanna Rustin provides a fascinating overview of feminist history in the UK from Mary Wollstonecraft to contemporary controversies over sex and gender. Throughout, she explores the tensions and challenges faced by successive generations of feminist writers and activists around what Wollstonecraft called "the distinction of sex". Whatever your views about whether biological sex or gender identity should be central to feminist analysis and activism, this book provides important insights into a currently contested issue.'

Dr Mary-Ann Stephenson, Director,
UK Women's Budget Group

'This important book navigates the history of feminism from Mary Wollstonecraft through the suffrage campaigns to anti-colonial socialism, peace movements and resistance to austerity at a time when the movement finds itself in opposition to an illiberal and regressive attack from the US right, Russia, Brazil and parts of eastern Europe on the rights of women, gender-nonconforming people, gays, lesbians, bisexuals and trans people. Admirably, Rustin has written for people who don't agree with her as well as those who do, and her book seeks broad alliances and welcome accommodations where there is currently ideological conflict. In doing so, it points up how feminist voices are often suppressed by the same forces that attack any and all disruptions to the status quo. This detailed, deft and fascinating exploration of writers, organizers, parliamentarians, campaigners and liberators, some famous, others unknown, from Mary Wollstonecraft to Stella Dadzie, Gail Lewis, Amrit Wilson, Hazel Carby and Jo Cox, reveals continuities no less than ruptures between generations of women and across economic and racial divides.'

Angelique Richardson, Professor of English,
University of Exeter

'This comprehensive chronicle of British feminism underscores how the material reality of being female has always played a key role in the history of women's rights and reforms. In an age where violence against women and girls is rampant, violent online pornography proliferates and prostitution is glamorized against a backdrop of rape convictions being at an all-time low, the salience of sex must be recognized.'

Tonia Antoniazzi, Labour MP for Gower

'*Sexed* argues that sex – sexed bodies – and not gender has always been feminism's fault line. Feminism touches the most difficult and, for Susanna Rustin, recalcitrant areas of our lives and times: reproductive technologies, motherhood, childcare, poverty and alliances with other groups. For these reasons and more, thinking about the "meanings of sex", Susanna Rustin reminds us, "is feminist work" that will always need to be done. *Sexed* offers a thoughtful guide to feminism's past and present.'

Sally Alexander, Emerita Professor of Modern History, Goldsmiths, University of London

'I love Rustin's attitude, unafraid to ask all kinds of questions with a calm, enquiring mind. How did we get here? Who says feminism comes in waves? A fascinating, illuminating and essential history of British feminism written in the eye of the hurricane around sex and gender raging right now.'

Samira Ahmed, journalist and broadcaster

'I know that libertines will also exclaim, that woman would be unsexed by acquiring strength of body and mind . . . I am of a very different opinion.'

Mary Wollstonecraft, 1792

'Whatever its philosophical vocabulary, feminism pushes the troubling question of sexual difference into the political domain.'

Sally Alexander, 1984

'This erasure of women's rights and protections is not going to happen in my lifetime, or at least I'm going to do everything I can to ensure it doesn't.'

Raquel Rosario Sánchez, 2023

Sexed

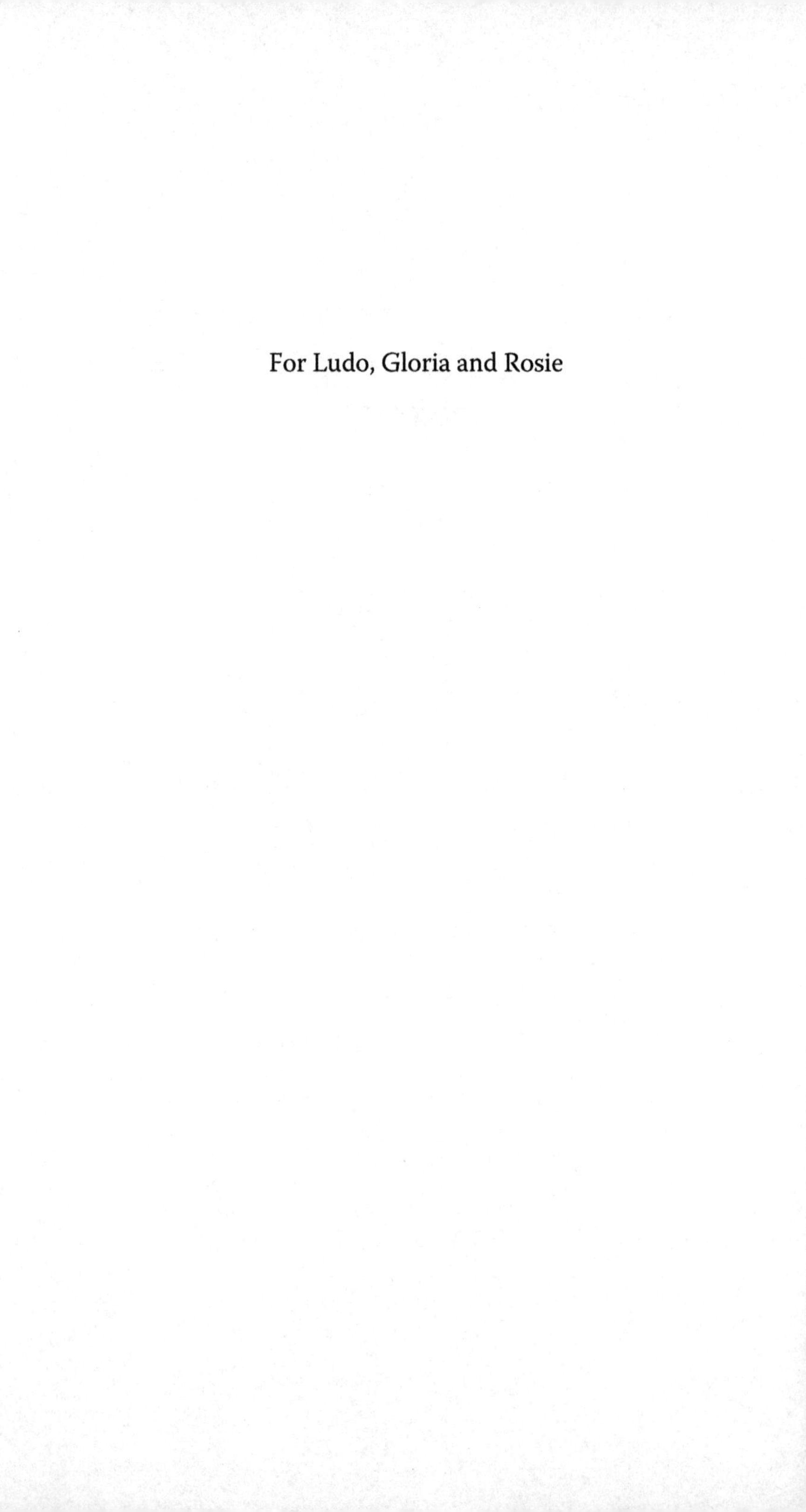

For Ludo, Gloria and Rosie

A History of British Feminism

SUSANNA RUSTIN

polity

First published by Polity Press in 2024.

Polity Press
65 Bridge Street
Cambridge CB2 1UR, UK

Polity Press
111 River Street
Hoboken, NJ 07030, USA

ISBN-13: 978-1-5095-5911-4 – hardback

A catalogue record for this book is available from the British Library.

Library of Congress Control Number: 2023949990

Typeset in 11 on 14pt Warnock Pro
by Cheshire Typesetting Ltd, Cuddington, Cheshire
Printed and bound in Great Britain by CPI Group (UK) Ltd, Croydon

For further information on Polity, visit our website:
politybooks.com

Contents

Illustrations

Acknowledgements

I wrote my first essay on women's rights, aged thirteen, in Princeton, New Jersey, where my family lived for a year. It was about the United States Supreme Court's decision in *Roe v Wade*, asserting the constitutional right to abortion. My mother helped me then, recommending articles and talking with me about them. I was so happy when she and my father said they liked this manuscript. Ludo, my husband, was the person with whom I confronted the realization that progressive gender politics, in its current form, is not for me. I couldn't have written this book without his love and support and that of our daughters, Gloria and Rosie.

It is a privilege to work for the *Guardian*, where I have had many opportunities – including thinking and writing about feminism for more than twenty years. The last few have been hard in some ways. But I have many fantastic colleagues, both on the leader writers' desk, where I work, and off it, and I am grateful to my bosses, Randeep Ramesh, Jan Thompson and Katharine Viner. To the sisterhood of *Guardian* and *Observer* women who, like me, believe that sexual politics is denuded of meaning when sex categories are relegated: I am proud to know you. The same goes for the other writers and campaigners I have met since I started paying attention to attempts to reorient feminism away from women.

This book had a bumpy beginning, and I am greatly indebted to the dynamo who is my agent, Caroline Hardman. Without her belief in the project, I would never have got to the end. I have been extremely fortunate, too, in my editor, Elise Heslinga, who is the right combination of firm and encouraging. The manuscript was hugely improved as a result of suggestions made by the anonymous reviewers who read it. Ellen Pasternack made helpful points about a section on evolutionary biology. Copy-editor Gail Ferguson was thorough and courteous. Thanks also to production editor Rachel Moore, publicist Emma Longstaff, the historians whose research I have drawn on and the librarians at Senate House, the British Library and my local library, Queen's Park in Westminster. About my generous interviewees, every one of whom I learned from, there are more details on p. 267.

I am lucky to know many thoughtful people, including plenty who don't share my views on sex and gender, none of whom has so far disowned me. Many women have paid a far higher price for expressing similar opinions to mine. This book is for them as well. I so appreciate my friends, family and everyone who has helped make me brave enough to write a book which goes against the grain of much recent feminism by emphasizing the biological reality of sex, and what this has meant historically.

Introduction: The Return of Sexual Politics

Over the past decade, a new feminist movement has grown up in Britain. It started in conversations conducted in person and online in Twitter messages, Facebook groups and Mumsnet discussion threads. It gathered strength in meetings as women organized themselves into volunteer-run associations and wrote about their ideas on the internet, in books and in magazines. Over the past five years, it has provided sufficient donations through crowd-funding appeals for more than a dozen court cases, and overturned a consensus shared by all the main political parties. The new movement's annual conference, held in venues from Glasgow to Portsmouth, attracts more than a thousand participants and has been running for longer than the national women's liberation conferences of the 1970s.

This resurgence of grassroots women's activism in Britain is among the most extraordinary political developments of recent years, particularly given what else has been going on at the same time (Brexit, a pandemic, an increasingly chaotic period of government). But while the movement has achieved a great deal, it hasn't received the recognition it deserves from either politicians or civil society organizations that claim to support women's rights. Instead, it has been traduced, attacked, ignored and misunderstood. This reaction is due to the form of feminism that it espouses. This is usually known as gender-critical feminism, or sex-based rights, though some activists prefer to be called radical feminists or, simply, feminists. What they have in common is a belief that biological sex remains relevant in politics and that women have specific needs, linked to their sexed bodies, that must be catered for by policy makers. They are committed to resist efforts to displace sex and sex discrimination with an alternative set of concepts: gender, gender identity, gender equality, and so on.

To an outsider, the difference might seem abstruse. But it is a crucial fault line. For sex-based rights activists, women's needs have a significant basis in the form of female bodies and the risks they are exposed to. For example, girls and women are far more likely than boys and men to be victims of sexual violence, bringing with it the possibility of unwanted pregnancy. With the recent explosion of online abuse and pornography, girls and younger women are particularly exposed to new forms of harmful treatment. Women also have different susceptibilities to various illnesses, including female cancers, and specific requirements from health systems, including birth control, fertility and maternity services. As women get older, they go through menopause as hormone levels drop and fertility ceases. Two-thirds of all people with Alzheimer's in the United Kingdom are female, partly because women typically live longer.[1]

Other needs are less directly associated with biological sex. Women are typically poorer than men, with lower incomes and less wealth, while black, Asian and ethnic-minority women are among the poorest people in society.[2] In 2022, the median hourly wage gap between men and women in the United Kingdom was 9.7 per cent,[3] while the pensions gap is estimated to be 35 per cent.[4] These kinds of inequalities are usually blamed on social norms that load the burden of unpaid care onto women. But they are also linked to women's role as mothers. While a 'motherhood pay penalty' opens up between women who have children and women who do not, no equivalent financial penalty is paid by fathers.[5]

Sex-based rights activists believe that women's lower wealth and status, and their vulnerability to specific kinds of harm, cannot be tackled without taking sex into account. This used to be an uncontroversial point of view, but in recent years it has brought them into fierce disputation with trans rights activists and their supporters, who hold a belief that contradicts theirs. This is the claim that everyone has a gender identity, or inner feeling of being male, female or neither, as well as a biological sex. According to this, either a person's gender identity matches their sexed body, making them cisgender, or it does not, making them trans or non-binary. It is a person's gender identity, and not their sex, that makes them a man or a woman. Various reforms derived from this premise have also been proposed, with the overarching aim of making society more inclusive for trans people. Sex-based rights activists do not necessarily oppose all these measures (for example, the increased provision of gender-neutral spaces) but strongly resist the shift away from language about sex and towards gender. It is perfectly possible to disagree fundamentally with trans activist aims while supporting the right of transgender people to be protected against discrimination.[6]

Arguments between feminists and trans rights activists have a long history. Differences of opinion about whether transgender women, who were formerly known as transsexual women, should be regarded as women formed part of a wider dispute about separatist and sexual politics in the 1970s and later. But whereas previously the expectation was that transsexual people would undergo a medical transition, usually involving hormones and surgery, more recently trans activists have asserted the right to be recognized in their acquired gender, regardless of any medical process and purely on the basis of self-declaration. Many activists in a wider progressive movement that is increasingly focused on personal identity and emancipation are supportive of these changes. To them, sex-based rights advocates are 'terfs' (trans-exclusionary radical feminists), an acronym frequently employed pejoratively.

Legal reforms over the past twenty years granted significant new rights to transgender people. The Gender Recognition Act 2004 enabled them to alter their birth certificates to reflect their acquired gender, while the Equality Act 2010 made gender reassignment a protected characteristic along with sex, race, age, disability, sexual orientation, religion or belief, pregnancy or maternity, and marriage. But over subsequent years activists argued that these measures were insufficient. They sought to change the Gender Recognition Act, making it easier for birth certificates to be altered by removing the requirement for medical evidence. This is the reform known as self-identification, which became one of the most bitterly contested issues in politics across the United Kingdom. Linked to it was the aim of making gender self-declaration a new social norm – so that individuals could decide whether they belonged in women's or men's sports and single-sex facilities, and would tell each other whether they wished to be addressed by male, female or neutral (they) pronouns when meeting each other.

British gender-critical feminists are not the only people to oppose these changes and the philosophy underlying them. Feminists in India, Ireland, Norway, Spain, the United States and many other countries have also mobilized in defence of sex-based rights and against the principle of self-ID.[7] Conservative authoritarian leaders and activists and far-right movements also oppose trans rights, albeit for different reasons. While lesbians are an important presence in the British gender-critical movement – because they are same-sex attracted and reject the idea of biologically male lesbians – on the American right, in Russia and in parts of Eastern Europe, attacks on trans rights form part of a wider, illiberal attack on the rights of women, gays, lesbians, bisexuals and others who reject sexist stereotypes.

Since Boris Johnson's government abandoned plans to introduce self-ID in 2020, British gender-critical feminists have found themselves in often uneasy agreement with his party on this issue. Under Rishi Sunak, the Conservatives turned opposition to self-ID, and support for women's single-sex spaces, into a prominent theme. This led some left-wing voices to warn that opposition to trans rights could be the thin end of a wider wedge of intolerance and bigotry. But polling data does not back them up. While support for self-ID has fallen in Britain, and only a small minority support the inclusion of transgender women in women's sports, in general British people's attitudes are more liberal than ever.[8] Labour, too, has decided against introducing self-ID, though it plans to make the legal gender recognition process easier.

The issue is international, but Britain is an outlier. Gender-critical feminism is stronger there than anywhere else. This has been commented on by opponents as well as supporters, with articles about 'terf island' appearing in the American, Australian and Irish press.[9] To understand why the pushback against gender advocacy has been so pronounced among British feminists is the purpose of this book.

It starts in 1792, with the revolutionary writer Mary Wollstonecraft, and ends with the sex-based rights movement of today. Each chapter describes a phase of what we now call feminism, but in the nineteenth century was called something else – women's rights, social reform, suffragism, a 'great crusade'. By examining how previous generations of women's rights activists thought about the place of sex in politics, the book seeks to establish connections between feminism as it is now and as it was then.

Writing and talking about sex-based rights in public has been extremely difficult in recent years. At one of the first gatherings organized by opponents of the proposed self-ID law, in

2017, a woman was physically assaulted.[10] Meetings organized by groups including Woman's Place UK, and events featuring gender-critical speakers, have repeatedly been the target of threatening attacks including smoke bombs, abusive chanting, and banging on windows aimed at drowning out speakers. Venues have refused bookings and cancelled at short notice. Most of the court cases referred to above relate to women who have been driven out of workplaces due to their gender-critical beliefs. While many of these are still in progress at the time of writing, discrimination claims have been upheld against Arts Council England and Garden Court Chambers.[11]

Since June 2021, the philosophical belief that 'biological sex is real, important, immutable and not to be conflated with gender identity' has been legally protected in the United Kingdom. This was the result of the landmark case brought by Maya Forstater, who lost her employment with a US-based non-governmental organization, the Center for Global Development, in 2019, and took it to court.[12] Forstater's victory meant that discrimination against holders of gender-critical views became illegal. But this doesn't mean that efforts to silence them have ended. In 2023, the movement's annual conference, organized by the charity FiLiA, narrowly avoided being cancelled at the last minute following complaints to the venue by trans rights activists, who proceeded to picket it, shouting insults at attendees. This book has been written in defiance of illiberal efforts to suppress sex-based rights feminism and to delegitimize it in favour of an alternative discourse of gender identity and gender – a highly contentious position that has been uncritically adopted by many human rights and feminist organizations as well as groups that advocate solely for trans rights.

Feminist history

There is no shortage of recent books about feminism. In the libraries I have visited, there are shelves and shelves of them. But most authors do not specifically address the movement in Britain. And though there is plenty of historical research, outside the academy general knowledge of feminism's past is lacking. The suffragettes and their direct-action methods remain a subject of fascination. However, white women in long dresses can be seen as problematic emblems at a time when progressive politics is strongly focused on intersectionality and decolonization.

Another factor is the way that feminism is viewed as a transatlantic phenomenon. The blurb on my paperback edition of Betty Friedan's famous polemic, *The Feminine Mystique* (1963), sums it up. 'Feminism began with the work of a single person: Friedan,' it declares. But this is untrue. *The Feminine Mystique* is a book about American women, and feminism long predates it. Researchers in England also studied women's lives in the post-war years, and Hannah Gavron wrote a book about them. Among her findings in *The Captive Wife* (1966) was that working-class fathers played a more active role in their children's lives than their middle-class counterparts.

Gavron did not have Betty Friedan's polemical pizzazz – and tragically took her own life before her book was published.[13] But it provides a crucial link between the women's liberation movement and an earlier generation of British feminists – one that is lost in accounts of second-wave feminism that start on the US east coast.[14] More recently, the American author Susan Faludi was credited with dragging feminism out of the doldrums. Published in 1992, her dissection of the rollback of feminist gains in *Backlash* is a deserved classic.[15] But when I reread it, I noted that the original subtitle, *The Undeclared War Against American Women*, had been altered for international editions. Had the backlash Faludi described actually happened in Britain? Or was there a cultural cringe in the tendency of British feminists to discard their own history in favour of America's?

Long-standing generational tensions within feminism have added to this historical amnesia. This pattern began when Mary Wollstonecraft was disowned by Victorian campaigners. Much more recently, the novelist Doris Lessing described the tendency of radical activists of all kinds to turn on past achievements: 'Many are the New Dawns that I have seen, and all of them are engineered by young people who have to hate their elders . . . Surely it doesn't have to be like this? For it is a wicked waste, this cycle, the new energies leaping up, demolishing what went before.'[16] Intergenerational disapproval does not flow only in one direction; older feminists have also been critical of younger ones. Such dynamics are as inevitable in social movements as they are in life. But as Victoria Smith and others have argued, they carry a particular charge between what are often called the 'waves' of feminism.[17]

This metaphor originated with the suffragists and was popularized in the 1970s, when activists seized on the description of themselves as a second wave. In the 1990s, American feminists launched what they called a third wave. It is not hard to see why the image caught on. Waves are dynamic and powerful, and oceans bring with them a rich language of crests, currents and so on. But no other social movement is conceptualized in this way and the image has also been called into question. One reason is the way it elides specific moments in particular countries' histories with what is at other times understood to be a global phenomenon.[18] Another is the emphasis it places on novelty at the expense of continuity, with many people sceptical about claims made in recent decades on behalf of a third, fourth or even a fifth wave of feminism. Generational differences like those that exercised Lessing are one aspect of the current schism between feminists, with younger activists more amenable to switching from sex- to gender-based politics. In looking for connections between a range of past campaigns, this book aims to provide a longer, more joined-up view.

Sex and gender

Since the meaning of sex and gender is contested, it is important to be clear about both terms. In UK law (The Equality Act 2010), sex is defined as a reference to 'a man or a woman', a man as 'a male of any age' and a woman as 'a female of any age'. For a small minority of people, differences of sex development make categorization more complicated.[19] But for the vast majority of people sex is straightforward, and refers to whether they are male or female. Sex was the word used throughout the nineteenth and most of the twentieth centuries to refer to the physical differences between men and women. These were widely held to exert more sway over women's lives than men's, which is why women were sometimes described as 'the sex', and the influence of their reproductive system was exaggerated (often wildly).

In the title of her most famous book, the French philosopher Simone de Beauvoir designated women and girls 'the second sex', as a way of describing the way that male thinkers and writers had cast themselves as the first one (as when God created Adam). The word 'unsex' was also used to describe what could happen when a woman gave up her traditional sex role or took on attributes traditionally seen as male. Mary Wollstonecraft was one of the first to elucidate the chauvinist threat made against women that they 'would be unsexed by acquiring strength of body and mind'.[20] She insisted that such strength was every woman's birthright. That she felt it necessary to make this argument illustrates how understandings of sex have for centuries extended beyond anatomy and physiology to incorporate psychology, intellect and behaviour.

The term 'gender' is harder to pin down. The *Oxford English Dictionary* records its first usage to signify male or female in 1474.[21] Almost four centuries later, a bill introduced to Parliament by a women's suffrage supporter proposed that election law should be altered so that 'words importing the masculine gender shall be deemed to include women' – thus enabling them to vote.[22] But the word was not used widely until the middle of the twentieth century, when the psychiatrist Robert Stoller and the psychologist John Money both applied it to people who experienced a mismatch between their sex and what Stoller and Money began to call their 'gender identity' or 'gender role'. Both men ran clinics attached to American universities and were pioneers in the field of transgender medicine.

Some other psychologists also used the word 'gender' around this time, and it soon began to be used more widely to express a distinction between nature (physical sex differences) and culture (social roles). This was the usage many feminist academics adopted, and of which the English sociologist Ann Oakley was among the pioneers. Her book *Sex, Gender and Society* (1972) included a discussion of Stoller and Money, and fieldwork on sex roles carried out by anthropologists.

These contrasting usages brought complications which were amplified by the work of the US philosopher Judith Butler and her followers, which proposed that gender should replace sex in liberatory politics. Amia Srinivasan, occupier of a prestigious chair in philosophy at Oxford, opened her bestseller *The Right to Sex* (2021) with a tribute to Butler, and the assertion that sex 'is itself already gender in disguise'.[23] Some natural scientists also questioned the usefulness of sex categorization. Anne Fausto-Sterling, a professor of biology and gender studies, once proposed that there are five sexes, not two, although she later said this had been 'tongue in cheek', and that her argument had been aimed at 'disrupting the silence around intersex' and improving the way that people with differences in sex development were treated.[24]

Examining how and why the term 'gender' came to replace 'sex' in so much feminist writing is one of the things I do in the second half of this book. To avoid anachronism, I will not use it much in writing about the nineteenth or early twentieth centuries. Although it is in my title, I will use the word 'feminism' sparingly in the early chapters for the same reason.

Two more notes on language. First, I have called this book a history of *British* feminism, but, as with most accounts of Britain, this one is dominated by England. It is not a history of English feminism, because Scottish, Welsh and Irish women – as well as women who moved to Britain from other countries – are in it. While I recognize differences in the feminist political traditions of the four nations of the United Kingdom, these are not described in detail.

The second point is about names. Mary Wollstonecraft is unusual among the women in this book in always being known by the same one. By contrast, Marian Evans was called during her lifetime and afterwards by several: Marian Evans, Mary Ann Evans, Marian Lewes, George Eliot, Mary Ann Cross. In between these two extremes lie many women who changed their names when they married – which is one reason why biographers often use first names. Some women, such as Barbara Leigh Smith Bodichon, are remembered to posterity by appellations that join maiden and married names together. In a book with lots of people in it, I have tried to keep things simple.

What follows is not a comprehensive account of everything that happened to British women in the past 230 years, or everything achieved by feminists in Britain. Many of the nineteenth-century campaigners I have written about were members of a wealthy, white elite. Not until the labour movement was established were working-class women able to assert themselves in political life, and black and Asian women become prominent only in the latter part of the twentieth century. The first black woman Member of Parliament (MP), Diane Abbott, was elected in 1987 – almost seventy years after Constance Markievicz became the first women elected to Parliament, as a Sinn Fein MP for Dublin.

I want this book to be useful. Around the world, the rights and freedoms of many – men as well as women – are under threat. But the situation facing women and girls is particularly bleak, with the United Nations warning that progress towards equality has gone into reverse.[25] Rising misogyny, including sexual violence, is part of the zeitgeist, and anti-feminism includes many men acting in what they believe to be rational self-interest. In 2020, a survey by the British charity Hope not Hate found that 50 per cent of boys and men aged 16–24 believed that feminism 'has gone too far and made it harder for men to succeed'.[26]

My view that sex-based rights are fundamental to feminism will be evident in what follows, but I will distinguish fact from opinion. I hope the stories and people in this book will interest those who do not agree with me as well as those who do. While some are already well known, others are less so. Ideas about sex and sexual politics are an important theme but not the only one.

While this is a book about divisions, particularly in attitudes to sex (and later gender), these should not be overstated. In the past, as now, feminists agreed as well as disagreed. Even in today's fractured landscape, most are united when it comes to issues such as health care, dismay at the prevalence of rape, and determination to reduce economic unfairness. I have been, and remain, disoriented by the turn that sexual politics has taken over the past decade. I am fearful about rising misogyny. At the same time, I think something remarkable is taking place with the renewal of grassroots women's organizing in Britain. It is my intention to explain how and why this happened, and what it means for women and girls today.

1

Rebels (1790s–1840s)

The organized women's movement started in the middle of the nineteenth century. But the women who ran it were not the first to notice or speak out about women's oppression. Uncovering the achievements of pioneers such as Mary Astell and Lady Mary Wortley Montagu – who wrote about the condition of women in the late seventeenth and early eighteenth centuries – has been an important feminist project. My starting point is 1792, when Mary Wollstonecraft – then a single, jobbing author of thirty-two – published *A Vindication of the Rights of Woman* and offered, in its opening paragraph, an insight that would become foundational for the women's movement. Women, she explained, had been hobbled by the 'specious homage' paid to them by men. While the elaborate courtesy shown them might look like respect, in fact this was a mask for something else. The truth was that men regarded females rather as women than as human.[1] Wives, daughters, mothers, sisters: none could escape the prism of sex.

Wollstonecraft, who lived from 1759 until 1797, was one of history's remarkable characters. Her father was the wayward son of an East London textile manufacturer, while her Irish

1 Portrait of Mary Wollstonecraft by John Opie

mother favoured her firstborn son over her daughters. The family did not prosper, despite an inheritance, and moved to Yorkshire where they failed at farming. Mary formed strong attachments and dreamed of building a life with her friend Fanny Blood, while struggling to get on with her sisters. Her father was sometimes violent, her education sporadic, and family life weighed down with losses, including the death of a brother, her mother and a baby niece. But in the 1780s, while in charge of a small school in Newington Green, then a village to the north of London, she found her way into a circle of radical intellectuals, most of whom belonged to the liberal, nonconformist denomination known as Rational Dissent (or Unitarians). She wrote a book on girls' education and endured a miserable spell as a governess before securing regular employment via the publisher, Joseph Johnson, who became her loyal patron. In France during the most tumultuous phase of the French Revolution, she produced the first English rebuttal of Edmund Burke's attack on it and, in 1791, over just six weeks, turned her observations on the oppression of women into a book. *A Vindication of the Rights of Woman* has been the mainstay of her reputation, and a pillar of woman-centred political philosophy, ever since.

In order to claim their natural rights as rational creatures, Wollstonecraft argued, women must first 'obtain a character as a human being, regardless of the distinction of sex'. To do this entailed confronting and disproving the false notion that women would be 'unsexed by acquiring strength of body and mind'[2]. Wollstonecraft wrote her furious thesis under extreme provocation. Her targets included Jean-Jacques Rousseau, the Swiss philosopher, whose limited prescription for girls' education she resented all the more because she regarded him as a mentor. Unless such prejudices could be overthrown, she feared, the world being ushered in by an age of revolution would be no better than the old one. For Wollstonecraft, who unlike her friends was not a Unitarian but adapted her Anglican faith to her personal philosophy, there was more at stake than political rights and personal freedom. Along with other Enlightenment radicals, she believed that the immortal soul was bound up with the power of reason. If women were not accepted as rational beings, equal to men, they were 'born only to procreate and rot'. Being sexed female, in a world ruled by men, meant being starved of the moral and intellectual capacity that was the 'emanation of divinity'.[3]

The dilemma facing Wollstonecraft, and echoed in the struggles of generations of women's rights advocates since, was whether to minimize what she called 'the distinction of sex' or to try to change what it entailed. In *A Vindication*, she negotiated a path between these alternatives, categorically rejecting the idea that intellectual or moral faculties were determined by sex, while accepting the division of labour and moral responsibility associated with women's role as mothers. Women, she argued, were trapped by their awareness of sexual difference, which negated their sense of themselves as human beings. 'The desire of being always women, is the very consciousness that degrades the sex,' she wrote. Education and independence offered the surest escape. 'Men are not always men in the company of women, nor would women always remember that they are women, if they were allowed to acquire more understanding.' She praised the Whig historian Catharine Macaulay on grounds that 'in her style of writing, no sex appears, for it is like the sense it conveys, strong and clear.'[4]

Repeatedly in *A Vindication*, Wollstonecraft links the 'illegitimate power' of sex with the gaudy trappings of hereditary privilege. In the less hierarchical future of which she dreamed, elaborate social distinctions between men and women would go the same way as unjust divisions of rank. Women would first have to be brought down from their gilded perches before being freed to attain their rightful place as equal citizens. At times she reached beyond her aim of persuading women to 'become more masculine', and imagined doing away with sex altogether. 'A wild wish has just flown from my heart to my head, and I will not stifle it, though it may excite a horse-laugh. I do earnestly wish to see the distinction of sex confounded in society,'[5] she wrote, explaining as she did so that she expressed this wish in defiance of mockery. In another passage she indicated – with an anxiety made apparent in frequent commas and hesitations, which give an impression of breathlessness – that she already had the case for women's enfranchisement in her sights: 'I may excite laughter, by dropping a hint, which I mean to pursue, some future time, for I really think that women ought to have representatives, instead of being arbitrarily governed.'[6]

Wollstonecraft was a romantic as well as a reasoner, who referred to her 'melancholy emotions of sorrowful indignation' in her book's opening sentence. She never wrote a promised sequel to *A Vindication*, which intended to discuss the law as it applied to women. But her posthumous, unfinished novel *Maria* (1798), to which she gave the subtitle *The Wrongs of Woman*, can be regarded as partially fulfilling this ambition. Through the dramatic histories of Maria and Jemima, the novel explores the extreme vulnerability of women of different classes to the grossest exploitation. It also articulates more clearly than any of Wollstonecraft's other books her belief in the force of maternal love, and rejection of the doctrine of wifely obedience, which entails the suppression of natural affection. 'Truth is the only basis of virtue; and we cannot, without depraving our minds, endeavour to please a lover or husband, but in proportion as he pleases us,' Maria explains.[7] Her integrity is her justification for leaving her vicious husband, even if the law refuses to recognize it.

Since it was unfinished, it is not known how Wollstonecraft would have concluded her novel. The happiest ending suggested in the surviving fragments is the establishment of an all-female household containing Maria, her rescued daughter, and Jemima as housekeeper-friend. The novel does not answer all the questions it raises about sexual politics and morality. But its endorsement of women's rebellion against oppression is clear, with spousal violence at one point compared to the abuse by West Indian masters of their slaves.[8] In the late twentieth century, Wollstonecraft faced criticism from some scholars for not having taken this analogy further. Intersectional feminists pointed to the limitations of a liberatory politics focused on sex, to the exclusion of the class and racial hierarchies that also structured Wollstonecraft's world.

More recently, Barbara Taylor has argued that the alliance between Maria and Jemima – traumatized women of different classes – makes *Maria* Wollstonecraft's most radical, sisterly work. But it is true that her visions of revolution – like those of her contemporaries – did not entail the total overthrow of the existing order. Wollstonecraft relied on servants all her life. The anti-slavery movement she supported (of which more later) had racist assumptions embedded within it.

Wollstonecraft died aged 38, in 1797, from complications following the birth of her second daughter, Mary (who would grow up to become the novelist Mary Shelley). Later readers learned much more about her life from the memoir published by her widower, William Godwin. Godwin's brief book culminated in a tribute to his wife's intelligence: 'I did not possess, in the degree of some other men, an intuitive perception of intellectual beauty . . . What I wanted in this respect, Mary possessed, in a degree superior to any other person I ever knew.'[9] But his sketch of his dead wife's mind was overshadowed by his account of her traumatic personal life. This included details of her abandonment by Gilbert Imlay, the lover who fathered her first daughter, Fanny, and of two suicide attempts – the second of which involved her hurling herself from Putney Bridge into the River Thames, from where she was rescued.

Mainstream opinion was scandalized by this material. Combined with her strong support for the French Revolution (although like other British radicals she supported the Girondins, not the Jacobins and their bloodthirsty Terror), it placed Wollstonecraft beyond the pale even for some former friends. Claire Tomalin, in her 1974 biography, suggested that the reaction against the radical 1790s would have so distressed her that it was perhaps almost as well that she died when she did. Amelia Opie, an anti-slavery activist who belonged to the same social circle, wrote a novel mocking her marriage. One admirer who did not immediately forsake her was Mary Hays. Born just a week after her more famous namesake, Mary Hays published her Wollstonecraft-influenced 'Appeal to the Men of Great Britain in Behalf of Women' in 1798. But she omitted Wollstonecraft from her multi-volume biographical dictionary of women. And her own reputation never recovered after a novel she wrote, which fictionalized her unrequited passion for a mathematician, saw her turned into an object of public ridicule.

By the time *A Vindication* was republished in a centenary edition, the women's movement had reclaimed it. But even then, an introduction written by the suffragist leader Millicent Fawcett conveyed uncertainty as well as pride. She began by stating that the changes in women's position are 'too powerful and too universal to be attributed to any particular individual' and went on to describe the author as 'the essentially womanly woman, with the motherly and wifely instincts strong within her'.[10] She ended by comparing Wollstonecraft's significance with Adam Smith's role in political economy. The message could hardly have been more contradictory: Wollstonecraft was both everywoman and genius.

Wrongly regarded as a libertine for much of the nineteenth century, Wollstonecraft was later lambasted for her politics and personality. As a book reviewer in my twenties, I was infuriated by one biographer's description of her attempted suicide as a 'huge failure in mothering'.[11] But while I rejected that unsympathetic judgement, there is no doubt that Mary Wollstonecraft's life story is part of what makes hers a difficult legacy. The death following childbirth of this brilliant thinker, who argued so forcefully against the 'distinction of sex' and in favour of female citizenship, was a tragic irony. 'Considering the care and anxiety a woman must have about a child before it comes into the world, it seems to be, by a *natural right*, to belong to her,' she wrote in a letter.[12] But such maternal advocacy was never an easy fit with arguments for equality. A campaign to memorialize her ended disappointingly in 2020, with the erection on Newington Green of a monument featuring an anonymous nude female figure on top of a much larger plinth.

The early socialists

Low as her reputation sank in the decades following her death, Mary Wollstonecraft was never without defenders. Her daughter's husband, the poet Shelley, was one. And in 1825 a book was published which declared in its opening pages its intention to 'have the honour of raising from the dust that neglected banner which a woman's hand nearly thirty years ago unfolded boldly, in the face of the prejudices of thousands of years'. William Thompson, the Irish radical who wrote this, went on to suggest that Wollstonecraft's *Vindication* was marred by 'narrow views'. He also criticized the 'timidity and impotence' of her friend Mary Hays. But such caveats aside, the book he co-wrote with his friend Anna Doyle Wheeler, which had the long title of *Appeal of One Half the Human Race, Women, Against the Pretensions of the Other Half, Men, To Retain Them in Political, and thence in Civil and Domestic, Slavery*, was intended to resurrect the audacious project of female emancipation that Wollstonecraft had begun.[13]

Thompson presented 'Mrs Wheeler' to readers as her worthy successor, explaining in an introductory letter that the book was written by them both. Portraying himself somewhat in the manner of a modern ghost writer, he had 'endeavoured to arrange the expression of those feelings, sentiments, and reasonings, which have emanated from your [Mrs Wheeler's] mind.' While 'a few only of the following pages' were actually written by Wheeler, the rest of the book should be regarded as their 'joint property'.[14] While Wollstonecraft's *Vindication* was a response to Rousseau, the *Appeal* was a rebuttal of another Enlightenment philosopher: the Scottish utilitarian James Mill. Mill wrote influential books on political economy, but the article which provoked Thompson and Wheeler's reply was in the *Encyclopedia Britannica*. This was a contribution to a wider debate about democracy, and to their dismay dismissed the idea that women should have political representation in just a few words. The reason Mill gave was that women's interests were 'included in those of others' – namely their fathers and husbands. Their *Appeal* attacked this argument on several grounds, among them the economically precarious position of single women. It also noted the tendency among men towards despotism over dependents and referred to such behaviour, in a vivid phrase, as 'mind- and joy-eradicating oppressions'.[15]

Domestic tyranny was something that Wheeler had herself experienced. Married by her own choice, and against her parents' wishes, when she was fifteen, she bore five children, three of whom died, before leaving her heavy-drinking and violent husband in 1812. In later years, her estranged daughter would

2 Anna Doyle Wheeler by Maxim Gauci

describe her as having been poisoned by Mary Wollstonecraft.[16] But whether or not the influence was direct, it is not hard to see connections between the two women's complaints about the state-sanctioned abuse of wives.

Already well read by the time she left her husband, and in correspondence with leading radical thinkers, Wheeler would go on to become a significant female voice on the early socialist left. From Ireland she moved to London and then northern France, where she joined the movement of freethinkers known as Saint-Simonians (after their founder, Count Claude-Henri de Rouvroy de Saint-Simon). Along with her friend William Thompson, she also absorbed the utopian theories of another French radical, Charles Fourier, and became a conduit between him and the Welsh socialist manufacturer and cooperative pioneer, Robert Owen.

There were differences as well as commonalities between these thinkers and the schemes in which they were involved. Robert Owen operated his cotton mill at New Lanark, near Glasgow, according to socialist principles, with the aim of transforming the condition of his workers and demonstrating how an egalitarian society could work. The Saint-Simonians became increasingly cultic, with one branch becoming absorbed in a search for the female messiah in Egypt. Fourier's more esoteric theories included a typology of the human passions. But all shared a recognition that the equitable reordering of society entailed an end to the sexual hierarchy which enabled men to rule over their families. It was Fourier's 'general thesis' that progress 'occurs by virtue of the progress of women toward liberty'.[17]

In all, there were seven Owenite communities established in Britain between 1821 and 1845. These experiments in communal living formed part of a broader radical revival, which had the expansion of the franchise and increased rights for working people at its heart. It also included the movement against slavery (the slave trade having been abolished in 1807) and, from the 1830s, the campaign against the protectionist Corn Laws. All these movements included female activists. Women were among the 300,000 people estimated to have joined the first boycott of slave-grown sugar in the 1790s and, when the movement revived in the 1820s, Lucy Townsend set up the first women's anti-slavery society in Birmingham. In 1828, the women's anti-slavery movement launched its own cameo, bearing the slogan 'Am I not a Woman and a Sister', as an alternative to the 'Am I not a Man and Brother' version created years earlier. Harriet Martineau, the political economist and journalist, became a prominent anti-slavery voice during a two-year visit to the United States.[18]

In 1840, the Sheffield Quaker and abolitionist Anne Knight was present when seven women who had come to London as part of the American delegation to the World Anti-Slavery Convention were barred from participating and placed behind a screen where they could listen instead. Three years later, the Scottish writer Marion Reid, who was also there, produced a pamphlet titled *A Plea for Woman: Being a Vindication of the Importance and Extent of Her Natural Sphere of Action*. This new 'vindication' was an attack on the ideology of separate spheres that sought to confine women to domestic activity. Reid began it with a quote, 'Can man be free, if woman be a slave?', attacked the male monopoly on property ownership, and held up the anti-slavery movement as an example for women's rights campaigners to follow.[19]

Women were also involved in pro-democracy campaigns. They had joined the demonstration preceding the massacre at St Peter's Field in Manchester, when cavalry charged protesters and killed an estimated eighteen, on 16 August 1819. And while the six demands of the pro-democracy Chartist movement – which arose in response to the limited extension of the franchise in 1832 – did not include votes for women, many joined in on behalf of their husbands, fathers and brothers. But as Barbara Taylor argued in her landmark book, *Eve and the New Jerusalem* (1983), it was the Owenite socialist women who showed the greatest radicalism in this period. Audiences at Owenite lectures on women's rights were regularly in the hundreds and sometimes in the thousands. Scores of letters were sent to the movement's newspapers, one of which, *The Pioneer*, had 'A Page for the Ladies' which was changed to 'Women' when it was pointed out that 'Ladies' was an overly grand term for its intended readership of working women.[20] Frances Morrison, an Owenite who wrote under the pseudonym 'A Bondswoman', was one of the first people to argue publicly in favour of equal pay.[21] Eliza Macauley used her position as manager of one of the London labour exchanges to highlight the particular difficulties faced by female workers, and in 1832 a Society of Industrious Females was set up to secure fair prices for a women's clothing cooperative.

Attacks on monogamy featured alongside the advocacy of free love and the prevention of pregnancy in the writings of socialists including Frances Wright (who was born in Scotland but emigrated to the United States). But female writers were in general more cautious than male ones when it came to sexuality. In a tract on marriage from 1838, Frances Morrison asserted that the responsibilities of husbands and fathers should be legally enforced until socialism had transformed society completely since the premature loosening of ties would leave women, especially mothers, dangerously exposed. Another Owenite lecturer, Emma Martin, spoke on divorce and was an early objector to male domination of female health care. She became a midwife when politics proved an insufficient source of income, and was said to have been reading a book by George Eliot when she died aged 39. Harriet Martineau contributed to the fund for her headstone.

Anna Wheeler's Irish landed background made her an unusual member of this company. But she was at the centre of the first efforts to conceive of an autonomous women's movement. In 1829, she gave a speech on women's rights at South Place

Chapel in Finsbury – the predecessor venue to Conway Hall. This emphasized the benefits to humanity overall from women's advancement, and urged men to give up what she called their 'debasing power'.[22] Four years later, Owen's newspaper, *The Crisis*, published her translation of a 'Call to Women', a manifesto demanding freedom and justice produced by a French group who called themselves 'New Women'. Wheeler's English version of this document was titled 'Only by Emancipating Women Will We Emancipate the Worker'.[23]

In the same year, a group described by Barbara Taylor as 'the first feminist separatist organization established in Britain' came briefly into being. Called the Practical Moral Union of Women of Great Britain and Ireland, it aimed to 'combine all classes of women', asserting the commonality of sex as an alternative to the divisions of rank, property and education.[24] England also had its own variety of female messianism, with one group of Christian millenarians adopting a heretical 'Doctrine of the Woman' or 'Woman Power'. The radical orator Eliza Sharples put her own spin on the story of Genesis, challenging an audience on their response to Eve taking the apple: 'Do you not, with one voice, exclaim, well done woman! LIBERTY FOR EVER!'[25]

Two reformers: Elizabeth Fry and Caroline Norton

Two more women who deserve a place in any account of feminism's forerunners are Elizabeth Fry (1780–1845) and Caroline Norton (1808–1877). While Mary Wollstonecraft and Anna Wheeler were radical thinkers who attacked the philosophical basis of male domination, Fry and Norton were reformers who sought practical remedies for the injustices they identified. Fry came from a wealthy Quaker background in Norfolk, with a family fortune built on textiles (her husband's came from tea and banking). The Quakers, or Society of

3 Engraving of Caroline Norton, campaigner for mothers' rights, by John Cochran

Friends, were highly unusual among Christian denominations in allowing women to speak at meetings. From her late teens, Elizabeth became an enthusiastic participant in religious and philanthropic life.

Prone to spiritual doubts, and troubled all her life by the pleasure she took in the trappings of privilege – expensive clothes, dancing, wine – Elizabeth found an outlet for her conscience and her energetic personality in 'DOING GOOD' (which she sometimes wrote in capital letters).[26] Initially engaged in educational and other local projects, in 1813 – by now married and living in London – she paid her first visit to Newgate Prison. So disturbed was she by what she saw that, over the next decade, she turned herself into Britain's leading penal reformer. The changes she oversaw initially at Newgate, where she opened a school in 1816 and persuaded the authorities to separate women from men, were widely copied. In 1823, largely as a result of her efforts, the law was changed so that prisons would be inspected and visited by chaplains, and female prisoners would have female guards. Following Fry's example, women-only associations of prison visitors were set up in Russia, France and Holland as well as Britain. Having honed her skills through her ministry, she became a celebrated public speaker, accustomed to addressing huge crowds. Her biographer, Jean Hatton, says that, royalty aside, she was the most famous woman in Britain.

Not all Fry's reforming efforts were woman focused. She visited convict ships, pressed for changes to the cruel system of transportation and argued against public executions. Like many Quakers, she also supported the movement to abolish slavery and worked closely with its evangelical leaders. But her advocacy on behalf of female prisoners, and her recognition of the sexualized nature of the abuse which they faced, set an important precedent. She also established the first hostels or halfway houses for released women prisoners, and was involved in an early project to train nurses.

Fry was an establishment figure who sought aristocratic patronage for her schemes, not a political radical. Rich relatives took pride in her efforts, which depended on the supply of family money. But she was frequently in dispute with her husband and eleven children, who resented the way that she put work over family commitments (even on foreign holidays she would visit prisons). While she was never hailed as a feminist foremother in the manner of Mary Wollstonecraft, Fry's uncompromising commitment to her work – as well as her practical achievements – made her another kind of role model. In the book about women's prisons that she published in 1827, Fry wrote that she rejoiced 'to see the day in which so many women of every rank . . . are engaged in works of usefulness and charity'.[27] Elizabeth Fry showed how a woman could, with sufficient resources and determination, not only carve out a niche in public life but become an expert. It was a lesson that later reformers took seriously.

As an aristocrat, the writer and mothers' rights campaigner Caroline Norton belonged to an even more exalted stratum, and the peak of her fame came a decade later. Caroline was a party to one of the most scandalous family law cases of the nineteenth century when, in 1836, her estranged husband sued the prime minister, Lord Melbourne, for £10,000 in damages, alleging adultery, which was then known as 'criminal conversation'. George Norton lost and biographers have tended to agree with the court that his wife was not unfaithful. But he did not accept the verdict, and the repercussions turned Caroline into a lifelong advocate for law reforms to benefit wives and mothers.[28]

Like Anna Wheeler, Caroline Norton had experienced domestic abuse. Her husband had become violent early in their marriage, when she gave birth to three sons by the age of twenty-five. Following the trial, the separated couple, who never divorced, fought a decades-long battle over money and their children. Wives, at this time, had fewer parental rights than unmarried mothers because husbands were entitled to make all decisions. George refused to allow Caroline to see her children and questioned their paternity, even changing one of their names. On one occasion, she travelled to where the boys were staying and attempted to leave with one of them, only for their father to order that they be physically dragged apart.

Norton was already a published poet and novelist, and her response to this disaster was to become a pamphleteer. Her first effort, *Observations on the Natural Claim of the Mother to the Custody of her Infant Children as affected by the Common Law Right of the Father* (1837), argued that married women should have the same guardianship rights over children aged under seven as unmarried mothers, and that courts and not fathers should make decisions about older children. This was followed by a further booklet, which was timed to coincide with a second attempt by her allies in Parliament at changing the law. A third polemic was pseudonymous and styled as *A Plain Letter to the Lord Chancellor on the Infant Custody Bill.* Caroline pulled all the strings she could to ensure it reached influential hands, including those of the Duke of Wellington. And in 1839, at the third attempt, a bill that increased the rights of mothers – but without equalizing them – was passed.[29] Since her children had been sent to live in Scotland, however, her husband was not obliged to comply with the new law. In 1842, the youngest boy, Willie, fell off a pony. Caroline arrived when the nine-year-old was already in his coffin.

Having won increased parental rights for mothers, she continued to advocate for married women's property rights. The doctrine known as 'coverture' meant that wives did not exist separately from their husbands, in legal terms, and were unable to own anything. Every penny earned from her prolific authorship thus belonged to her husband. Caroline spent much of her life in castles, and could expect replies when she sent poems and letters to Queen Victoria. She also knew Mary Shelley, who faced a similar situation when her father-in-law threatened to take her son away after she was widowed. But inherited wealth and friends in high places could not prevent Caroline Norton from losing access to her children.

Questions of sex

Radical Unitarian circles continued to provide a home for women's rights advocacy in the 1840s. The writer Mary Leman Grimstone, for example, advocated communal housing and childcare. Unitarians were among the first to omit the bride's promise 'to obey' from the marriage service, and campaigned against what they called the 'Great Social Evil' of prostitution. In 1846 an organization called the Whittington Club was established for the purpose of mixed-sex socializing, after women complained about their exclusion from existing clubs.

Like the female abolitionists who drew attention to sexual exploitation in the slavery business, Elizabeth Fry was a pioneer of a woman-centred reform politics. Caroline Norton's pamphlets and personal lobbying initiated another strand in women's activism – for the enhanced rights of wives and mothers. Neither woman was egalitarian in outlook. With her elite background, Norton could even be regarded as a prototype of the white, western feminist whose concerns about social justice do not extend much beyond her personal interests. But to take this view of her achievements would be to ignore their radical aspects. Although it was not revolutionary, such advocacy challenged the status quo, while single-sex anti-slavery and prison reform societies marked a crucial stage in the development of an autonomous women's movement.

In the decades after her death, when the English literary world largely looked on Mary Wollstonecraft as a reprobate, translations of her *Vindication* were still being produced by rebellious women across Europe. The American anti-slavery and women's rights activist Lucretia Mott kept a copy on her table. Anne Knight, the Quaker abolitionist, saw in such foreign connections a source of hope, and wrote to American friends about Marion Reid's polemical *Plea for Women* that 'these things ought to be sent darting off like lightning to all the world'.[30] While the European revolutions of 1848 did not spread to Britain, and an Irish rebellion was quickly suppressed, Knight and others saw their efforts to launch a women's movement as part of an international uprising. The year 1848 was also that of the world's first women's rights convention at Seneca Falls in New York.

'The mind has no sex,' in the words of the Scottish-American socialist Frances Wright. Women's rights activists in this period mostly shared the view that sex differences were misunderstood and exaggerated. But not all agreed that minds were unsexed, or that 'the distinction of sex' (in Wollstonecraft's phrase) was limited to reproductive functions. The political meaning of the female body, and how to reconcile recognition of its capacities and vulnerabilities with demands for equality, was among the questions she and others struggled with. Another was how disparities in power between men and women corresponded to other injustices, such as the vast gulf that divided rich from poor, and the barbaric slave system. In the next chapter, I will show how a later group of women's rights campaigners confronted some of the same problems and came up with their own set of answers.

2

Organizers (1850s–1860s)

In later life, Barbara Leigh Smith Bodichon dated her interest in setting up a women's college to 1848, when her brother Benjamin became a university student. 'Ever since my brother went to Cambridge I have always intended to aim at the establishment of a college where women could have the same education as men,' she explained in a letter.[1] This was the year of her twenty-first birthday, when her father made her financially independent with an income of £300 a year (worth around £30,000 today), greatly assisting her wish to escape a social world in which, in the words of her first biographer, 'the holding of original opinions was deemed as unfilial as it was unwomanly.' Even the personal ownership of a dog, by a girl, could be frowned upon because it suggested too great a degree of independence.[2]

Barbara's Unitarian upbringing strayed far from such stultifying conventions. The granddaughter of a prominent anti-slavery campaigner, she was taught at home by a teacher brought in from Robert Owen's school at New Lanark. In 1848, she was cutting her teeth as a journalist, writing for a newspaper in Hastings, the seaside town where she lived when she was not in London. Already she had a sophisticated grasp of the way in

4 Barbara Bodichon by Samuel Lawrence, 1880, after an original painting

which the denial of education to women was rationalized. In an article headed 'The Education of Women', she pleaded with her readers not to suppress their daughters' curiosity: 'Women in the ordinary cant of the day, are supposed to have a *mission*. They are not the human creature itself, but attendants sent in some way to refine and elevate man. They are supposed to be a sort of abstract principle of the world, and the prominent appearance of intellect is thought to mar the impression.'[3]

Like Mary Wollstonecraft, Barbara and her friends loathed the deliberate fostering of ignorance. Even the roughly 25,000 governesses in England often had little to offer pupils since they were barely educated themselves. In 1848, Queen's College in London became the first institution to offer academic qualifications to women. The following year, Barbara attended drawing classes at another new institution, the Ladies' College in Bedford Square (later renamed Bedford College). Barbara described herself in the 1851 census as a 'scholar at home',[4] but it is neither as an intellectual nor an artist that she is chiefly remembered. Instead, Barbara Leigh Smith – who became Barbara Bodichon when she married – is known as a leading light of the Langham Place group of reformers, who campaigned for women's property rights, education and jobs, and played an important role in the early days of the women's suffrage movement.

There are two blue plaques bearing her name – one in Hastings and another at Girton College, Cambridge, which she co-founded with Emily Davies. But Barbara Leigh Smith Bodichon is nowhere near as well-known as Mary Wollstonecraft or the leading suffragists. If the general neglect of women's political history is one reason for this, another is her nationality. Madame Bodichon, as she was known after her marriage in 1857, is a French name, and after her marriage Barbara lived partly in Algeria, where her husband was a doctor. Legally speaking, Barbara Bodichon *was* French since the law of the time altered a woman's nationality to match that of her husband. Thus anyone seeking to describe Barbara as a British or English feminist, or proto-feminist, must first reclaim her (the same is true of her friend Madame Mohl, another radical English woman with a French husband).

Barbara was also prone to self-effacement, a trait which may have been linked to the question mark that hung over her background. Her parents never married, for reasons that biographers have struggled to explain. As a result, she and her siblings were illegitimate. Although Barbara led a busy life, and enjoyed some success as a painter, she was not fully accepted by polite society. Her famous first cousin, Florence Nightingale, did not acknowledge her as a relation.

Committee women

Described by her great friend, Bessie Parkes, as having an 'initiative mind',[5] from her youth Barbara was sociable and keen on women-only activities. Parkes was another daughter of prominent Unitarians (her great-grandfather was Joseph Priestley, the radical theologian and scientist whose home was torched by a mob due to his support for the French Revolution), and the pair set up a book club. The French writer George Sand, known for dressing in traditionally masculine attire, was one writer the young women admired. Others were Elizabeth Barrett Browning and Charlotte Brontë, whose novel *Jane Eyre* (1847) included an impassioned denunciation of the shortcomings of girls' education. Their circle of acquaintance also included Anna Jameson, an art historian who made her living from writing after separating from her husband. Harriet Martineau was another role model, as Parkes described: 'She was the first, she has helped on by her example all the others. Twenty years ago its [sic] a bold thing of a woman to write on political economy'.[6] Marian Evans (who adopted the pseudonym of George Eliot in 1859) became both a friend and mentor.

Barbara's first practical scheme was the progressive co-educational primary school that she opened in 1854 in London. That summer, she and Bessie went on holiday to Snowdonia, where they swam in a lake 'in the most utterly crazy Diana-like way with no Actaeon save a mountain mutton or two who came and stared and thought we were literally two very odd fishes'.[7] As well as wild swimming, the two friends spent their days editing the proofs of their first books: Bessie Parkes's *Remarks on the Education of Girls*, and Barbara Leigh Smith's *A Brief Summary, in Plain Language, of the Most Important Laws Concerning Women*. The year 1854 also saw the publication of Caroline Norton's fourth pamphlet, *English Laws for Women in the Nineteenth Century*, and a review essay by Marian Evans titled 'Woman in France: Madame de Sablé', published anonymously in the *Westminster Review*. (In an irony of publishing history, the same year saw the first appearance of Coventry Patmore's narrative poem 'The Angel in the House', which helped to popularize the Victorian ideal of selfless womanhood.)

As discussed in the previous chapter, and as Barbara explained in her *Brief Summary*, everything belonging to a woman became her husband's when she married, and from a legal point of view she ceased to be a separate person, unable to sign a contract or take a case to court. There was a twist, however, which meant that wealthy wives sometimes were able to hold on to assets. This was due to the existence of the Court of Chancery, which had functioned in parallel to the common law courts since the Middle Ages (and is the setting for the famously interminable case of *Jarndyce v Jarndyce* in Charles Dickens's *Bleak House*). In the Court of Chancery, property worth more than £200 (around £20,000 in today's money) could be settled on a wife by her father, enabling her to act as a 'feme sole' or spinster in regard to her own possessions. The coexistence of two systems was a source of confusion as well as injustice, as had been recognized by campaigners including Caroline Norton.

In 1855, Barbara hosted a meeting in her family home at 5 Blandford Square, just north of Marylebone Station in London. The purpose was to form a committee and start a petition in support of a proposed new law that would extend property rights to women who did not meet the Court of Chancery threshold. Those present included Barbara, her younger sister Nannie, their friends Bessie Parkes and Anna Mary Howitt, Anna Mary's mother Mary Howitt – a writer and translator – and Anna Jameson. The committee was not the first women's rights pressure group in England. A Practical Moral Union of Women had briefly existed two decades earlier, as had women's anti-slavery and prison reform groups. In 1851, Anne Knight formed a Sheffield Female Political Association to press for women's suffrage. But the petition gathered in support of the Married Women's Property Bill marked the start of a period in which women became progressively more organized.

Parliament was not their only target. In 1855, Barbara was among the donors to a new Society of Female Artists. A year later, her friend Anna Mary Howitt exhibited a picture of Boudicca, and was crushed by a letter from John Ruskin, in which the eminent critic commanded her to 'leave such subjects alone'.[8] Barbara responded by setting up a new society called the Portfolio, where women could discuss their pictures and encourage each other. Barbara and Bessie also contributed, along with Isa Craig, a Scottish writer they knew, to an Edinburgh-based fortnightly women's newspaper called the *Waverley Journal*. In 1857, Bessie became its editor but was dissatisfied with the arrangement, and negotiations were begun for Barbara to buy it. This she did, forming a company in order to do so, and jettisoning the magazine's Scottish heritage in favour of a new identity as the *English Woman's Journal*.

This became the group's house magazine, and important as an outlet for their writing and a way of drawing attention to subjects that concerned them. It carried articles on education, employment, poverty, factory conditions, prostitution, the arts and comparisons of British women's situation with that in other countries. It reported on the married women's property rights campaign, which continued after the bill they had petitioned for was rejected. Instead, legislation passed in 1857 altered the divorce laws and transferred jurisdiction from the ecclesiastical to the civil courts. For the first time, women were allowed to petition to dissolve a marriage.

Elizabeth Blackwell, who was Bessie Parkes's cousin, addressed her letters around this time to the 'Reform Firm'. This was how the group saw themselves, as they sought through various means to influence policy makers and public opinion. The 1851 census had revealed the existence of half a million single or 'surplus' women, who were supported neither by husbands nor other male relatives, and one scheme promoted women's emigration to New Zealand and other British colonies. From 1859, Jessie Boucherett, another of their associates, led a Society for Promoting the Employment of Women. This sought to widen the range of possible occupations from teaching and sewing, and reduce the likelihood of women being forced into prostitution, by training them as clerks, printers and hairdressers. Emily Faithfull, another of the Society's members, started a Victoria Printing Press, which had the contract to print the *English Woman's Journal* and hired female apprentices.

From 1859, the *Journal*'s offices at 19 Langham Place, between Regent's Park and Oxford Circus, contained reading and dining rooms, accessible for an annual membership of one guinea. This was as an attempt to give women who could afford it the same opportunity for single-sex socializing as men had long enjoyed. Like many of their other projects, this one was also aimed at asserting the presence of middle-class women in public space. The limitations of such liberal feminist schemes have often faced criticism. But the formal and informal ties that connected the Langham Place women with each other provided crucial support at a time when their creative efforts, as well as their political ideals, drew hostile reactions.

'Is there a plague of Egypt worse than the strong-minded woman? . . . However, we do not fear that this species of vermin will ever infest English drawing-rooms,' is how one reviewer described Bessie's pamphlet on girls' education in the anti-feminist *Saturday Review*. The phrase was echoed in an attack on Barbara's subsequent effort, *Women and Work* (1857), which raged against 'strong-minded women', while disparaging her on grounds that 'women are fatally deficient in the power of close consecutive thought'.[9] Not all critics and editors were as unsympathetic as these. When Barbara met Marian Evans, she was working for John Chapman, the publisher of the *Westminster Review*. He hosted regular literary parties at the building in the Strand which was his home as well as the magazine's office. The 'woman question' was debated there, and the Swedish novelist and women's rights campaigner Fredrika Bremer was among Marian's acquaintances. (Although married, Chapman attempted to start an affair with Barbara, who although she was in love with him declined.)

Many Victorians cherished female companionship. But Barbara and Marian's bond relied on a distinctive combination of intellectual encouragement and moral support. While Marian was older and more confident, she was pained by the ostracism that followed her choice to live with a man who was married to someone else. George Henry Lewes was separated from his wife, but for financial reasons never sought a divorce, and while Marian called herself Mrs Lewes, many people refused to see her socially. In their letters, the two friends likened themselves to Scheherezade, the storyteller from *The Arabian Nights* (Marian) and Dinarzade, her sister and co-conspirator (Barbara), while Barbara – who was saddened by her childlessness – sometimes referred to their books as 'children'. When Marian's first novel, *Adam Bede*, was published in 1859 under the pseudonym George Eliot, Barbara detected the truth of its authorship straightaway and wrote to her in excitement that she had 'read one long extract which instantly made me internally exclaim that is written by Marian Evans, there is her great big head and her wise wide views'. When she told the secret to her sister, Nannie, Barbara wrote again to Marian, joyously, that 'She was so enchanted! She congratulated me with tears in her eyes – that a woman had done it – a friend – you. I wish you had seen her!'[10]

The *English Woman's Journal* lasted five years from its launch in 1858, and towards the end became riven with personal and religious conflicts. One of the editors, Emily Faithfull, became embroiled in a divorce trial in which she was suspected of being the lover of a married woman – and was more or less written out of the history of the women's movement as a result. So was Matilda, also known as Max Hays, the novelist and translator of George Sand who became the *Journal*'s penultimate editor. Hays, who dressed in what were then regarded as men's clothes, had a succession of close partnerships with women, one of which was described by Elizabeth Barrett Browning as a 'female marriage', entailing 'vows of celibacy and eternal attachment'. But the couple broke up, and such private sorrows were one factor in the *Journal*'s closure.[11]

College women

Barbara Bodichon had tried running her own co-educational school before her marriage. Another member of the group, Elizabeth Whitehead (who became Malleson when she married), was its head teacher. But the paucity of elementary school provision was only one of the issues that concerned female education reformers, and the Langham Place women became closely involved in one campaign in particular – that for a women's college in Cambridge. In 1860, Barbara gave a paper bemoaning the low standards of girls' education to the recently formed National Association for the Promotion of Social Science (also known as the Social Science Association). Two years later, she joined with Emily Davies, a former editor of the *English Woman's Journal*, and Isa Craig in setting up a Committee for Obtaining Admission of Women to University Examinations in Art and Medicine.

Their immediate aim was to offer support to Elizabeth Garrett, who Davies knew well, having met her when Garrett visited Davies's home town of Gateshead. Garrett wanted to train as a doctor, and worked as a nurse in London's Middlesex Hospital while attending lectures and dissections. There was already one doctor in the Langham Place circle. Elizabeth Blackwell, Bessie Parkes's Bristol-born cousin, had obtained her medical degree in New York. After the law was changed in 1858 to admit doctors trained abroad, she became the first woman on the British General Medical Council's register. But she encountered difficulties in London, where she spent a year working at St Bartholomew's Hospital. Like the Owenite midwife, Emma Martin, Blackwell was troubled by the control exerted by men over women's reproductive health care. 'Every department [at St Bart's] was cordially opened to me, except the department for female diseases,' she noted. At another time, she wrote to her sister of the malicious stories told about her: 'I am glad I, and not another, have to bear this pioneer work. It *is* hard, with no support but a high purpose, to live against every species of social opposition.'[12]

Garrett was refused admittance to multiple medical schools, including Glasgow and Edinburgh, and in 1862 was studying privately as a member of the Worshipful Society of Apothecaries, whose charter did not allow them to exclude women. In London, she met Blackwell, who became a mentor, and with the support of friends finally managed to obtain a licence to practise medicine (coming top of her class) from the Apothecaries in 1865. The Society then changed its rules, meaning that another young would-be doctor, Sophia Jex-Blake, was forced to try her luck elsewhere. She chose Edinburgh but encountered fierce resistance – on one occasion protesters shoved a sheep after her into an anatomy lecture – and eventually qualified in Switzerland.

But the group's ambitions went beyond medicine. They envisioned a general opening up of educational opportunities and, with this in mind, in 1863 Emily Davies secured permission for eighty-three girls to sit the School Certificate in Cambridge (a rough equivalent of modern GCSEs). The following year, Elizabeth Malleson founded a College for Working Women in central London – as a counterpart to the Working Men's College opened a decade earlier. In 1865, Davies gave evidence to a government appointed Schools Enquiry Commission, focused on middle-class secondary education, and succeeded in altering its terms of reference so that girls would be considered as well as boys. At her side, when she gave evidence, was Frances Buss, the pioneering headmistress of the North London Collegiate School (and later the Camden School for Girls). The pair seized the opportunity to make arguments for teacher training, regular inspections, endowments for girls' schools, and post-school training to equip young women for employment, although her anxiety about speaking in public left Buss close to tears.[13]

The issues of girls' schooling and women's higher education were closely connected since once there was a university college, there would need to be schools to prepare girls for entry.[14] In 1866, Davies published a book, *The Higher Education of Women*, and founded a London Schoolmistresses' Association with others, including Elizabeth Malleson. At a time when male tutors in Cambridge and Oxford were obliged to relinquish fellowships if they married, and scholarship retained associations with monasticism, there was nothing to be taken for granted about the idea that women should be able to get degrees. But Davies and Bodichon were a determined partnership, canvassing for support and gradually gathering subscriptions. They found a site at Girton, then a village just outside Cambridge, and Barbara set a generous example, donating £1,000 at the start, followed up by a £10,000 gift in her will (worth around one million pounds today). Girton's first five students arrived at temporary premises in Hitchin in 1869, although it would be many decades before Cambridge's women were allowed to matriculate on equal terms with men. One year later, elementary schooling was made compulsory.

The Langham Place group believed that women, especially unmarried women who did not have domestic responsibilities, should have opportunities as men did. Their methods were those of other reformers – lobbying, public speaking, fundraising. In the various committees and societies they were

5 Girton blue plaque © The Mistress and Fellows, Girton College, Cambridge

involved in, they built a distinctive culture of mutual support. Their wider circle of friends included artists and intellectuals, but they were primarily institution builders, not philosophers. Since there was no radical movement in the 1850s and 1860s to compare with the one described in the previous chapter, the main challenge to their liberal worldview came from conservatives who favoured the status quo.

There were disagreements. Some of these were personal and religious, with Emily Davies's Anglicanism unpalatable to some in Barbara's network. Others concerned tactics, with Davies anxious to remain on good terms with the male-dominated establishment. Another argument concerned the approach that should be taken to existing differences in educational provision. Davies never wavered from the view that Girton's students must follow exactly the same syllabus as Cambridge's other colleges. If they did not, they would be judged inferior. Another group of campaigners, who established a North of England Council for Promoting the Higher Education of

Women in 1867, included women who took a more flexible approach. Anne Clough, for example, who had run a school in the Lake District, opposed compulsory Latin and Greek, and thought that, given the limitations of girls' schools, easier exams could provide a stepping stone.

This was partly a pragmatic point about how quickly the level of women's education could be raised, but there was also an implicit question about whether women's colleges might, rather than imitating the existing curriculum, decide to do things differently. This was the path initially chosen by Newnham College, which opened in Cambridge two years after Girton, with Clough in charge. Another row erupted when Davies made up her mind to punish a group of students for cross-dressing in order to play male parts in a performance of scenes from Shakespeare.[15] The students were furious and threatened to leave, but were persuaded to back down by Barbara who smoothed things over by explaining that any adverse publicity could jeopardize funding. While Davies was concerned with her college's reputation, the episode also shows how equalitarian views like hers could coexist with restrictive attitudes to dress codes and behaviour.

Another significant figure in the field of women's education and employment was Florence Nightingale – although she avoided being associated with Barbara and did not get on with Elizabeth Blackwell either. The mythology that grew up around Nightingale's role as a nurse in the Crimean War (1853–56) for a long time obscured other aspects of her life and career. But Nightingale was a pioneering statistician, who translated Homer and Plato in her teens, conducted her own analysis of the first modern census (in 1841) and regarded the prospect of a life of leisure, either as a wife or with her parents, as akin to suicide. The essay she wrote in her early twenties, *Cassandra*, is among the bitterest attacks ever penned on the social code under which Victorian women 'accustomed themselves to consider intellectual occupation as merely selfish amusement', while good manners required them, when in company, 'to make a remark every two minutes'.[16]

Cassandra was not made widely available until after Nightingale's death, when it appeared in 1928 as an appendix to *The Cause,* Ray Strachey's history of the women's movement. In her lifetime, Nightingale held herself apart from other campaigners and cultivated her own high-level contacts, including government ministers, in order to influence policy in the areas that interested her – primarily nursing but also military and public health more widely. The Nightingale Training School for Nurses opened at St Thomas's Hospital in 1860 and was the first institution of its kind. But Nightingale did not support women's access to medical training. While she sometimes seemed to side with her critics in dismissing 'ministering angel nonsense',[17] her vision of a sex-segregated health workforce, and of nurses as missionaries of sanitation, conflicted with the efforts of contemporaries who were trying to break down the division of labour and gain entry to the male-controlled field of medicine.

Anti-slavery activity, mainly focused on the southern United States, continued alongside these other initiatives. Sarah Parker Remond was a black American anti-slavery activist who came to England partly in order to access education. She attended London's Bedford College, as Barbara had done, and toured Britain giving lectures to thousands of people between 1859 and 1861. Her speeches highlighted the sexual brutality which was part of the slave system, and she urged British women to 'demand for the black woman the protection and rights enjoyed by the white'.[18] Remond also trained as a nurse, and later moved to Italy where she became a doctor. In London in 1863, she joined Harriet Martineau, Elizabeth Malleson and others in establishing a Ladies' Emancipation Society to advance understanding of the Union cause in the American Civil War.

American women's suffrage and anti-slavery activism were closely linked, and in Britain too there were connections.

6 Sarah Parker Remond, a black American anti-slavery activist, gave lectures across Britain 1859–61 and attended Bedford College in London

Charlotte Manning was on the Emancipation Society's committee, and in 1865, when the American civil war ended, she turned her home into a base for a group that backed votes for women. The Kensington Society's fifty or so members included

7 Photograph of women's suffrage advocates John Stuart Mill and Helen Taylor, his stepdaughter, *c.*1860

many of those who had signed the married women's property petition. Dorothea Beale, the head of Cheltenham Ladies College, joined, as did Helen Taylor, the daughter of Harriet Taylor Mill and stepdaughter of John Stuart Mill (whose famous essay *The Subjection of Women* had been written but not yet published). Barbara Bodichon was among the Society's first speakers, giving a paper in response to the question, 'Is it desirable for women to take part in public affairs, and if so, in what way?', on 21 November. Her answer, an emphatic yes, was a plea for women's enfranchisement.

The petition in support of women's suffrage that ensued was officially based at the home of Elizabeth Garrett on the grounds that, as an unmarried doctor, she belonged to the class of women – single, female taxpayers – who were thought to have the strongest case. There was disagreement over whether the committee should be women only, or include men. Barbara favoured the latter and regarded herself as a less-than-ideal choice as the campaign's secretary, 'being legally a Frenchwoman and having a French name'.[19] But she accepted the role, and the petition of 1,521 women's signatures presented in Parliament by Mill, a Liberal MP for Westminster, on 7 June 1866 was described as coming from 'Barbara L. S. Bodichon and others'.[20] In the same year, her paper, 'Reasons for the Enfranchisement of Women', was read aloud at the Social Science Association where a botanist from Manchester, Lydia Becker, was in the audience. After returning home, Becker convened the first meeting of the Manchester Woman's Suffrage Committee and went on to launch the *Women's Suffrage Journal.* (I return to the story of the suffragists in chapter 4.)

Strong-minded women

In 1851, an article by Harriet Taylor Mill, setting out a case for female suffrage, appeared in the *Westminster Review.* Titled 'Enfranchisement of Women', it praised the resolutions passed at a recent Women's Rights Convention in Massachusetts and proposed that the equalization of rights and privileges would enable more partnerships of the type she valued between 'a strong-minded man and a strong-minded woman'. Taylor Mill believed brute force lay behind the custom of women's subjection, and she attacked the male-chauvinist preference for women with weak minds. 'Until very lately,' she wrote, 'the rule of physical strength was the general law of human affairs.' Anatomy aside, she did not dwell on 'alleged differences in physical or mental qualities between the sexes'.[21] One of her footnotes proposed that what were regarded as typical male or female traits of character or intellect could be attributed to upbringing.

That differences between men and women existed was not in dispute. Men's greater average physical strength was recognized and assumed by women's rights activists to be the source of their power; while pregnancy and motherhood were understood to make particular demands on women's bodies and minds. But not everyone agreed with Harriet Taylor Mill that the divergence in typical male and female behaviours was solely due to training. In 1854, Marian Evans began her 'Woman in France' essay, a hymn of praise to the literary achievements of seventeenth- and eighteenth-century French women, with the assertion that 'a certain amount of psychological difference between man and woman necessarily arises out of the difference of sex, and instead of being destined to vanish before a complete development of woman's intellectual and moral nature, will be a permanent source of variety and beauty.'[22] By the end of the decade, Evans was well on her way to becoming one of the intellectual leading lights of her age. Between 1859 and 1866, writing as George Eliot to disguise her sex, she would publish five novels – an incredible work rate – and create some of the most memorable female characters in literature. Hester Burton, who was Barbara Bodichon's first biographer, argued that George Eliot's fiction surpassed anything that her more practically minded friends achieved. 'Eliot's contribution to the emancipation of women lay in her own career, and in the creation of characters like Dinah Morris, Maggie Tulliver and Dorothea Casaubon – heroines utterly unlike the vapid young ladies of the average Victorian novel,' she wrote of *Adam Bede, The Mill on the Floss* and *Middlemarch*. 'They had minds; they had ambitions; they had souls. These three girls with their troubles and their courage and their dignity found a way into many more English homes than the pamphlets from Langham Place, and had a far more lasting effect on the minds of her generation.'[23] Such assertions, of the value of art over activism, are impossible to verify. But Burton's point is echoed by the reminiscences of Simone de Beauvoir, who wrote of the impact that Maggie Tulliver had on her when she read *The Mill on the Floss* as a teenager: 'I resembled her, and henceforward I saw my isolation not as a proof of infamy but as a sign of my uniqueness.'[24]

Evolutionary theory was one influence on Evans's thinking. Before setting up home with George Lewes she had been in love with Herbert Spencer, the scientific philosopher-sociologist who coined the phrase 'survival of the fittest' – and who rejected her. This interest in biology was shared with Lewes, and Evans was reading an advance copy of Charles Darwin's *On the Origin of Species,* which presented the evidence in support of natural selection, on the day in 1859 that it came out. One of the crucial questions for Evans, and others who were interested in the Darwinian science of sex, was whether it would reinforce the assumptions of male superiority that were integral to a western worldview grounded in Christian theology. Many readers, along with Darwin himself, took the view that it did. But Evans detected male bias in such interpretations, making her one of the first 'feminist' Darwinians. While she drew on evolutionary ideas in her fiction, her characterizations challenged Victorian stereotypes – which persisted in scientific literature – of women as vessels for male desires and strategies, and of mothers as paragons of selfless devotion. In stories such as that of Hetty Sorrel, the country girl who commits infanticide in *Adam Bede,* and Princess Alcharisi, the opera singer who gives her son away in *Daniel Deronda,* Evans demonstrated an understanding of human nature that went far beyond most of her peers, and took on board that women – like men – have their own interests that are distinct from anyone else's.[25]

Early critiques of Darwinian science from a female point of view were largely stifled. It is worth bearing in mind that Evans/Eliot also believed in phrenology, differentiating between 'Gallic' and 'Teutonic' physical types. She was far from immune to error. But to contemporaries she was an enormously influential mentor. 'To me one of the morals of your work is [to] help the highest education of women,' Barbara wrote to her in 1871.[26] To another friend, Barbara wrote that 'when I was reading the other day Mozart's letters I was struck with the fact in his life that his sister would probably have had as great a musical career as himself if she had been allowed the same advantages.'[27] Virginia Woolf seems unlikely to have come across this observation since it was made in personal correspondence. But had she done so it could have provided a model for her own famous riff, in *A Room of One's Own* (1928), about Shakespeare's uneducated sister: 'She had the quickest fancy, a gift like her brother's, for the tune of words. Like him, she had a taste for the theatre. She stood at the stage door; she wanted to act, she said. Men laughed in her face.' That women's creative and intellectual capacities had for centuries been stifled, and must in a liberal age be allowed to develop, was among the core beliefs of Barbara Bodichon and her friends.

Unlike the Owenite women, these reformers mostly belonged to an elite, and their activities must be differentiated from working-class and radical politics. One article in the *English Woman's Journal* referred dismissively to 'the wildness of the Wollstonecraft school and all its ultra-theories'.[28] But Barbara Bodichon and Marian Evans were also among those who kept Wollstonecraft's memory alive. One of Evans's early essays compared a book by the American writer Margaret Fuller with *A Vindication of the Rights of Woman*, and she saw a resemblance between her own life and Wollstonecraft's, in that a painful experience of romantic rejection had been followed by a rewarding partnership.[29] While Evans was not a strict equalitarian, committed to the elimination of differences between men and women in the interests of justice, nor was she a sex-role conformist. In the essay mentioned above, she backed Fuller's plea on behalf of girls and women who were drawn to activities such as wood carving that were considered 'not proper for girls'. Indeed, her whole life can be viewed as a rebellion against such restrictions. Like Harriet Taylor Mill, she believed fervently that the poor state of female education was holding back human progress.

Evans's participation in the Langham Place campaigns was mostly limited to signing petitions and making donations. I have written about her here because I think her career, and friendship with Barbara, were an important adjunct to the practical achievements of these years. The Langham Place women were not committed separatists. Barbara and others were active in mixed-sex groups (such as the Social Science Association) alongside their women-only ones. But the personal and political bonds they established between each other held the first women's lobby together in what Barbara called a 'united sisterhood'.[30] Despite fallings out and failures, the support they offered each other was crucial to their efforts. And while these were predominantly aimed at improving the prospects of middle-class or gentlewomen, there were glimmers of the more expansive sex consciousness that lay ahead. In August 1869, Barbara declared herself encouraged by the presence of 'all sorts and conditions of women' at a large public gathering in London of suffrage activists.[31]

Barbara Bodichon predicted, correctly, that she would be dead by the time women won the franchise. 'You will go up and vote upon crutches,' she said to Emily Davies, 'and I shall come out of my grave and vote in my winding-sheet.'[32] Davies was eighty-eight on 14 December 1918 – the date of the first general election at which women could vote – and in the 1860s still had decades of suffrage activism ahead of her.

But another campaign lay between the Langham Place group and the heyday of the 'votes for women' movement. The taboo surrounding public discussion of prostitution was about to be broken in the most spectacular style.

3

Crusaders (1870s–1880s)

Josephine Butler, who led the campaign to repeal the Contagious Diseases Acts mandating the compulsory genital inspection of prostitutes, called her memoir *Personal Reminiscences of a Great Crusade* (1896). It was as crusaders that Butler and many of her allies conceived of their efforts to help the women who sold sex, either on the streets or in one of the seven thousand brothels that are estimated to have existed in Britain in the 1870s. Deeply religious since childhood, and profoundly altered in mid-life by the death of her five-year-old daughter after a fall, Butler drew inspiration from her faith as well as her radical, suffragist politics. Halfway through the sixteen-year campaign to repeal the Acts, Butler wrote a biography of the fourteenth-century saint, Catherine of Siena.[1]

This campaign was narrower in scope than the movement for education, employment and property rights discussed in the previous chapter. It was much briefer than the long struggle for the vote which is the subject of the next one. Prostitution had been subject to state regulation in parts of Europe since the start of the century, when Napoleon licensed brothels and, with them, the police in charge of checking prostitutes for

8 Josephine Butler in 1876. Photo by Hayman Seleg Mendelssohn

disease. The Contagious Diseases Acts introduced in Britain in the 1860s followed this model and gave the authorities the power to carry out genital examinations of women – but not men – as a way of controlling the spread of venereal infections, especially in the armed forces. When the campaign against this legislation launched in 1870, the repealers attracted fierce hostility, manifested in physical assaults and even arson.

Yet, while Butler is recognized among the grandees of Victorian feminism, a good deal of ambivalence surrounds her life's work. (These days, students of feminism would be far more likely to think of Judith, the American philosopher, than Josephine, if quizzed about the famous 'J. Butler'.) Equivocation with regard to her achievements is not surprising. Prostitution and the wider commercialization of sex and reproduction remain highly contested issues. The Christian morality that animated the repeal campaign – as well as the temperance movement that coexisted with it and the 'social purity' one that followed – is not a comfortable fit with modern, secular feminism.

But the story of Butler's crusade is a crucial one, not only because it was the moment when the British women's movement took a public stand on sexuality and decisively rejected the reticence and modesty that were then supposed to be the natural condition of respectable women. This campaign was also the testing ground for the radical direct-action tactics and separatist organizing that were taken up by the suffrage movement. And it formed part of a wider, late nineteenth-century debate on personal morality, which included the advocacy of free love, as well as restraint.

Rescue and repeal

The women who campaigned to repeal the Contagious Diseases Acts were not the first social reformers to raise concerns about prostitution. Mary Wollstonecraft had railed against the miserable condition of women reduced to selling sex through the lack of any other means of providing for themselves. By the 1850s, the increasingly visible trade had become known as 'the Great Social Evil', and the first issue of the *English Woman's Journal* included an article by Anna Mary Howitt about a penitentiary for fallen women in Highgate.[2] 'Rescue work' among prostitutes was an established form of social welfare activism. Nor were critiques of the sale of sex limited to formal transactions. The socialist utopians of the 1830s and 1840s had dismissed marriage as legalized prostitution, on grounds that wives were legally obliged to submit to husbands' desires. While such views were never mainstream, in the 1880s they would be taken up by sexual libertarians.

But from 1870 the campaign against what repealers regarded as state-sponsored sexual exploitation became the centrepiece of the British women's movement. After the National Association for the Repeal of the Contagious Diseases Acts excluded women from its first meeting, a Ladies' National Association (henceforth the LNA) was swiftly formed. As governor of Malta, Sir Henry Storks had been responsible for introducing a Contagious Diseases Act there, and Josephine Butler took the lead in an audacious campaign to prevent his election to Parliament, as the Liberal candidate in a by-election in Essex. As a garrison town, Colchester was one of the areas where the compulsory genital inspections, which had been introduced in 1864 and extended in 1866, were in force. Butler spent two weeks trying to visit the local lock hospital where prostitutes were confined, speaking to prayer groups, and finally escaping from a public meeting through a window, in disguise, after an angry, mostly male crowd surrounded the building.

Storks was defeated, but the stunts continued alongside more conventional tactics. Campaigners walked the streets wearing sandwich boards and handed out satirical verses. Butler was assaulted in Glasgow, and in Manchester excrement was thrown at her. In 1872, a by-election in Pontefract, Yorkshire, presented another chance to attack the legislation. The candidate this time was Hugh Childers, also a Liberal, who had overseen the Acts' implementation in Plymouth and Portsmouth. A hay loft on the edge of town was the only venue that repealers could find to hold a women-only meeting. Stones were thrown, breaking the windows, and bales of straw set alight below.

Childers won. But Butler and her allies were undaunted and hired agents to bolster their campaign. She was a much-admired speaker who attracted fierce loyalty and was often described as beautiful by contemporaries. Like her, other members of the LNA's executive were typically women in their forties. Many of them came from the kind of radical, nonconformist backgrounds that shaped the culture of earlier women's activism, and some had links to early socialism. Emilie Venturi, for example, was the daughter of William Ashurst – a prominent anti-slavery campaigner who was also Robert Owen's lawyer. Elizabeth Wolstenholme Elmy, who proposed that Butler should lead the repeal campaign, was a dissident against Victorian social mores who modelled herself on Mary Wollstonecraft. She cohabited with her lover until she became pregnant, when friends persuaded them to marry. More than a century before it was made a crime, she also spoke out against rape within marriage, describing the criminal code of 1880 which defined rape as 'the act of a man . . . having carnal knowledge of a woman, who is not his wife, without her consent', as reducing wives (who were excluded from the law) to the condition of slaves.[3] In 1898, either she or her husband authored the first article defining feminism in a British publication. This appeared in the *Westminster Review* under the pseudonym of Ellis Ethelmer, which was used by both of them.[4]

Butler and other LNA propagandists specialized in the kind of heightened language that compelled attention. In her public appearances, she made reference to Wat Tyler, leader of the Peasants' Revolt of 1381, who was fabled to have taken revenge on behalf of a victim of sexual assault. The instruments used to conduct genital examinations were described and held up for audiences' horrified inspection (cervical screening for cancer was not introduced until a century later, and the insertion of a speculum into a woman's vagina was likened to a form of torture). Pamphlets referred to 'enslaved wombs' and the 'medical lust of handling and dominating women'.[5] Butler referred to the coalition of legal, police and military interests ranged against them as a 'diabolical triple power'.[6]

Like the female prison visitors of the 1820s, members of the LNA carried out voluntary work alongside their campaigning. Local groups in Belfast, Bristol and elsewhere organized regular trips to the lock hospitals in which infectious women were forced to stay for months at a time. Butler opened her own home to prostitutes who were either dying from venereal disease or seeking to leave the sex trade, and also established a refuge for destitute women discharged from the workhouse. But the relations between the middle-class women of the repeal movement and the prostitutes they were seeking to protect from state coercion were not straightforward. Much like alcoholics who did not want to be reclaimed by temperance reformers, prostitutes who rejected attempts to save them were sometimes dismissed as members of an undeserving underclass.[7] Butler and her closest associates saw the sex trade primarily in economic rather than moral terms. Far from single-issue campaigners, they supported women's suffrage and other causes. Butler's first published article was a pamphlet called *The Education and Employment of Women*. In 1867, she became president of the North of England Council for Promoting the Higher Education of Women, where she worked alongside Anne Clough (the future principal of Newnham). But within the repeal campaign, moralistic, repressive attitudes coexisted with liberal, compassionate ones.

Not all women's rights advocates opposed the Contagious Diseases Acts. As a doctor with an interest in public health, Elizabeth Garrett backed them. Nor was repeal the only public health campaign in this period. From 1871, Barbara Bodichon was involved, along with Frances Power Cobbe, in a spin-off from the Social Science Association called the National Health Society. It used the motto 'Prevention is better than cure' and issued pamphlets offering advice on diet. It also trained the first health visitors and secured the opening of school playgrounds during holidays. But as attempts were made to extend the Acts far beyond their original, limited remit to encompass a far wider population and geography, opposition was ramped up. This was particularly pronounced in the regions, where many people objected to what they saw as overreach by a too-centralized state (provincial antipathy to London was also a dynamic of other Victorian social movements). Some supporters of the Acts proposed that military wives should be inspected, although soldiers and sailors had been exempted on grounds of the risk to morale. A bill published in 1872 proposed to apply the legislation across the British Isles.[8] In evidence to the House of Lords, one police commissioner said that officers should be free to apprehend 'any woman who goes to places of public resort'.[9] Interpreted in such broad terms, the Acts were not only harmful to prostitutes but a more general threat to women's freedom.

Given that the Acts' strongest support came from the aristocratic and military establishments, and placed working-class girls and young women at greatest risk, Butler saw working-class men (their fathers and brothers) as natural allies. In 1876, a partnership with the Working Men's National League was formalized, and joint discussions were held. The medical evidence for the Acts had by this time been revealed as weak since venereal disease had not been wiped out, and in 1883 an opportunity arose when a Liberal MP, James Stansfield (brother-in-law of Emilie Venturi), secured a parliamentary debate. The Liberals were not then in government, but the repeal campaign, which maintained its independence from political parties, had gained in strength, numbering more than a hundred local LNA branches.[10] On 20 April, a hall in the Westminster Palace Hotel was the venue for a packed prayer meeting. Butler spent her time shuttling back and forth between it and the House of Commons and was upstairs in the Ladies' Gallery, where women were allowed to watch from behind a screen, when the result of a vote was announced after midnight. A cheer went up as the Acts were suspended.

Success and scandal

If the furore around the Colchester by-election, and the explosion into public life of a subject that had hitherto been discussed mainly in whispers behind closed doors, meant that the campaign led by Josephine Butler had a shocking start, this was nothing compared with the scandal at its end. Anxious that the suspension of the Acts would be reversed, distrustful of Parliament, and preoccupied by reports of the pimping of children, by 1885 Butler and her allies had the raising of the age of consent in their sights, along with repeal of the Contagious Diseases Acts, which had so far only been suspended. Just as frustrating was the trial of a Chelsea brothel-keeper whose wealthy clients included King Leopold II of Belgium. This ended with the damp squib of a £200 fine. Determined to break the impasse, Butler and the editor of the *Pall Mall Gazette*, William Thomas Stead, hatched a plan.

The result was a series of articles titled 'The Maiden Tribute of Modern Babylon', published in the newspaper over several days in July 1885. To prove that the sex trafficking of girls into brothels – given the lurid name of a 'white slave trade' – was not a figment of imagination, Stead decided to buy a teenager and announced this on advertising hoardings bearing the slogan 'Five pounds for a virgin warranted pure'. Using the services of Rebecca Jarrett, a former prostitute, Stead bought a thirteen-year-old girl known as Eliza Armstrong (and given the pseudonym of Lily) from her mother for five pounds. She was examined to confirm her virginity, dosed with chloroform and taken to Paris.

Crowds besieged the newspaper's offices in the days following publication, and the 'Maiden Tribute' was taken up around the world. Within days, the Criminal Law Amendment Bill's second reading was rushed through, and it became law a month later, raising the age of consent from thirteen to sixteen. Even this did not satisfy the popular ire that had been aroused by the events described, and on 22 August a huge demonstration was held in Hyde Park.

This was one of the most audacious newspaper stunts ever attempted. It was also unethical, not least in the pressure applied to the vulnerable characters selected to carry it out. The initial triumph curdled when the plot's principal actors, including Stead but not Butler, were charged with abduction and assault. Following a trial that drew yet more headlines, Stead and three others were jailed. But such calamitous personal consequences aside, and spurred on by prurient coverage, the 'Maiden Tribute' marked a shift in the temper of the times. By the time the Acts were finally repealed, in 1886, charitable interest in helping women to exit the sex trade was on the way to being overtaken by a more coercive approach. The National Vigilance Association (NVA) established by Stead in 1885, along with the White Cross Army – a men's purity organization set up by the Christian feminist, Ellice Hopkins – took sexual morality campaigning in a more conservative direction. Prosecutions of brothel-keepers and drives against streetwalking sharply increased. Obscene books were burned.

The repeal campaign had always had a puritanical aspect. From 1880, the children of prostitutes could be legally removed from their care and placed in industrial schools. Butler's socio-economic analysis of the sex industry led her to reject such measures. She and her allies objected to the persecution of prostitutes by the sex trade's opponents as well as by its supporters. 'Leave individuals alone,' while attacking the structures underpinning sexual exploitation, was their guiding principle. Barbara Bodichon agreed, and she drew apart from her old friend Elizabeth Blackwell when Blackwell became a vigilance campaigner. Butler joined the executive of the National Vigilance Association when it launched, as did Millicent Fawcett (Elizabeth Garrett's married younger sister), who would soon become leader of the suffragists. But Butler was soon issuing warnings to 'Beware of Purity Societies' and an alternative, feminist group dedicated to upholding women's bodily autonomy was formed. This called itself the Personal Rights Association and, as the rift with vigilance campaigners grew, it derided them as 'stampers' on vulnerable people.[11]

But it was not in Butler's power to impose her humanitarian vision on the anti-vice movement, and in the 1880s she turned her attention abroad. Laws similar to the Contagious Diseases Acts remained in force in British-governed territories, and when it was revealed that recruiting sergeants in India had instructions to purchase 'young and attractive women' for the use of British troops, a new repeal campaign began.[12] The distressing case of a fourteen-year-old runaway, who a magistrate ruled should be forcibly reunited with the man who had bought her, was offered as evidence of the present system's inhumanity. But it was not enough to persuade the colonial authorities that Indian girls and women were at risk of being trafficked. It would be several more years before the sale and examination of Indian prostitutes was outlawed. This phase of activism was, however, significant in that it saw British women seek to extend their sphere of influence to the empire. Known by historians as 'maternalist imperialism', this is a form of politics I will return to in chapter 5.

Education and jobs

The campaign against the Contagious Diseases Acts took a massive effort and attracted many of those already involved in women's causes, as well as those with a specific interest in sexual exploitation and civil liberties. Josephine Butler and her allies catalysed a particular energy, and developed techniques that would later be imitated by suffragettes, but their campaign was not separate from the rest of the late nineteenth-century women's movement. Indeed, there was so much crossover between activism against the Contagious Diseases Acts and for 'votes for women' that some suffragists worried lest their cause should become muddled up in the public mind with the issue of prostitutes.

Suffragism aside, the main campaigns of the mid-Victorian years remained unfinished. The one on behalf of married women begun in Barbara Bodichon's sitting room in 1855 had momentum behind it, and it achieved its aims in stages, with Married Women's Property Acts passed in 1864, 1870 (when wives were granted ownership of their own earnings and inheritances) and 1882 (which extended the principle to anything else they owned). The 1878 Matrimonial Causes Act made divorce more accessible to middle-class women, though working-class wives were for financial reasons mainly limited to seeking separation orders made by magistrates – meaning they were unable to remarry. The position regarding unequal guardianship continued to improve. In 1886, a new law granted mothers guardianship, or at least joint guardianship, of any child whose father had died – meaning that a woman's in-laws no longer had the right to exclude her from her child's life, as Mary Shelley's father-in-law had threatened to.

The Co-operative Women's Guild was launched in 1883, at a congress in Edinburgh (initially under a different name), as a wing of the wider cooperative movement. From 1889, when Margaret Llewellyn Davies became president, it took up more strongly feminist positions, including support for women's suffrage. While its activities included highly localized mutual aid, such as maternity bags for new mothers, it also investigated the conditions of women's work. Women in the northern textile areas had been established in the workforce for decades. But elsewhere employment options were extremely limited. Efforts to promote apprenticeships and other forms of training continued alongside the promotion of women's emigration – another example of a feminist project that was also an imperialist one.

Throughout the nineteenth century, a series of Factory Acts had imposed limits on the employment of children, and from 1844, starting with a twelve-hour day, these began to be extended to women. The argument in favour of such protective legislation, as it was known, was that women like children were easily exploited, lacking trade unions, and that the risks associated with pregnancy and maternity meant they required safeguards. But feminists including Josephine Butler regarded such laws as protectionist rather than protective, and aimed at ensuring men's preferential access to jobs. As with prostitution, a regulatory framework devised by men ran contrary to women's interests. Women's vulnerability in the workplace was undeniable, however, and 1874 saw the launch of a Women's Protective and Provident League which aimed to address this. Emma Paterson, its secretary, was another sceptic about protective legislation, who believed unions and not sex-specific laws were the solution to women workers' problems. The new organization won the support of Harriet Martineau, among others, and Paterson became one of the first-ever female delegates to the Trades Union Congress, though her early death cut her career short.

The League became the Women's Trade Union League, and this was soon joined by a Women's Industrial Council. Both took the role of promoters and recruiters for the unions that women were joining in increasing numbers, and also conducted research on working conditions with a view to influencing policy makers. Since many existing unions were designed to exclude female workers, who were generally lower paid with fewer skills, this process caused friction in the labour movement. But by the 1890s the number of female trade unionists had risen to around 118,000 – which, while a significant number, was still less than 8 per cent of total union

9 The Match Girls' Strike Committee with Annie Besant (centre), 1888

membership.[13] The cause célèbre of this early phase of women's labour activism was the Match Girls' Strike. Annie Besant, a middle-class activist, wrote an article titled 'White Slavery in London' about the dismal conditions of the young workers at Bryant and May's factory in Bow, East London. Around 1,400 women workers were involved in the walkout, which began in July 1888 in protest against low pay, harsh management and dangerous working conditions that saw them exposed to cancer-causing yellow phosphorus (the disease it caused was known as 'phossy jaw'). Three weeks after the stoppage, their employer granted some of their demands – the first time unskilled workers in the capital had won such concessions by striking.[14]

Battles over protective legislation continued. Women had been banned from working down mines in 1842 but continued to work around pitheads, loading and sorting coal. In 1886–7, the pit brow lasses, as they were known, successfully resisted an attempt to outlaw this. The 1890s saw the first of several attempts to ban or restrict women from working in bars, while the 1891 Factory Act forbade employers from letting women work for four weeks after giving birth. Efforts to extend access to education, and raise its quality, were also ongoing. In 1873, the college that had absorbed so much of the energy of Barbara Bodichon and Emily Davies finally moved from its temporary base in Hitchin to Girton, just outside Cambridge. But neither Girton and Newnham, nor Somerville and Lady Margaret Hall in Oxford – which opened in 1879 – initially awarded degrees. The first women to obtain degrees in England did so in Liverpool and London in 1888.

Campaigns around dress reform, and the popularity of bicycles in the 1880s, contributed to a more general loosening of ties. In the case of middle-class women's fashions, these ties were literal and advances included the casting off of underwear that restricted breathing. Progressive educationalists including the housing reformer Octavia Hill, who ran a school with her sisters, encouraged girls to spend more time outdoors, and from 1891 women were allowed to train as gardeners at Swanley College in Kent. While much of the social and poverty alleviation work carried out by middle-class women continued to be voluntary, rather than professional, the range of paid work done by them also grew.

Sexuality and sisterhood

Josephine Butler saw prostitution as primarily an economic issue. When women have no means of support and nothing else to sell, they will sell themselves. But her motivation was spiritual as well as humanitarian. She drew on the example of Christ as her authority for believing in 'the equality of all men and women'. A Christian commitment to alleviate suffering, and promote the development of the individual conscience, lay at the core of her ethic of care. Butler described herself as 'possessed with an irresistible desire to go forth and find some pain keener than my own – to meet with people more unhappy than myself . . . and to say (as I now knew I could) to afflicted people, "I understand. I, too, have suffered".'[15] Her biographer, Jane Jordan, has argued persuasively that private grief for her lost daughter lay at the heart of her female-centred philanthropy.

But the late nineteenth-century campaign against male sexual entitlement, and the state's role in upholding it, was not reducible to one woman's personality. The leadership of the LNA was dominated by women in their forties, and the movement encompassed a more general impulse towards what we would now call safeguarding. Until 1969, the age of majority was twenty-one, so in the nineteenth century (and for most of the twentieth) older teenagers did not have the same rights as adults. Before 1885, the age of consent was just thirteen. Research on prostitutes from this period shows that many were aged 18 and 19, with orphans over-represented in the records.[16] While coercive and puritanical attitudes to sex among the poor were present in the repeal movement, the women (and men) who were its activists can also be viewed as early advocates for girls' rights and child protection.

'We are human first; women secondarily,' was Butler's conviction. But while she was determined to advance women's equal claim to humanity, she was not an equalitarian minimizer of sex differences. On the contrary, she celebrated them, arguing in a book of essays, *Women's Work and Women's Culture* (1869), for an extension of 'home influence' (by which she meant women's) into wider society.[17] This belief in women's distinct, moral character was one of the arguments used in favour of women's suffrage – although other feminists opposed it. But the view that male sexual culture was unethical, and in need of reformation, was widely shared. As well as targeting the worst excesses of the present, campaigners against the Contagious Diseases Acts advocated an alternative code of behaviour under which men would embrace chastity before marriage and self-restraint afterwards.

Euphemism had not been done away with. When the Acts were suspended in 1883, the *Women's Suffrage Journal* chose to refer obliquely to 'this painful subject' rather than tell readers what had actually happened.[18] But after the repeal campaign it became far harder for women to be corralled into rival encampments of saints and sinners – with the former obliged by the rigid codes of female behaviour to feign ignorance of the latter's existence. Feminists, including Frances Power Cobbe, also began drawing attention to domestic violence (which then as now often had a sexual aspect). In parts of Europe, Englishmen had a reputation as wife-beaters, and the connection of violence with drunkenness was one of the themes of the temperance movement.[19] Cobbe complained about what she called the 'halo of jocosity' surrounding the abuse of wives,[20] and recounted the shocking case of a woman who had appeared in court without a nose, 'and told the magistrate she had bitten it off herself'.[21]

In another piece, for the *Women's Suffrage Journal*, she described the horrific murder and mutilation of a woman by a former lover, who chopped her body into sixteen pieces, and asked: 'Why are these particularly revolting murders always committed against women?' Cobbe was also among the first to highlight the double standard whereby women are judged more harshly for violence against spouses. When a woman named Isobel Grant was sentenced to death for killing her husband in a drunken fight, in the same week that a man who had murdered his wife was sentenced to one week in prison, she ran a campaign to highlight the discrepancy.[22]

The dominant view among repealers was that male and female sexual interests were in conflict, and girls and women needed protecting from dangerous male appetites (this included the risks to wives from repeated, undesired pregnancies, as well as harm to prostitutes and unmarried victims of seduction). But from the 1880s, a different kind of critique of Victorian social mores began to emerge in counterpoint to the social purity movement. As discussed in the previous chapter, the Langham Place circle included female couples and romantic attachments, though the possibility of erotic ties between women was barely acknowledged. But in the late nineteenth century, alternative family structures, increased sexual freedom and pleasure began once again to be spoken about (although same-sex love remained taboo). While such ideas were not new, evolutionary theory was a fresh ingredient in a debate about sexuality and progress which also encompassed the first, tentative advocacy of 'preventive checks' (birth control) and sex education.

Annie Besant, who had supported the Match Girls' Strike, was one participant in these discussions. She was prosecuted in 1877 for her role in distributing a birth-control tract, and lost custody of her daughter as a result. The Scottish feminist Jane Hume Clapperton was another. She proposed that a 'modern moral code' – of which she produced versions from the mid-1880s – should replace Christian sexual ethics, and saw family planning as a way to end poverty. Clapperton was a member of Edinburgh's suffrage society, but her libertarian attitude to sexuality set her apart from most female peers. While she never married, and was probably celibate, Clapperton saw libido as 'a legitimate human instinct, comparable to eating and drinking'.[23] Her novel *Margaret Dunmore* (1888) proposed communal living as preferable to patriarchal family life, and its final section described a birth-control conference. A novel by another Scot, Lady Florence Dixie, told the story of a girl who, disguised as a boy, went to Eton and Oxford before becoming prime minister.

Clapperton cited the free union entered into by Mary Wollstonecraft as an inspiration, and had friends in common with Marian Evans. By contrast, the majority view among feminists was that birth-control devices served male sexual interests, while the weakening of marriage bonds could encourage desertion. 'What would become of wives over 40 . . . if they could be thrown to one side like broken toys?' asked a *Daily Telegraph* letter-writer in 1888.[24] When a handful of women were invited to join a new, mixed-sex discussion group where relationships would be analysed, they were so alarmed by the proposed name of the Wollstonecraft Club that they vetoed it. Instead, the group was called the Men and Women's Club, and in the late 1880s it became the forum for some vigorous exchanges. Karl Pearson, the statistician and eugenicist, was the dominant figure, and the historian Lucy Bland has shown how feminist members, even well-known 'New Woman' writers such as Olive Schreiner, were frustrated by its masculinist agenda. But the fact that such a group existed at all shows how sexual culture was changing.

As mentioned above, prosecutions linked to prostitution rose after the Contagious Diseases Acts were repealed. Anxieties about unlicensed sex and venereal disease, as well as alcoholism, became associated with fears of national decline. The brutal Ripper murders of five women in East London in 1888 fuelled a sense that women were under threat in a vice-ridden urban landscape. For all her compassionate eloquence, Butler was also capable of describing the inhabitants of workhouses as 'human weeds'.[25] Prejudice against the poor was lent a pseudo-scientific justification by social Darwinism.

In the early twentieth century, eugenics would be widely endorsed by liberals and socialists convinced that selective reproduction could have progressive advantages. But already in the 1880s, feminist and reactionary currents were intertwined. A homophobic amendment added in a late-night sitting to the 1885 Criminal Law Amendment Act outlawed 'gross indecency' between men, and this became the law under which gay men, including Alan Turing, would suffer cruel punishments. This was not a measure sought by feminists, whose primary interest in the bill was the lowering of the age of consent, and they can hardly be blamed for the actions of an all-male parliament. But it is notable that child protection and the persecution of gay men were from this point linked in law, and this shows how efforts to prevent abuse and cruelty could become mixed up with repression and bigotry.

Elements of the racist discourse that gained ground towards the end of the century – as European powers engaged in a murderous 'scramble for Africa' – also echoed the rhetoric of the repeal and vigilance movements. The use of the word 'slavery' to describe the condition of women, and particularly the poorest women, has a long history and should not be dismissed out of hand. In the nineteenth century, some wives were put up for sale, husbands were legally entitled to demand sex, and 'slavey' was a widely used term for the most menial, downtrodden servants. The phrase 'white slave trade' was originally used to differentiate European sex trafficking from the black slave trade (which was formally abolished in the British Empire in 1807, though brutally coercive labour practices continued). But given that the Atlantic slave trade had featured sex trafficking on a vastly larger scale, with millions of black women and girls sold into sexual and reproductive exploitation, the emphasis placed by Victorian and Edwardian campaigners on 'white slavery' was a distortion of reality and a perverse form of appropriation. The racist erasure of black women's suffering, combined with the fixation on the victimization of the white, female body, would become a persistent feature of white supremacist ideology.

The campaigners against the Contagious Diseases Act did not share an identical outlook. Even among Butler's own circle there were divergences that defy easy pigeonholing. Some contemporaries were critical of her separatism, while she once criticized Emily Davies as being among the 'masculine aiming women'.[26] Elizabeth Wolstoneholme Elmy advocated free unions, while Ellice Hopkins, the evangelical social purity leader, saw marital sexuality as a means of approaching divinity.[27] While many of its leading figures were religious, the movement's character was not sectarian. Anglicans and non-conformists worked together, and in 1885 a Jewish Association for the Protection of Girls and Women was formed. Where beliefs and aims varied, activists united around the conviction that compulsory genital inspections must end. The way that the LNA seized the initiative, on this issue, was unprecedented. So were Josephine Butler's style of leadership and the campaign's use of propaganda, direct action and the press. Underlying it was a powerful ethic of female solidarity. 'Courage, my darlings, you are women, and a woman is always a beautiful thing. You have been dragged deep in the mud, but still you are women,'[28] was how Butler expressed this. Her assertion of the need for bravery, her pride in womanhood, and the possibility of redemption through suffering would all find echoes in the suffrage battles that lay ahead.

4

Suffragists (1860s–1920s)

The struggle for the parliamentary franchise is the most dramatic episode in the history of the women's movement, and no history of feminism would be complete without it. The denial of women's right to vote was understood to be the greatest obstacle to their full participation in society and the clearest sign of their subordinate status. The suffrage movement was a significant extra-parliamentary force in British politics for several decades and, unlike some of the other campaigns covered in this book, it is widely celebrated. Its key characters, and above all the three powerful Pankhurst women – Emmeline and her daughters, Christabel and Sylvia – are historical celebrities. Many people are familiar with the main aspects of the story, which was turned into a BBC serial, *Shoulder to Shoulder*, in 1974 and more recently a feature film, *Suffragette* (2015), starring Meryl Streep.

The centenary in 2018 of the Representation of the People Act 1918, which granted the vote to around eight million women over thirty (roughly two-thirds of the adult female population), prompted a new upsurge of interest. Millicent Fawcett, who led the constitutionalist, non-militant branch of the movement, was honoured with a statue holding a banner bearing her famous slogan 'Courage calls to courage everywhere,' thanks to a campaign led by the feminist writer and activist Caroline Criado Perez. Books and exhibitions drew out previously neglected stories, such as that of Princess Sophia Duleep Singh, the daughter of an exiled Indian maharaja whose suffragette activities led to long-term surveillance by the police. A new statue of Emmeline Pankhurst (often known as Mrs Pankhurst) was erected in St Peter's Square, Manchester – making her one of a tiny handful of women to have more than one. Diane Atkinson's book *Rise Up, Women!*, published to mark the anniversary, includes an extraordinary amount of detail about almost two hundred militants, who ranged from nurses and small-business owners to actors, teachers and postal workers.[1]

Differences in interpretation between historians, echoed in the wider culture, have tended to focus on the question of militancy. The strategy of the Pankhurst-led Women's Social and Political Union, which involved causing extensive damage to property including arson and bombings, followed by hunger strikes once women were imprisoned, has long been a subject of fascination. But at the time and since, the suffragettes – as they were dubbed by the *Daily Mail* before adopting the label themselves – drew disapproval as well as admiration. I have called this chapter 'Suffragists' because it is a broad term that encompasses all those campaigned for votes for women. 'Suffragettes' refers only to militants.

Another theme of suffrage studies is the relationship between class and sexual politics. The early women's suffrage movement had close links with both the Liberals and the Independent Labour Party. Keir Hardie, who would become Labour's first leader, was a key early supporter, and working women's organizations, particularly in Lancashire, were important bases of support. But as successive attempts to promote legislation were thwarted, and the Women's Social and Political Union abandoned pressure-group politics in favour of direct action, militant suffragism increasingly conceived of itself as a force outside, and distinct from, political parties and the class interests they represented. Sylvia Pankhurst's refusal to abandon socialism in favour of a sex-based struggle was the reason for the painful rift with her mother and elder sister.

As discussed in earlier chapters, the movement can be traced back to Mary Wollstonecraft's anxious suggestion that 'women ought to have representatives' (in 1792), and to Anna Wheeler and William Thompson's rebuttal (in 1825) of James Mill's assertion that they ought not. On 3 August 1832, the radical MP for Preston, Henry Hunt, presented the first women's suffrage petition to the House of Commons on behalf of 'a lady of rank and fortune' from Yorkshire. This woman, known only as Mary, sought an extension of the franchise to unmarried, propertied women like herself in the year that the so-called Great Reform Act explicitly restricted the franchise to male persons for the first time.

In 1839, a Female Political Union in Ashton-under-Lyne, Lancashire, wrote an open letter to the women of Britain and Ireland, proposing that they should point out to their husbands and friends their hope of securing 'the elective franchise as well as our Kinsmen'.[2] Just over a decade later, the Quaker anti-slavery activist Anne Knight recruited a group of female Chartists to a Sheffield Female Political Association and persuaded the radical Earl of Carlisle, a government minister, to present another petition, this time to the House of Lords. But it was in the final third of the nineteenth century that the suffrage movement became the force that it would remain until its aims were met.

Growth and division: 1867–1903

Members of Parliament were reported to have rushed back from dinner in order to be present when the Liberal MP for

Westminster, John Stuart Mill, gave a speech in the first parliamentary debate on women's suffrage, in June 1867. Such was the expected entertainment value of the topic, led by a speaker once described as 'the man who wants to have girls in parliament.'[3] Leading suffragists had campaigned for Mill in the general election of 1865. Their petition of 1,521 signatures (described in chapter 2), from 'Barbara L. S. Bodichon and others', had been presented. Now, Mill proposed an amendment striking the word 'man' out of the franchise reform bill that was then before MPs, and replacing it with 'person' – so that women would be included. Like his dead wife Harriet Taylor Mill, John Stuart Mill believed that the domination of women by men was harmful to both, and a brake on social progress. Millicent Fawcett was upstairs in the Ladies' Gallery on this momentous occasion. From behind the screen through which women were permitted to observe, she judged Mill's speech a 'masterpiece'.[4]

But receptive as some listeners may have been, Mill's amendment was rejected. As had happened in 1832, the Second Reform Act of 1867 enlarged the franchise significantly – from around one million to around two million of a total adult male population of seven million – but did not give it to a single woman. Outside Parliament, suffragists responded by intensifying their efforts. A Manchester society already existed, with Lydia Becker (who had been inspired by Barbara Bodichon) among its founding members. Edinburgh, Birmingham and Bristol formed their own groups, while in London the petition committee renamed itself the London National Society for Women's Suffrage, but remained divided over whether to be mixed or single-sex. Helen Taylor (Mill's stepdaughter) was in favour of women only. Barbara Bodichon tried and failed to persuade her that 'we shall get it [the vote] ten years quicker' by including men.[5]

Manchester suffragists soon spied an opportunity for a stunt. A widow called Lily Maxwell, who ran a crockery shop, was accidentally included on the electoral register. In November 1867, Lydia Becker went with her to the polling station, where she cast her vote in a by-election while members of the public cheered. In the following months, thousands of women attempted to follow this example by claiming a legal right to vote. Richard Pankhurst, who would become Emmeline's husband, was the lawyer in a case that reached the High Court. He lost, but the campaign marked a significant broadening of tactics and a recognition that there were other targets than Parliament and other methods than petitions.

Millicent Fawcett gave her first public speech on women's suffrage in Brighton, where her husband was the MP, in July 1869. As previously outlined, the following decade was a decade of vigorous activism against the Contagious Diseases Acts. While many women supported both causes, the combination caused unease among some suffragists,[6] and Millicent was among those who kept her distance from the repealers – though she would go on to write a book about Josephine Butler in later life. But women including Rhoda Garrett, who was her cousin and the first woman to run an interior design business, were active in both movements, and suffragism was understood as part of a broader programme for women's advancement.

'Vote for the man who favours justice to women, be his political creed, in other respects, what it may,' was the direction offered by the launch issue of the *Women's Suffrage Journal* in 1870.[7] In time this ethos of feminist non-partisanship would be taken up by both militant and non-militant activists. But in the 1870s and 1880s it was not the mainstream position. In the stronghold of Manchester, the initial hope was that pro-democracy Liberals, also known as Radicals, would take up the women's cause. William Gladstone, who served four separate terms as prime minister, was against votes for women, but his party was also that of John Stuart Mill, Millicent Fawcett's husband Henry and other sympathizers. But hopes were dashed in 1884 when the franchise was again extended, this time to encompass around 60 per cent of men – but still no women. The Pankhursts were among those who turned away from the party and towards the labour movement.

Keir Hardie, the Scottish trade unionist and politician, was a strong supporter and the Pankhursts' close friend (he would later become their daughter Sylvia's lover). When the Independent Labour Party – predecessor of the modern Labour Party – was formed in 1893, Emmeline and Richard were closely involved. Richard had already stood twice, unsuccessfully, for Parliament. But the Pankhursts' hope that the pro-democracy workers' rights movement would provide a natural home for women's suffrage activists faded as tensions between class and sexual politics emerged. The suffragist demand for women's equality was widely understood to mean that propertied women would gain the vote first – since these were the terms on which men qualified. But this did not have the unanimous backing of working-class women, let alone men. Like their Chartist predecessors, some socialist and trade unionist women thought that the exclusion of their class from the franchise was the more urgent problem than the exclusion of their sex. They recognized that the enfranchisement of women on property-based terms could further entrench power in the hands of the wealthy at the expense of the poor. Indeed, this was the explicit aim of some Liberal women, who rejected full adult suffrage not on the pragmatic grounds that it was unachievable and would need to be won in stages, but because they did not believe in it.

As discussed in the previous chapter, the last decades of the nineteenth century saw an upsurge in trade union activity involving women, including strikes by the London match girls but also cigar makers in Nottingham and jute workers in Dundee. One female trade unionist described Manchester workers as worn down by 'the crushing and numbing force of the bare struggle for life',[8] and women's lack of political rights was recognized as a problem. But the question of the order in which the men and women excluded from the franchise should be added was a vexed one. Margaret Bondfield, who would go on to become the first Labour woman in the cabinet, opposed what she called 'ultra-feminist suffragists' for arguing 'the specific woman point of view'. While she was clear that class took priority,[9] other left-wing women found themselves torn between a male-led labour movement and a female-led women's one. In 1893, a committee aimed at broadening the suffrage movement's base of support referred to the rights of women 'in the factory and workshop',[10] and more meetings started to be held in public places rather than middle-class drawing rooms.

But the labour movement also included opponents of women's suffrage. The Victorian ideology of separate spheres – and the principle of women's confinement to domestic tasks and settings – was never limited to the middle classes. The trade unionist Henry Broadhurst was cheered when he defined the aim of the labour movement as being 'to bring about a condition of things, where wives could be in their proper sphere at home, instead of being dragged into competition for livelihood against the great and strong men of the world'.[11] Bruce Glasier, the chairman of the Independent Labour Party, once recorded in his diary that in a meeting with Emmeline and Christabel Pankhurst he lost his temper, and accused them of 'miserable individualistic sexism'.[12] Others were less explicit about objections that did not sit easily with their pro-democracy, anti-elite commitments. But what one socialist woman described as a 'a curious half-defined antipathy' to feminism was widely noted.[13]

Unmarried female rate-payers were widely seen as having the strongest claim to the vote. They did not face the barrier of the 'coverture' doctrine, whereby a wife's legal existence was subsumed into that of her husband, and they had already gained the local franchise. But, as time went on, some of the married women who were simultaneously campaigning for wives' property rights became dissatisfied with the prospect of a suffrage bill that would exclude them. Elizabeth Wolstoneholme Elmy, one of Josephine Butler's close allies, scathingly referred to any measure enfranchising single women only as a 'spinster and widow bill'. Along with Emmeline Pankhurst and Ursula Bright, she was among the founders of the first breakaway group from the main suffrage movement, which they called the Women's Franchise League, in 1889.

In 1897, seventeen suffrage societies from around the country, including Scotland and Wales, came together in a federation they called the National Union of Women's Suffrage Societies (the NUWSS or National Union). Millicent Fawcett chaired the first meeting, though she did not acquire the formal title of president for another ten years. The National Union's strategy was to demonstrate as much support as possible for the cause, and by doing so to persuade Parliament to act. From subscriptions and donations it raised the money to fund organizers' salaries, and a series of petitions from working women were collected. Selina Cooper and Ethel Derbyshire, both of whom had worked in cotton mills, helped set up the first working women's suffrage organization, the Lancashire and Cheshire Women Textile and Other Workers' Representation Committee. But decades on from the first women's suffrage petitions, and supported by only a handful of MPs, legislation remained a distant prospect.

Marchers and militants: 1903–1918

On 10 October 1903, Emmeline Pankhurst, now a widow, called the first meeting of a new organization, the Women's Social and Political Union (the Women's Union), in an attempt to inject new life into what she and her allies had decided was a moribund suffrage movement. Their demand was for 'complete equality with men, both social and political'.[14]

Initially conceived as a ginger group, or internal lobby, within Independent Labour, the Women's Union (WSPU) sought to move beyond the Liberal-supporting, pressure-group tactics of mainstream suffragism. While the National Union's committee included prominent men, the new organization would be for women only, though an exception was made for the husband of Emmeline Pethick-Lawrence, Frederick, mainly on the grounds that the couple were generous donors (he was not a member as such but was allowed to share his wife's duties as treasurer). Emmeline Pankhurst later recalled that this meeting was when the group decided that 'deeds, not words, was to be our permanent motto'.[15]

Initially, meetings and speaking engagements continued much as before, although now with the central aim of winning over Independent Labour. But after a bill that would have enfranchised a limited number of women was talked out by MPs in May 1905, Women's Union members decided to protest rather than retreat. This impromptu gathering in Westminster was described by Emmeline as 'the first militant act'.[16] A few months later, Christabel Pankhurst and Annie Kenney unfurled a 'Votes for Women' banner at a Liberal Party meeting at Manchester's Free Trade Hall, and challenged the politicians on the platform, including Winston Churchill (who was then a Liberal), about what the government planned to do. After Christabel spat at a police officer, both she and Kenney were arrested and charged. When they chose to go to prison rather than pay a fine, the women's challenge to the forces of law and order was begun.

The term 'suffragette' was coined by the *Daily Mail* in January 1906.[17] This was the month of a general election in which the Women's Union campaigned against the Liberals who had so enraged them. The movement's most hopeful result was in Wigan where a trade unionist, Thorley Smith, stood as a women's suffrage candidate and came second. But the Liberals were returned with a large majority. That summer, suffragettes went to the home of the chancellor, Herbert Asquith, and were arrested. Three, including Annie Kenney, went to prison. The following year, Emmeline quit Independent Labour, as did Christabel, and presided over the first 'Women's Parliament', a public gathering aimed at driving home the message that the Westminster Parliament was for men. After tearing up a draft constitution, Emmeline told the Women's Union's members that they belonged to an army, while their new newspaper, *Votes for Women*, instructed: 'Do not leave any of your womanliness behind when you come into this movement . . . If you have any class feeling, you must leave that behind.'[18] In 1908, the first windows were smashed, in Downing Street, and the tricolour colour scheme was launched – green for hope, white for purity, violet for dignity. (The National Union also had a colour scheme – green, white and red – though it never gained the currency of the suffragette colours. As Diane Atkinson has pointed out, colour photography would have transformed later impressions of the suffrage movement.)

In 1909, jailed suffragettes began going on hunger strike in protest against their treatment as criminals rather than political prisoners, and direct action grew more flamboyant. As well as attacks on property, there were numerous direct contacts with senior politicians. One group followed Asquith – who was now prime minister – on holiday to Devon, questioning him in church and festooning his garden with signs. A car was painted in suffragette colours and in 1910 a fire engine was driven along Oxford Street. On what became known as Black Friday, 18 November, demonstrators attempted to gain entry to the Houses of Parliament and were viciously assaulted by police, with many women complaining of having their breasts twisted and pinched, as well as being beaten and shoved.[19] Four days later, Christabel made what she called a declaration of war on the government, and around 200 women marched to Downing Street, smashing the windows of government departments on their way. Ethel Smyth's suffrage anthem, 'The March of the

Women', was premiered the following year and became the welcome chorus sung when prisoners were released.

The new energy brought by the militants was initially welcomed outside their ranks. Near the start of the campaign, in 1906, Mrs Fawcett wrote to the *Times* that the Pankhursts and their allies had 'done more during the last twelve months to bring it [women's suffrage] within the realm of practical politics than we have been able to accomplish in the same number of years'.[20] But violent direct action was soon causing disquiet. Actions such as spitting at police officers and vandalizing property, it was feared, could alienate public opinion, which constitutionalists hoped to bring over to their side with peaceful displays, such as the 1907 Mud March – which took its name from the rain-soaked ground on which the marchers' skirts dragged.

The increasingly autocratic leadership style of Mrs Pankhurst and her eldest daughter, Christabel, was also criticized. It was this that led to the first of several splits from within the Women's Union's ranks, when a group left to set up the Women's Freedom League in 1907. But while these and later divisions were important, members of different factions also worked together. Cicely Hamilton's propagandist play, *The Pageant of Great Women*, for example, toured Britain in 1910 with a range of backers. Smaller groups, including the Actresses' Franchise League and Women's Emancipation Union, coexisted with the main ones. There were supporters of women's suffrage in every political party, although fewer on the right than on the left. From 1903, it was the official policy of the mass-membership Co-operative Women's Guild. In the summer of 1911, a procession to mark the coronation of George V and Mary was conceived as a show of unity by the movement's militant and law-abiding wings.

But when the hopes invested in a 'conciliation bill', produced by a cross-party committee, were dashed, suffragettes stepped up their campaign of vandalism. On 21 November

1911, window-breakers moved beyond their original targets of government buildings and smashed the glass fronts of shops, post offices, a hotel and the *Daily Mail.* In 1912, windows were broken in Dublin and Scottish suffragettes travelled to London to join the protests. On what was described as a day of rage in March, hundreds of shopfronts and other buildings were damaged, as a result of which around 150 women were sent to prison. Mrs Pankhurst, who with two other women smashed the windows of 10 Downing Street, was charged with conspiracy and incitement to riot, alongside the Pethick-Lawrences. Christabel fled to Paris. 1912 was also the year that Labour finally adopted women's suffrage as a policy. This convinced the Fawcett-led National Union to abandon its earlier policy of political neutrality, and an Election Fighting Fund to support pro-suffrage candidates was set up. But for the Pankhursts, a pro-suffrage majority in Parliament had long ceased to be a viable strategy. The suffragettes were 'absolutely independent of all men's parties and movements', as Christabel put it.[21] Their one object was to force the government to act.

It is a pity that more films have not been made about suffragism. The final phase of the story is so dramatic that it hardly seems real. Disguises and aliases were commonplace, particularly after the 1913 Prisoners (Temporary Discharge for Ill-health) Act, popularly known as the Cat and Mouse Act, allowed for the release of prisoners who were malnourished, and re-arrest when they had recovered – if they could be found. Lilian Lenton, a dancer nicknamed 'the Elusive Pimpernel', dressed as a boy and was once whisked away from Dover in a yacht. But while some activists relished this cloak-and-dagger aspect, it did nothing to diminish the horror of force-feeding, which involved the use of metal gags and tubes, and left multiple women with lasting injuries. One suffragette was force-fed 232 times in three months and, while most strongly associated with Holloway, the practice spread as far as Perth, where prisoners were fed through their rectums.[22] In 1912, George Lansbury, the suffrage-supporting Labour MP who himself endured force-feeding, told Asquith: 'You will go down in history as the man who tortured innocent women.'[23]

In February 1913, four postmen were injured in Dundee when poisonous chemicals were placed in postboxes. Two months later, Emmeline Pankhurst was jailed for her part in a conspiracy to bomb a house belonging to the Liberal chancellor, David Lloyd George. On 6 June, the forty-year-old suffragette Emily Wilding Davison ran on to Epsom racecourse in front of a horse owned by the king, dying in hospital of her injuries a few days later – in a protest thought by historians to have been an individual initiative, as many militant actions were. Mrs Pankhurst was arrested, meaning she missed the funeral procession of 6,000 women and ten brass bands that accompanied Davison's coffin to a church in central London, from where it was taken by train to Northumberland.

A few days later, the constitutionalists launched one of their most ambitious demonstrations. The 'Great Pilgrimage' saw marchers drawn from the National Union's 300 branches set off from six locations in England and Wales, converging several weeks later at a 50,000-strong rally in Hyde Park. As well as a show of strength in numbers, and geography, the pilgrimage was an opportunity for members to disassociate themselves from the suffragettes' escalating destruction, which included arson and acid attacks, the slashing of paintings and vandalism of a tea house in Kew Gardens. Photographs reveal placards declaring the pilgrims to be 'law-abiding'. Disquiet about the militant strategy directed by Christabel, with her mother's backing, had by this time spread to the very top of the Women's Union. After pleading with Christabel and Emmeline for some modification, the Pethick-Lawrences were ejected in October 1912. Over the following months, Sylvia too grew restive and sought to distance herself from the elder Pankhursts' 'sex war' rhetoric.

The sexual double standard, and the harm caused by the combination of male sexual licence and the expectation of chastity and obedience in women, had long been recognized as a feminist issue. As discussed in the previous chapter, most feminists believed men should demonstrate restraint, and wives should be able to escape abuse, while a libertarian minority placed their hopes for a happier future in birth control and alternatives to marriage. From 1912, two suffragist newspapers, *Votes for Women* and *Vote*, carried court columns that criticized the lenient sentences handed to abusers. Edith Watson became a full-time legal correspondent for the Women's Freedom League, which also recruited volunteers to attend hearings. In one case, a magistrate was reported to have said of the abuse of a three-year-old girl that such crimes were 'just one of those things that the very best people in every class of life were apt, in an unguarded moment, to commit'.[24]

Along with equal pay and access to employment, prostitution was understood as being among the issues that a female electorate would force Parliament to address. But 1912 marked a change, as Christabel and Emmeline Pankhurst threw themselves into the social purity movement, and their separatist ethos took on a sharper, anti-male edge. Christabel wrote a series of articles which in 1913 were gathered in a pamphlet, *The Great Scourge and How to End It*, and adopted the slogan 'Votes for women and chastity for men', while Emmeline made public statements about the 'white slave traffic'.[25]

Whiteness had figured in suffragette iconography since the start of the militant campaign, when activists had been encouraged to wear white dresses, and the movement included some vocal imperialists. Frances Swiney, a suffragist in Cheltenham, was the author of a book arguing that British women were the most advanced in the world and describing Queen Victoria as the 'Great White Queen'.[26] A celebratory empire float was included in 1911's suffragist coronation procession. But in the years leading up to the First World War, the links between a purity-focused suffragette movement and a rising nationalist mood – with its embedded racial and class hierarchies – became more pronounced.

To socialist, internationalist Sylvia, this was anathema. Her position was closer to the Fawcett-led National Union, and its pact with Labour, than to her family. She was concerned too about the harsh treatment of militant young activists in prison, while Christabel made the most of her exile in Paris. Initially, Sylvia tried to stay within the Women's Union's orbit with the launch of a new, East End branch as a vehicle for the kind of locally based, mixed-sex organizing that she and her allies were committed to. But 1913 saw a series of arguments, including over her use of the word 'suffragette' in the name of the East London Federation of Suffragettes. The painfully public ending was a press statement of her expulsion in February 1914. The youngest Pankhurst sister, Adela, emigrated to Australia around the same time.

In a global empire like Britain's, domestic policy issues could never be entirely separated from foreign and imperial politics, and in the 1910s suffragists faced a series of tricky negotiations around the movement for Irish home rule (self-government within a United Kingdom of Britain and Ireland). In her radical youth, Emmeline Pankhurst had been a home-rule supporter, while Millicent Fawcett opposed it. But when Labour and Irish nationalist politicians chose to remain loyal to Asquith's Liberal government because they supported its pro-home-rule policy, despite its broken promises on women's suffrage, the two movements came into conflict. In 1912, George Lansbury resigned his seat rather than toe the Labour Party line, and fought and lost a by-election as a women's suffrage-supporting independent. When the leader of the Ulster Unionists, Sir Edward Carson, refused to commit to women's suffrage, suffragettes began an arson campaign in Northern Ireland.

Given that both militants and non-militants relied on fundraising, as well as the willingness of thousands of women to take action, it is clear that the positions taken by the leadership commanded support. But suffragists had a range of views on many issues. While it is beyond the scope of this book to examine the grassroots in detail, and for reasons of space and storytelling I have focused on the movement's leaders, this diversity is important to note. The trade unionist and suffragist organizer Ada Nield Chew, for example, was one of first to argue publicly for state-funded nurseries.[27]

After her initial praise for the militants' energy, Millicent Fawcett became critical both of their strategy and the confrontational politics underpinning it. 'As long as mothers have sons and fathers daughters there can never be a sex war,' she wrote in 1910. 'What draws men and women together is stronger than the brutality and tyranny which drives them apart.'[28] Separatism was both ideology and strategy for the militant suffrage movement, with the hostile, misandrist rhetoric that Fawcett disliked becoming more prominent over time. While some in the movement minimized sex differences – as equality-focused feminists always had done – others sought to emphasize what

10 Millicent Fawcett addresses a suffrage rally in Hyde Park, 1913

Teresa Billington-Greig (who left the Women's Union in 1907) called the militants' 'injured innocence'.[29] Coralie Board, who wrote for the suffragette press, proposed that sex or birth strikes should replace window-breaking and other vandalism as a tactic on grounds that the latter were 'men's methods' – and suffragists ought to develop their own.[30] Hunger strikes and force-feeding turned the figure of the female prisoner, at the mercy of a vicious male state, into an icon. Joan of Arc was adopted as a mascot and at Emily Wilding Davison's funeral a silk banner proclaimed her reputed last words: 'Fight on and God will give the victory.'

The outbreak of war heralded a new split and divided the movement across its militant and gradualist wings, as Irish home rule had done. Unlike class feeling, which had long been officially prohibited by suffragettes (though this mainly applied to working-class women, as women from the already enfranchised classes did not confront the same conflict), nationalist sentiment was celebrated by them. Militancy was suspended, and Emmeline Pankhurst forged a remarkable new alliance with the government, including her former nemesis, Lloyd George. With large numbers of women recruited to the war effort, including munitions factories, it was finally accepted by ministers that some women at least would have to be granted the franchise when hostilities ended, along with the men returning from the front who did not qualify under existing laws. Millicent Fawcett was also among the war's enthusiastic backers, and in 1915 the National Union split when a group of pacifists and anti-imperialists, including the future Labour MP, Ellen Wilkinson, left to join the Women's International League for Peace and Freedom.

But the argument in favour of a limited extension of the franchise was, by this time, almost won. With the support of both wartime Liberal prime ministers, Asquith and Lloyd George, a compromise was hammered out at a Speaker's Conference in 1916. When the House of Commons voted on it, on 19 June

1917, the bill granting the right to vote in general elections to some, but not all, women passed by 385 votes to 55.

Ten more years: 1918–1928

On the day the Representation of the People Act was passed by the House of Lords, 11 January 1918, the novelist Virginia Woolf recorded in her diary: 'Another sedentary day, which must however be entered for the sake of recording that the Lords have passed the Suffrage Bill. I don't feel much more important – perhaps slightly so. It's like a knighthood; might be useful to impress people one despises. But there are other aspects of it naturally.'[31] The sense of anti-climax described by Woolf, who had once volunteered in a suffrage office, was perhaps inevitable after four years of war. The suffragette Jessie Kenney recalled that she and Christabel Pankhurst heard the news of the bill's passage while 'huddled in our coats over a tiny fire'.[32] Exhausted by war work, they had long given up on the victory procession they once dreamed of. Others, including Sylvia Pankhurst, were actively dismayed. Inspired by events in Russia, she thought propertied women had been co-opted by the state as a bulwark against revolution.[33]

This is where many stories of the suffrage movement stop. By contrast with the fireworks of militancy, the women's movement of the 1920s gained the reputation of what one historian described as an 'exhausted volcano'.[34] If a sense of anti-climax is one reason for this lack of interest in what came next, another is disappointment. The general election held in December 1918 delivered a bitter blow to suffragists, several of whom stood as parliamentary candidates. As so often, the movement had divided over tactics. At a conference convened by the Labour-aligned Standing Joint Committee of Industrial Women's Organisations (the Standing Joint Committee), Millicent Fawcett agreed with the majority that 'the line of sex division' should be rejected in favour of mixed-sex politics. But delegates from the Women's Union, which was in the process of turning itself into a Women's Party, disagreed. While their organization was 'in no way based on sex antagonism', they said, women needed a party of their own.[35] Christabel became its sole candidate, and lost to Labour by just 775 votes at Smethwick in the West Midlands. While the Women's Party slogan was the staid 'Victory, National Security and Progress', its radical manifesto included proposals for equal pay and parental rights, cooperative housing and means-tested childcare. Other defeated female candidates included the trade unionist Mary Macarthur, who stood for Labour and came third in Stourbridge, suffragettes Charlotte Despard (Labour) and Emmeline Pethick-Lawrence (Labour), and the suffragist Ray Strachey (Independent). It seems unlikely that these women were helped by the slogan adopted by Labour in its campaign, 'No sex in politics'.[36] Also in 1918, the Women's Labour League, which had campaigned for women's suffrage, dissolved itself and formed the women's section of the Labour Party.

Constance Markievicz, the only woman elected, had been active as a suffragist in Ireland and England, and was sentenced to death for her part in the Easter Rising. Released during the war, she refused to take her seat (as Sinn Fein policy decreed), and feminists had to wait another year to see a woman in Westminster. What difference it might have made to British politics if Christabel Pankhurst or another suffragist had been elected in 1918 is an intriguing question. Instead, the first woman to enter the House of Commons was the Conservative MP for Plymouth, Nancy Astor, following a by-election called when her husband, the sitting MP, inherited a peerage. Eton- and Oxford-educated Waldorf Astor was the heir to a fortune built on Manhattan property, and Nancy, his American-born wife, understood very well that she was not the woman feminists would have chosen to carry the suffrage torch into Parliament.

11 Nancy Astor on the campaign trail in Plymouth, 1919

But complicated as Nancy was in her attitude to many things, there was nothing half-hearted about her embrace of politics. The costume she adopted, of a black suit, white shirt and black hat, became iconic. The author and MP Harold Nicolson wrote that 'from the very day of her introduction, [Nancy] taught her contemporaries that the expansion of woman's liberty could be achieved, not by mute acquiescence, but by voluble pugnacity.'[37] Having lost two brothers to alcoholism, she gave a maiden speech on controlling the sale of drink, and her Private Member's bill outlawing the sale of alcohol to children remains on the statute book. She also played a crucial role in the second legislative stage of women's enfranchisement.

Having turned itself into a political party, the Women's Union no longer existed. But with around five million women still excluded from the franchise, suffragists had a substantial hurdle to clear, and after the election questions of strategy continued to be debated. The National Union was split over whether to concentrate on votes for women or adopt a broader programme. It resolved to do both, and in 1919 Eleanor Rathbone replaced Millicent Fawcett as president and a new name was adopted: the National Union of Societies for Equal Citizenship (which I will keep calling the National Union). Local societies underwent their own reorganizations. The London Society for Women's Suffrage, for example, reconstituted itself as the London Society for Women's Service with a focus on 'economic equality'. Its president was Philippa Fawcett, a mathematician and Millicent and Henry Fawcett's only child. (In 1953, another name change would turn it into the Fawcett Society, which still exists.) In 1920, the suffragist newspaper *Common Cause* was relaunched as the *Woman's Leader*, and was soon joined by a new feminist weekly, *Time and Tide*.

The arrival of female MPs, starting with Astor, who was soon joined by a Liberal, Margaret Wintringham, meant that suffragists no longer had to rely on male allies to do their parliamentary work. At least one franchise bill was presented every year between 1919 and 1927, while debate over what the *Daily Mail* nicknamed 'the flapper vote' (because women in their twenties were the key demographic still without it) raged in the press. One of the arguments used against franchise equality before 1918 had been that if all women were able to vote, the existing sex imbalance in the electorate would tip the other way because so many men had been killed in the war. But as time went on, the pressure increased, and Labour included a franchise bill in its 1923 manifesto. The first three female Labour MPs were elected that year, and Dorothy Jewson used her maiden speech to second a Private Member's bill that would have granted the vote to women on the same terms as men. It was lost when that government fell.

Stanley Baldwin, the Conservative prime minister from 1924, was personally supportive, and Nancy Astor helped ensure that a public pledge by his home secretary, William

Joynson-Hicks, that there would be an equal franchise before the next election, was not forgotten. But the Tories were divided. In particular, they feared the electoral consequences of granting the vote to miners' wives. 'My own view is that in the industrial districts Labour will score heavily . . . In our pit villages the women are far wilder than the men – and they are hopeless to argue with,' recorded Cuthbert Headlam, the Conservative MP for Barnard Castle, in his diary. Winston Churchill was vehemently opposed, as was the *Daily Mail*, and in 1926 the National Union described the lack of progress as 'depressing'.[38]

In 1925–8, as part of a renewed push, some of the techniques of the earlier suffrage movement were brought back. Letter writing was stepped up and politicians bombarded with questions. Lady Rhondda (Margaret Mackworth), a wealthy former suffragette and hunger striker who had inherited her father's title and business interests in Wales, briefly tried to orchestrate a comeback for Mrs Pankhurst, who was now the proprietor of a French tea shop. But the scheme came to nothing. Instead, feminists were active alongside trade unionists amid a much wider radical mood, which reached its peak in the general strike of May 1926.

The Labour Party's male leadership was still capable of being obstructive. It sabotaged a link between the National Union and the trade unionist Standing Joint Committee by blocking the latter's involvement in suffrage rallies. But in April 1927, Baldwin told MPs that a bill enfranchising everyone over twenty-one was on its way (there had been discussions about a voting age of twenty-five, meaning that some younger men would have seen their votes taken away). When it was debated, Nancy Astor referred back to the time when she was the lone female MP and colleagues 'thought that I was rather a freak'.[39] She also drew attention to the recent increase in legislation dealing with women and children, which she saw as proof of the beneficial effects of women's presence. Emmeline

12 A corner in the Ladies' Gallery, House of Commons, by Harry Furniss, 1888. Parliamentary Archives, HC/LB/1/112/248

Pankhurst watched from the Ladies' Gallery, but hoped soon to join Nancy in Parliament. She had returned to London and was preparing to stand as a Conservative in the next election. But in the spring of 1928, her health suddenly declined, and by the time the Equal Franchise Act received royal assent on 2 July, she was dead.

Since female citizens of the Irish Free State had been granted the vote on the same terms as men in 1922, this act – unlike the 1918 one – did not apply there. In an unsigned article, the feminist weekly *Time and Tide* paid tribute to the militant campaign Mrs Pankhurst had led:

> It is very easy for the descendants of those who twenty years ago had not the courage to allow themselves to be thought violent and outrageous, or the insight to realise that the time had come when that sacrifice was demanded of them, to suggest today that it was they, who through thick and thin remained sweetly reasonable, who *really* won the vote . . . But the vote was not won by sweet reasonableness, it was won by self-sacrifice and courage, and – above all – by that most difficult of all forms of courage, the courage to appear violent, unreasonable, ugly.[40]

Others saw things differently. Ray Strachey argued in *The Cause* (1928) that the law-breakers were only ever backed by a minority. Eleanor Rathbone went further, arguing that the militants 'came within an inch of wrecking the suffrage movement, perhaps for a generation'.[41] Conflicting interpretations of the movement, in other words, were firmly in place by the time that equal suffrage was won, on terms set by those who had adopted contrary strategies in the first place.

Sisterhood and separatism

The demand for the vote might appear straightforward. But, from the beginning, women offered different answers to the question of whether they should be enfranchised because they were the same as men, or because they were not. The argument made by Mary Wollstonecraft, and often reiterated, was that sex differences had been so grotesquely exaggerated by a male-led culture that women's true nature and capacities could barely be discerned. In the nineteenth century, Liberals including Harriet Taylor Mill sought to demonstrate that the exclusion of women from public life harmed not only them but society as a whole.

John Stuart Mill agreed, explaining in 1861 that he took 'no account of difference of sex' in making the case for women's suffrage, considering it 'irrelevant'. Only, and in a pattern that recurs in later feminist arguments, this was not entirely the case. After dismissing sex, he went on to contradict himself with the assertion that 'if there be any difference women require it [good government] more than men, since being physically weaker, they are more dependent on law and society for protection.'[42] In his landmark 1867 speech in Parliament, Mill referred again to this asymmetry and the violent abuse by husbands of wives. At moments, he clearly regarded men's capacity to dominate their households by force, due to their size and strength, as an argument in favour of women's rights.

These tensions were present throughout the campaign for votes for women. Suffragism drew on arguments about civil rights, derived from constitutional law, and the universal, natural rights declared by Enlightenment thinkers. It made the case for women's enfranchisement with reference to the common good, principles of equality and democracy, and the welfare of children. It also articulated ways in which women's political interests were shaped by nature, including their role in reproduction. More than any campaign before it, the suffrage movement became the crucible for the development of sex consciousness, as a form of political consciousness, and a vehicle for women's entry into political organizations and activities focused on their rights.

Many people have seen a huge amount to admire in the physical courage of the suffragettes, their defiance of unjust law and heroic invasions of public space. Martyrs such as Emily Wilding Davison exert a particular fascination. But Susan Pedersen, the historian, believes there is also a troubling aspect to suffragette iconography, with its insistent emphasis on brutalized female bodies.[43] In a world where violence against women is so prevalent, I think she is right that we should be cautious about endorsing this kind of political spectacle, even in retrospect. Other historians have criticized various aspects of suffrage politics, particularly the jingoism of the war years. The rightward political trajectories of Christabel and Emmeline Pankhurst mean they are often contrasted, unfavourably, with socialist internationalists including Sylvia and Ellen Wilkinson. Mary Richardson, who in 1914 attacked Velázquez's painting, *The Toilet of Venus* (known as the *Rokeby Venus*), with a meat cleaver in the National Gallery, went on to hold a senior role in the British Union of Fascists.

The class composition of the movement is also controversial and, as reliable membership data do not exist, will continue to be so. Writers including Diane Atkinson and Helen Lewis have challenged the stereotype of the upper-middle-class suffragette. June Purvis has pointed out that Emmeline Pankhurst remained committed to 'equal industrial justice and equal

13 Leading figures in the WSPU (left to right): Flora Drummond, Christabel Pankhurst, Annie Kenney, unknown, Emmeline Pankhurst, Charlotte Despard, *c.*1906–7

social justice' after rejecting left-wing parties and politics.[44] Meanwhile, the movement's leading liberal, Millicent Fawcett, was also a vigilance campaigner, a Unionist and an imperialist. The suffrage movement defied easy categorization on a right–left or conservative–liberal–radical spectrum at the time, and still does. Not least because the greatest willingness for confrontation with the state came from the movement's separatist authoritarians – not its democratic socialists. It is another salutary fact, for those seeking to celebrate women's suffrage as part of a more general march of progress, that the textile industry that incubated working-class women's political organization was in the process of ruining manufacturing in India with its exports.

5

Legislators (1920s–1930s)

By the tenth anniversary of the first suffrage act, twelve women had been elected to Parliament – although not all were still there. Constance Markievicz's Dublin constituency was abolished in 1922, when the Irish Free State gained its independence. Three more Conservatives were elected in the 1920s. They were the former musical comedy actor Mabel Philipson, the Anglo-Irish aristocrat Gwendolen Guinness, Countess of Iveagh and MP for Southend, and the Scottish anti-suffragist Katharine Stewart-Murray, Duchess of Atholl, who became the first female Tory minister. All these women, apart from Markievicz, took over seats formerly held by their husbands.

The first three Labour women, elected in 1923, were Margaret Bondfield, Dorothy Jewson and Susan Lawrence. Jewson lost her seat a year later, but Bondfield and Lawrence appear in a photographic portrait made in 1929 of the nine Labour women who were victors in that year's general election. Arranged on steps, they are mostly smiling, wearing a lot of black (except Ellen Wilkinson) and matching Mary Jane shoes. While several had long careers in labour organizing behind them, the Scottish miner's daughter Jennie Lee was just twenty-four (and thus unable to vote herself) when first elected. Lee would go on to become a doyenne of Labour politics as Aneurin 'Nye' Bevan's wife and a minister under Harold Wilson. In this photograph, she looks diffident and amused at one end of the front row, where she is placed despite being among the tallest.

Nancy Astor and Margaret Bondfield had one thing in common, besides being pioneering politicians: they each had ten siblings. But otherwise, a gulf in incomes and experience divided these women. The astronomically rich Astors owned a palace, Cliveden, that featured a room transported from a French chateau and a balustrade from the Villa Borghese in Rome.[1] Bondfield, by contrast, was the daughter of a Somerset lacemaker and had grown up in a cottage where the light came from candles and water from a well. After leaving school at fourteen, she was apprenticed to a Brighton dressmaker and moved on to shopwork in London. In the 1890s, she joined the Women's Industrial Council and then the Independent Labour Party, acting as a kind of undercover agent, moving around jobs in order to investigate shopgirls' working conditions.

Under the dashing pseudonym of 'Grace Dare' (Dare was her mother's maiden name) Bondfield penned articles for the union press on the bullying and unjust treatment these young women and teenagers were subjected to. At twenty-four, she gave her first speech and in 1898 became a full-time officer for the Shop Assistants Union. The following year, she was the sole female delegate to the TUC conference in Plymouth. Her friend and fellow trade unionist, Mary Macarthur, described being bowled over by Margaret's 'brilliant gifts and vital energy' at their first meeting.[2] But while her work as a trade unionist, travelling all over the country, made her a champion for working-class women, it did not draw her into the campaign for the vote. She opposed any property qualification for female voters, believing along with others, including Macarthur and Sylvia Pankhurst, that this would further entrench power and privilege in the hands of the wealthy.

It took three attempts for Bondfield to reach Parliament: she came second in what would become her Northampton seat twice before winning it in 1923. By then, she was well into middle-age: single, politically experienced, well known in the labour movement, with an energetic public-speaking style that involved emphatic hand gestures. Ramsay MacDonald, the prime minister at the head of a minority Labour government, gave her a job as a junior minister. When he became prime minister again in 1929, she advanced, aged 59, to become secretary of state for employment – Britain's first female cabinet minister and privy councillor. But her cabinet career was short-lived, and her reputation never recovered from her decision to support cuts to unemployment benefits, including removing married women's entitlement, in the panic that followed the 1929 financial crash. It is intriguing to wonder how differently she might have been remembered had Virginia Woolf accepted an invitation to write her biography.

An abyss lay between the life experiences of the men on the Labour and Conservative benches also. But what makes this early group of female MPs fascinating is their awareness of their pioneering status, and the duty it brought with it to represent women's interests from the dingy shared office by the river that they sometimes called 'the tomb'. They disagreed about a great many things, and some actively opposed feminist legislation. But with the Liberal Mrs Wintringham, as she was known, in the role of informal coordinator, there were issues on which they worked as a cross-party group – sometimes at the prompting of the female constituents and other women who sent them a vast quantity of letters. The rest of this chapter describes how the women's movement adjusted to their presence in Parliament and considers the feminist legislation of these years (apart from the 1928 suffrage act, which was dealt with in the previous chapter). It also discusses the role of pressure groups and a debate that developed between 'new' and 'old' feminists.

Unfinished business

From the early 1920s, there was broad agreement, in feminist circles, that while the campaign for equal suffrage must continue, their movement must raise its ambitions. The agenda of the relaunched National Union of Societies for Equal Citizenship (formerly the National Union of Women's Suffrage Societies), under Eleanor Rathbone's leadership, included equal pay, the right to enter the professions, guardianship rights for mothers and an end to the sexual double standard that mandated chastity for women but not men. None of these demands was new, but after the first suffrage act they were regarded as requiring more attention. A new feminist campaign group, launched by the Welsh former suffragette and industrialist Lady Rhondda and known as the Six Point Group, announced a parallel set of demands along with its intention to help more women get elected.

After the 1918 law allowing women to stand for parliament, the next legislative success was the Sex Disqualification (Removal) Act of 1919, which allowed women to enter the professions. This law was frowned on by some feminists because it was introduced with the aim of squashing a rival bill that would have given more women the vote. But while the unbarring of the law, medicine and civil service to women did nothing obvious for the majority of people, for middle-class girls and women who wanted to earn their livings it was hugely significant. Virginia Woolf looked back on 1919 as 'the sacred year' on account of the new opportunities it opened.[3]

The Act carried particular significance for one feminist. Lady Rhondda had inherited her father's title and property and wanted to take over his seat in the House of Lords. The Sex Disqualification Act stated that 'a person shall not be disqualified by sex or marriage from the exercise of any public function', and in a series of hearings she and her lawyers argued that such functions included the role of peer in the legislature. With the

14 Margaret Mackworth (born Haig Thomas), 2nd Viscountess Rhondda

backing of Viscount Astor, Nancy's husband, and a committee vote in her favour, she came closest to her prize in 1925. But she had a steadfast opponent: the Tory Earl of Birkenhead, who was also Lord Chancellor. On one occasion, explaining his opposition, he described women as 'conduit pipes' for the next generation due to their role in reproduction (Rhondda had no children).

Equal guardianship, granting mothers the same parental rights as fathers, had been the aim of feminists since Caroline Norton in the 1840s. Eleanor Rathbone described as a 'monstrous legal fiction' the law giving a husband 'sole control of his children',[4] and from the early 1920s this became an issue around which female MPs organized. As well as their objection, on principle, to a situation in which fathers could overrule mothers' wishes with regard to their children's lives, campaigners were familiar with notorious examples of painfully severed ties. When marriages failed, husbands were entitled to do with the children as they chose, which sometimes included breaking all contact. Nancy Astor was the first to try to change the law with a Private Member's bill, but it took two more failed attempts and a major lobbying effort before Labour was persuaded to adopt the measure, which passed in 1925.

The introduction of widows' pensions was another victory – and was argued for by Ellen Wilkinson in a maiden speech which also referred to votes for women. The lack of any public support for bereaved wives meant that they were frequently left in desperate straits. If they had young, dependent children and were unable to go out to work, they were forced to rely on the Poor Law and sometimes ended up in the workhouse. Feminists saw this as unjust, given that the state provided old-age pensions, unemployment and sickness benefits to support those who had no income for other reasons. After 1925, new benefits were offered to widows and orphaned children, and wives were enabled to seek financial support from husbands before separating – a measure designed to protect those who needed to leave homes where they had been abused.

While, initially, female MPs, the National Union and the Six Point Group did not have birth control on their agendas, this was another area in which campaigning stepped up. Marie Stopes was among the pioneers, and in her case support for birth control, although not abortion, was part of a broader campaign to improve women's sex lives. Her book *Married Love,* which drew extensively on her personal experiences and experiments, sold 400,000 copies between 1918, when it came out, and 1923. After the prolonged and painful separations caused by war, and millions of bereavements, there was a great deal of interest among the public in the linked ideas that marriage could be made more satisfying to both partners, and family size limited.

Stopes was an egotistical character whose snobbish attitudes and support for eugenics mean her legacy is frowned on as well as celebrated. But she was sincere in her commitment to the public understanding of sex, about which many people, especially young women, were astoundingly uninformed. For married women who could afford to pay doctors, this situation could be partially remedied with advice, at least for those bold enough to seek it. But working-class women had no such resource, and this was the gap that Stopes sought to fill with the London clinic she opened in 1921 with the backing of a former suffragette, Lady Constance Lytton. Three years later, Rose Witcop and Guy Aldred were prosecuted for publishing Margaret Sanger's pro-birth-control book *Family Limitation*. Their legal costs were paid by supporters, including the economist Maynard Keynes. Labour remained extremely cautious, partly for fear of alienating Catholic supporters. But in 1924 Dorothy Jewson was among the founders of the Workers' Birth Control Group, following a resolution at one of her party's women's conferences.

Children's health was another topic in which female MPs took an active interest, and the subject of the first-ever speech by a Labour woman in the House of Commons. A former Conservative who had been converted to socialism by the low pay of school cleaners, Susan Lawrence had been to prison as part of a campaign against unjust rates. She described school food as 'one of many things for which we felt women to be especially needed in the House'.[5] Other legislation championed by feminists during this period included the removal of a secrecy clause in incest cases, and of a defence enabling child sex abusers to escape punishment if they believed their victims to be older. The death penalty was removed from the statute in cases of infanticide where mothers were deemed to have not 'fully recovered from giving birth' (in other words, suffering what we would now call postnatal depression or psychosis).[6]

In 1925, Ellen Wilkinson argued vociferously against a new silk tax which Winston Churchill, who was then chancellor, had included in the budget. She and her party believed it unfairly penalized younger women, who lacked the vote and did not deserve to be deprived of silk stockings. In 1927, a Private Member's bill from a Tory woman, Mabel Philipson, led to the registration of nursing homes, which was part of a longer process whereby female-dominated nursing and care work became regulated. What was new in the 1920s was the way in which these issues were brought together, along with the continuing struggle for an equal parliamentary franchise, as the diverse components of a feminist platform.

Feminist economics

If one issue besides equal-franchise suffragism can be said to have dominated interwar British feminism, it was the campaign for family allowances. Eleanor Rathbone championed a range of causes over her lifetime – including women's suffrage and the rights of refugees. But the campaign for family allowances, which are the payments by the state to mothers now known in the United Kingdom as child benefit, was hugely significant in expanding the role of the state in women's lives. Rathbone's background was in philanthropy and local politics in Liverpool, where she was the first woman elected to the council. The daughter of one of the city's wealthiest families – a mercantile dynasty and importer of slave-grown American cotton – she was educated at Somerville College, Oxford, where she ran a women's group called Associated Prigs (or APs).[7] Her father was a Liberal MP with the charitable commitments shared by many rich nonconformists. His grandfather had been among the founders of the Liverpool Society for the Abolition of the Slave Trade. But it was in Liverpool during the First World War that Eleanor Rathbone, then in her forties, had the experience that transformed her politics. Placed in charge of dispensing the separation allowances paid to servicemen's wives, as compensation for lost income, she was shocked by the desperation she encountered, as women in filthy housing, lacking food and heat, engaged in a daily struggle to survive.

The endowment of motherhood, as family allowances were also known, was debated in Fabian circles, with a pamphlet published in 1908, and a Mother Allowance Scheme in south London among the Fabian Women's Group's first projects. The Swedish feminist Ellen Key was another pioneer of the idea that women should be paid by the state to raise children, and argued this case in her book *Love and Marriage* (1911). But such arguments were not part of the British feminist mainstream, and discussions that emphasized women's role as mothers too strongly were viewed by some as anti-feminist. When the writer Edith Nesbit, author of *The Railway Children* (1905), argued in a talk to the Fabian Women's Group that women were 'predominantly creatures of sex' whose strongest needs lay in family life, she aroused a storm of protest.[8]

Eleanor Rathbone saw no conflict between the need of the vast majority of housewives for increased economic independence, and the aspirations of educated, unmarried women such as herself. On the contrary, she saw it as her vocation to champion working-class women's entitlement to a greater share of the nation's resources. The wage system in the industrialized world, she thought, had been designed with insufficient regard for women and children, who were therefore 'disinherited' by the state. An initial attempt to get family allowances onto the agenda of the National Union in 1921 was blocked. So Eleanor began to gather data, comparing the situation of British (mainly English) workers and their families with those in France, Germany and Australia. Published in 1924, her book *The Disinherited Family* described how children in industrialized countries had gradually been removed from the labour force, starting in the north of England. Where in an agrarian and artisanal economy, women and children had once been engaged in productive activity alongside men, in many cities and towns (although less so in Lancashire) families were now reliant on the wages of a single breadwinner – the man of the house. Particularly when families were large, or when there were issues of illness or ongoing dependency, men struggled to earn sufficient wages to support them.[9]

The problem, as Rathbone saw it, was one of faulty distribution. While the wage system treated all workers on a given pay grade the same, the fact was that at certain stages of life, and depending on family size, some households needed more money than others. To raise wages across the board, on the model of the living wage demanded by trade unions, would entail remunerating workers for the upkeep of non-existent children. The unaffordability of this would in turn, she thought, make it harder for women to win equal pay. For this reason, she called the living wage a 'clumsy, mis-shapen' policy, and proposed allowances paid to mothers as an alternative. These allowances would either be spent on food and housekeeping or on childcare, enabling mothers to go out to work. The twinned aims of the policy were to end wives' dependence on husbands and to reward their labour in the home.

Rathbone was scornful of the way in which women's poverty had been neglected, and opened her book by asking 'whether there is any subject in the world of equal importance that has received so little and articulate consideration as the economic status of the family'. The entire discipline of economics was, in her view, guilty of behaving as if mothers did not exist. 'I do not think it would be an exaggeration to say that, if the population of Great Britain consisted entirely of self-propagating bachelors and spinsters, nearly the whole output of writers on economic theory during the past fifty years might remain as it was written, except for a paragraph or phrase here and there, and those unessential to the main argument,' she declared in one passage.[10]

Rathbone knew it would take time to persuade others. Conservatives predictably objected to such a radical expansion

15 Eleanor Rathbone, leader of the National Union of Societies of Equal Citizenship, addresses a crowd from a vehicle, 1922

of the state's obligations. So did Liberals, including some feminists. At a crucial 1925 meeting of the National Union council, Millicent Fawcett stated her opposition to family allowances on grounds that they were a 'step in the direction of practical socialism'. There was truth in this: Rathbone's analysis developed themes discussed by Friedrich Engels as well as Ellen Key and the South African socialist Olive Schreiner.[11] But trade unions were also suspicious of endowment policies, which they regarded as a means of suppressing wages – the needs of workers' families being one of their strongest bargaining chips in negotiations with employers. Experience elsewhere suggested that such fears were justified. In France, family allowances were pioneered in the textile industry and overseen by employer groups with church involvement. Keeping costs down to preserve competitiveness (and profits) was among this system's stated purposes. Rathbone's preferred option was for the state, not industry, to take charge of a British endowment system and fund it through taxation. But she understood that her advocacy on behalf of working-class women and children was a challenge to the labour movement, as well as to the image of men as benign providers. While unions and the Labour Party saw themselves as the authentic vehicles of working-class interests, she saw them as biased in favour of men.

Entering Parliament as an Independent MP in 1929 for the constituency known as the Combined English Universities (its electorate was made up of graduates of Durham, Liverpool, Manchester and five other universities), she faced attacks from both right and left. The Labour MP and former miner Rhys Davies was a bitter opponent, deeply angered by the view she offered of male workers lording their financial muscle over dependent wives. Rathbone was never a separatist in the mould of Christabel Pankhurst, and her anti-poverty work was aimed at raising the living standards of large families overall, not just wives. But Davies was correct in identifying a distrust – and perhaps also a fear – of male sexuality that ran through her politics.[12]

Eventually, and having taken their time to absorb Rathbone's arguments, key figures in both the Liberal and Labour Parties overcame their objections. Ellen Wilkinson was an important supporter – particularly since on some other issues, where feminists and Labour disagreed, she took her party's side. William Beveridge read *The Disinherited Family* soon after it came out, when he was director of the London School of Economics, and introduced one of the first schemes of family-linked payments for its staff. But after a flurry of interest, and in the much less progressive climate of the 1930s, resistance to Rathbone's analysis grew stronger. It was not until 1942 that the Labour Party and TUC offered their backing.

'New' and 'old' feminisms

After the financial crash of 1929, campaigns against poverty increasingly occupied some of those on the left who were also active in feminist causes. Inequalities rose sharply and, in many cases, agonisingly. Formally abolished in 1930, workhouses continued to operate in much the same way under the new name of public assistance institutions. Ellen Wilkinson's personal friendship with Nancy Astor continued, despite political disagreements. But the priorities of feminists from different parties began more sharply to diverge. A women's committee chaired by Nancy Astor, which had functioned as a bridge between civil society groups and Parliament, broke down in 1928. In October 1936, Wilkinson helped to organize the 300-mile 'Hunger March' of 200 unemployed men from Jarrow to London. Intra-feminist arguments over protective workplace legislation also recurred, and gained a new sting in an era of falling incomes and rising unemployment, since men feared being replaced by cheaper female workers. In the late 1920s, the feminist Open Door Council and trade unionist Standing Joint Council traded arguments in rival pamphlets. While Open Door opposed protective laws on the grounds that their real purpose was to protect male economic interests, the Council took the Labour and TUC line that female employees required special treatment.

Feminist policy initiatives did not come to a standstill. The Workers' Birth Control Group had set itself up to counter the eugenicist policies of middle-class reformers, and in the run-up to the 1929 election worked with the National Union to overcome Labour hostility to feminist-socialist coordination. After the election, the rules on contraceptive advice were altered, and in 1930 the Family Planning Association was formed. A few years later, the mass-membership Women's Co-operative Guild passed a resolution in favour of legalizing abortion, and in 1936 an Abortion Law Reform Association was set up.

Two years later, a doctor, Aleck Bourne, was prosecuted for performing an abortion on a fourteen-year-old who had been raped by off-duty soldiers. His defence relied on the risks to the girl's physical and mental health, and campaigners celebrated when he was acquitted.

The issue of equal pay also remained live. Ellen Wilkinson and a Conservative MP, Thelma Cazalet, were among those who spoke on the subject in Parliament. But as the international picture darkened, with Mussolini at the head of a police state in Italy and Hitler's ascent to the chancellery of Germany in 1933, British politics became increasingly focused on foreign threats. While this suited the interests and expertise of some women, the tilt away from domestic affairs did not favour them electorally. At the 1935 general election, the number of women in Parliament fell from fifteen to five. Cazalet recalled that male colleagues used to point her out 'as though I were a sort of giant panda'.[13]

Meanwhile, the women's movement outside Parliament was marginalized and divided, with the National Union's membership in decline and feminists a 'beleaguered band'.[14] Factions had always existed. But increasingly, in the post-suffrage period, they struggled to identify common ground. While Eleanor Rathbone sought to give feminism an alternative, materialist basis with the campaign for family allowances, groups including the Open Door Council wanted to keep the focus on equal rights. In the 1920s, partisans on either side of this debate gave themselves labels of 'new' and 'old' feminists. In a revealing exchange in the *Yorkshire Post*, Winifred Holtby, who belonged to the latter group, attacked 'suggestions for sex warfare' and blamed new feminists for stirring them up. New feminist Eva Hubback, a close ally of Rathbone's, hit back by accusing Holtby and her ilk of being hidebound purists who resisted any effort to dilute what she called the 'pure milk' of equality – the phrase carrying a hint that they were babyish. Rathbone, similarly, compared her opponents to little sisters desperate to join the boys: 'The new feminists, as we sometimes call ourselves, . . . scoff at this other school by calling them . . . the "Me too" feminists. Are women, we ask, to behave for ever like a little girl running behind her big brother and calling out, "Me, too"?'[15]

Observant as they were of the toll on women from large families, new feminists shared an interest in health care with birth-control campaigners. Maternal mortality in this period hovered at around one death per 250 births, a level of risk that had hardly reduced since the nineteenth century. Rathbone was among those outraged by the lack of progress. As they wrote about and lobbied on this and other issues, new feminists saw themselves as pioneers of an innovative, woman-centred politics. As Rathbone saw it, 'all the factors in the problem of women's wage have their root in the one set of facts common to women as apart from men, viz. their function as child-bearers and housewives.' More than any other politician of the period, she was determined to expand the scope of feminist activity by reaching into areas of life (notably working-class family finances and reproductive health) that it had barely touched. 'We can demand what we want for women, not because it is what men have got but because it is what women need . . . to adjust to the circumstances of their own lives,' she wrote in the *Woman's Leader* in 1925. On another occasion, she told the House of Commons, 'I am 100 per cent feminist.'[16]

But other influential figures disagreed. That women were men's equals was the bedrock on which liberal feminism was built. While Rathbone saw childbearing as the key to understanding the ways in which women were disadvantaged, other feminists thought that emphasizing motherhood would hold them back. (Perhaps Lady Rhondda heard an echo of Lord Birkenhead's offensive description of 'conduit pipes' in Rathbone's speeches on motherhood.) The conflict was shaped in part by differences in circumstances. Many of the middle- and upper-class women involved in feminist politics and journalism at this time were unmarried – unsurprisingly, since married women were expected to give up work. Eleanor Rathbone was one such; her lifelong companion was another woman, the Scottish social worker Elizabeth Macadam. But she was preoccupied with the situation of wives, mothers and widows in a way that some of her peers were not.

This debate was not limited to Britain, and British feminists clashed on international stages as well as domestic ones.[17] In 1926, a row erupted at a conference of the International Women's Suffrage Alliance in Paris, when the American National Women's Party was blocked from affiliation on the grounds that its aims were in conflict with another affiliate, the League of Women Voters. While the League was engaged in social work with mothers and children, and also favoured protective legislation, the Women's Party was equalitarian and more individualist. (Its campaign for an Equal Rights Amendment to the American Constitution would later be adopted by second-wave feminists.)

Allied with the League, Rathbone found herself pitted publicly against a furious Lady Rhondda, who regarded the American Women's Party, and not the social workers, as the true allies of suffragists. In an angry speech, Rhondda attacked women who chose to 'putter away at welfare work', spoke of dividing sheep from goats, and said the dispute had 'shown us who are feminists, feminists first and last . . . we are one body, the feminists of the world'.[18] In 1927, some of those unhappy with the direction taken under Rathbone resigned, and in 1928 the organization split itself in two, creating a National Council for Equal Citizenship and a National Union of Townswomen's Guilds that bore similarities with the Women's Institute. A few years later, the National Union's journal, the *Woman's Leader*, folded and was replaced by *The Townswoman*.

In the 1930s, Rathbone became involved in a related dispute over India's female electorate. How to respond to Indian demands for independence was a huge issue during this period and took up a great deal of parliamentary time. Having sent a delegation to lobby the British government during the First World War, Indian women had been granted the vote on the same terms as men in nearly all provincial legislatures. But the franchise was restricted, with property and income qualifications, and in the 1930s a rift opened up over proposals to extend it. Rathbone, who set up a British Committee for Indian Women's Franchise in 1933, wanted reserved seats for Indian women. She thought guaranteed representation was the best way of ensuring that the kinds of feminist, humanitarian causes she was concerned with would be taken forward when India was granted either dominion status, like Canada and Australia, or full independence.

In 1929, the Duchess of Atholl had given the first speech in the House of Commons on female genital mutilation (which she called 'the circumcision of girls') in Kenya. Rathbone's view was that wherever they were in the world, elected female politicians were the trustiest advocates for women's rights. But the main Indian women's organizations and their leaders, including Muthulakshmi Reddi (the first female legislator in India) and Amrit Kaur (president of the All India Women's Conference), disagreed with her proposals. They objected to quotas partly on anti-sectarian grounds since their main use was in allocating seats to religious minorities. They were also against voting qualifications and the gradualist approach that such measures represented. For Kaur, the goal was 'adult suffrage or nothing' – along with full independence for India.[19]

In India, as in other colonial and post-colonial contexts, feminist and nationalist (and religious, class, caste and race) politics intersected in new ways. Exploring the full range of these is beyond the scope of this book. But it is important to note that Indian feminists confronted similar political challenges as British ones, as well as different ones. Just as Eleanor Rathbone's adversaries in Britain were equalitarians who rejected the emphasis she placed on sexual difference, her opponents in India believed that political rights must take precedence over social improvements, even ones designed to benefit women. They regarded strict equality as part of the anti-colonial package – and preferable to any special treatment proffered by imperialists.

Maternalist feminism, as this mother-focused form of advocacy became known, was always something of a high-wire act, mandating as it did a prominent role for motherhood while simultaneously demanding enhanced public entitlements. Then, as now, it risked alienating women who were not mothers or did not want to think of their lives as circumscribed by biology. Others regarded ideas about women's distinct capacities and needs as too easily derailed by their resemblance to old-fashioned sexism. In the 1920s, Rathbone gave as good as she got, carefully assembling a mountain of evidence for her policy of family endowment, and dismissing the 'sugary phrases' of pro-natalists as humbug. She fought publicly with Rhondda over what feminism meant. But in the 1930s feminists were forced onto the back foot, and such debates became hard to sustain. Ray Strachey wrote in 1936 that modern women 'show a strong hostility to the word feminism'.[20] In her 1938 polemic *Three Guineas*, Virginia Woolf described a fantasy in which she wrote it on a piece of paper and set it on fire (giving modern writers one reason to be careful whom we retroactively label feminists).

In the context of a world threatened by fascists, maternalist policies in particular became difficult to defend. The Nazi cult of *Kinder, Küche, Kirche* (children, kitchen and church) carried clear echoes of the Victorian ideology of separate spheres. Increasingly, the threat of war crowded out other issues and divided feminists – as it had done in the 1910s. Nancy Astor was firmly and shamingly in the pro-appeasement camp, her poor judgement facilitated by her anti-Semitic and anti-Catholic prejudices. Lady Rhondda opposed fascism and supported the Spanish government, but dreaded war which she feared would mean 'the end of feminism *and* Western civilization for generations to come'.[21] Rathbone, by contrast, looked forward to Churchill's leadership of a national government, in spite of his anti-feminism. She became involved in efforts to rescue refugees from Franco's Spain and correctly foresaw that failures in western diplomacy would lead to a Hitler–Stalin pact. The day before Chamberlain returned from Munich in 1938, crowing about his capitulation to Hitler, Ellen Wilkinson wrote the leading article in *Time and Tide* and 'howled' over a glass of brandy.[22] Her fury at the government was shared by the Duchess of Atholl, who had travelled to Spain with her and Rathbone as a civil war observer. Now, the Duchess's refusal to toe Chamberlain's line triggered a by-election in which she stood, bravely, as an anti-appeasement independent. Mocked as 'the Red Duchess',[23] she lost narrowly.

'Here is a complication'

In total, thirty-nine women served in the House of Commons between 1918 and the start of the Second World War, though the maximum at any one time was fifteen. Feminism is not reducible to legislation now, and was not in the 1920s and 1930s. But the direct participation of women in the law-making process marked a seismic shift – as did the creation of the first space for female legislators. The campaign for family allowances paved the way for a century of feminist economics, but, though a painting of Eleanor Rathbone hangs in the National Portrait Gallery, she is less well remembered today than she should be. Partly this is because she was elected as an Independent. This means there is no political party with an interest in turning her into an icon – the kind of treatment given to Labour heroines such as Ellen Wilkinson and Barbara Castle, or Conservatives Nancy Astor and Margaret Thatcher. Lady Rhondda would be better known outside Wales had she succeeded in her quest to become a legislator herself (women were not admitted to the House of Lords until 1958).

British feminism in this period is thus something of a paradox. The passage of the Equal Franchise Act in 1928 was a moment of triumph. Three months later, Virginia Woolf gave the speech in Cambridge that would become her book *A Room of One's Own* – a polemic against anti-woman prejudice to rank alongside Mary Wollstonecraft's and one of the most famous feminist essays ever written. At *Time and Tide*'s Fleet Street office, Lady Rhondda presided over a pioneering all-female board. In magazines, books and lecture halls, intellectuals such as Jane Harrison and Rebecca West shared investigations of politics, mythology and psychology, while novelists including Woolf, Jean Rhys and Elizabeth Bowen broke new ground in their fiction. Yet despite all this activity, and that of the first women in Parliament, there was also the sense of anti-climax captured in the historian's image of a spent volcano[24] – or the more familiar one of a wave that had crashed.

Labour had been the only party to back votes for women in 1912. But, once elected, female Labour MPs often distanced themselves from a too explicitly feminist agenda. Patricia Hollis, the Labour politician who wrote Jennie Lee's biography, argued that the term became something of a dirty word in the 1920s, when 'virtually all the women MPs insisted that they were not feminists'. Lee (who was an MP for two years, 1929–31, and again after the war) had a particularly prickly relationship with women's rights; Hollis calls her the 'most socialist' and 'least feminist' of the early Labour women. Along with Ellen Wilkinson, who became education minister in 1945 and the second Labour woman to serve in a cabinet, Lee is regarded as a trailblazer. She wore a tie with a skirt suit to party conferences, and was known to walk out of evening parties rather than follow the convention of ladies leaving the table after dinner. When a journalist asked her later in life if she considered herself a feminist, Lee replied 'that's a damned stupid question', and added 'I am the oldest living example of liberated womanhood.' But she was not particularly interested in the campaigns for family allowances or birth control. Her interests lay in mining, housing and foreign policy.[25]

There were active feminists on the Labour benches: Dorothy Jewson (elected in 1923) and Wilkinson (in 1924) were both suffrage organizers before they became MPs. By the end of the decade, the party had around 1,800 women's section groups as well as a separate women's conference. But Marion Phillips, a key figure as secretary of the trade unionist Standing Joint Committee and an MP from 1929 to 1931, declined an invitation to join the women's committee, chaired by Nancy Astor, and opposed single-sex women's organizations on the grounds that they could put women 'in danger of getting their political opinions muddled'.[26] Tensions between sex-based and class-based politics periodically erupted, as in the clashes over protective legislation. Anti-militarist, socialist–communist and anti-colonial currents coexisted with the efforts of Rathbone and others to create a role for themselves as advocates for colonized women – the form of politics described by historians as 'maternalist imperialism'.[27] In 1929, Ellen Wilkinson offered Rathbone an eloquent statement of her opposition to their efforts in a letter giving her reasons for declining to sign a proposed letter to the *Times* about Indian child marriages. She explained:

> I think the danger when you have one country governing another, such as is the case of either Ireland or India, however well-intentioned the people of the governing country and however necessary the reform may be, is that it tends to make the governed elevate the abuse into a principle to be maintained against the oppressor, as they consider it . . . such a letter could be positively harmful.[28]

These arguments coexisted with the disputes between new and old feminists about the importance of sex in the framing

16 Nine of the first eleven women Labour MPs, 1929 (from left to right): Cynthia Mosley, Marion Phillips, Susan Lawrence, Edith Picton-Turbervill, Margaret Bondfield (in front row): Ethel Bentham, Ellen Wilkinson, Mary Agnes Hamilton, Jennie Lee. © National Portrait Gallery, London

of women's politics. Nature, wrote Virginia Woolf in *Three Guineas*, was the 'familiar accomplice' of sexist argument.[29] In a less well-known essay from around the same time, the writer and former Labour MP Mary Agnes Hamilton noted drily that 'certain Feminists' shared the view of anti-feminists that 'they had a contribution to make that would save the world.' Hamilton briskly dismissed such grandiosity. But, like John Stuart Mill, who had declared sex differences irrelevant in politics, only to propose that maybe they were not after all, she looped back to the idea that perhaps, after all, there was something distinctive about women. She even proposed that this might be not the result of conditioning, or life experience, but innate: 'Few among them [women] can wholly forget or leave out of the picture the other human beings with whom their lot is cast, though many can show a high and rare self-forgetfulness. This incapacity has, of course, been encouraged by tradition and training and general expectation. Yet its roots would seem to lie deeper . . . Here is a complication.'[30] Even Ellen Wilkinson, equalitarian in many of her attitudes, was inclined to think that men were more inclined to militarism, and that the enfranchisement of women could help bring about a more peaceful world. 'Where men dream of the glory and prizes of war, women see the mutilated bodies of their sons,' she wrote in a magazine article in 1929. 'International peace will be the great gift to the world of the mother enfranchised.'[31]

Thus the question about the significance of sex remained crucial. While equal pay stood for an attack on the old and wrong idea that women were inferior, the endowment of motherhood brought up questions of dependence and mutuality. Winifred Holtby's view was that, since there was so little likelihood of 'sex differentiation' ever being underestimated, forward-thinkers should look past it, keeping their eyes on the prize of parity between the sexes. That the female reproductive system drove behaviour in ways that the male one did not was the belief at the core of sexist political philosophy. Collapsing the division of labour which dictated that public life belonged to men was unfinished business; the next step should be for fathers to get more involved in childcare and housework.

Holtby was a humanist internationalist as well as a feminist. She looked forward to a day when feminism would no longer be needed by 'a society in which there is no respect of persons, either male or female, but a supreme regard for the importance of the human being'. That meant transcending the old roles and definitions of what it meant to be a man or a woman, and finding new ways to live. While others regarded a conflict of interest between the sexes as a fact of life, Holtby imagined and expected that such divisions would one day be obsolete. In the book she wrote about Virginia Woolf, published in 1932, Holtby became one of the first feminist writers to propose substituting the word 'sex' with the word 'gender' on grounds that the former was too weighted down with the kinds of biological connotations that dragged women down. 'We ought, when talking about the difference between men and women, to be allowed to use some such neutral word as "gender" instead of "sex"', she argued. 'For "sex" has been associated so closely with the amorous and creative instinct, that its convenience has been destroyed, and its meaning lent an emotional significance which may be quite alien to our purpose.'[32]

It would be several decades before the idea of substituting gender for sex caught on. It is a move strongly associated with feminism's second wave, and I was astonished when I came across Holtby making it. Her humanitarian optimism was admirable – all the more so given her own chronic illness, which killed her aged 37. Almost a century after her death, the rapid advance of technology and changing nature of work mean that the differences between men and women in wealthy countries such as the United Kingdom have, in some ways, diminished as she predicted. Nevertheless, I think she was misguided in her conviction that something as fundamental to human life as sex could ever become politically irrelevant.

6

Housewives (1940s–1950s)

Any account of twentieth-century Britain breaks down into before and after the Second World War, and this is as true of feminism as of anything else. There was no women's movement in the period covered by this chapter to rank with the all-consuming campaigns already described. But this does not mean that there were no feminists. In Parliament and outside, there were women who continued to advocate for sex equality in law and for women's improved access to social goods such as education and health care. This chapter describes some of their achievements.

But it is different from the rest of the book in that it focuses less on specific feminist issues and characters, and more on broader societal changes. I see it as a hinge that links the pre-war movement (often described as the first wave of feminism) to the women's liberation movement of the 1970s and 1980s. I will also use it to highlight a paradox about post-war Britain, which is that the period generally remembered as the most progressive in our nation's recent past – that of the creation of the National Health Service and the rest of the welfare state – is also seen as one of the least feminist.

Woman power

The fragmented pre-war parliamentary feminist lobby regrouped in wartime and made women's employment its dominant theme. Aware that female workers had been forced to give up their jobs to returning soldiers after the First World War, female politicians set about preventing a repetition and formed a Woman Power Committee in Nancy Astor's home. As well as looking ahead, feminist MPs and their allies were concerned about the government's treatment of women during wartime. After the introduction of compulsory registration for war work in 1941, effectively home-front conscription, ten out of the fourteen serving female MPs spoke in a House of Commons debate that marked one of the high points of wartime parliamentary feminism.

A personal injury scheme was a particular grievance since men were compensated more generously than women, even if injuries such as the loss of a limb were sustained during compulsory fire-watching. Irene Ward, the Conservative who had won Margaret Bondfield's seat from her (and would go on to become the longest-serving Conservative woman MP), had 'never been known as a feminist', she told the House of Commons. She went on to attack the higher wages paid to men in war-work training centres, the lack of women at the highest levels of government, and the disrespect for women revealed by the low status granted to the leaders of the nursing profession and Auxiliary Territorial Service (the women's section of the army).[1]

Another Conservative, Thelma Cazalet, began by saying that 'If we had forty or fifty women Members of Parliament instead of the present small number, I doubt whether this debate would have been necessary.' At least the position of women in Britain was better, she observed, than in the 'Hitlerized countries'. The Liberal Megan Lloyd George (daughter of the former prime minister and the first Welsh woman MP) called on ministers

17 Women MPs celebrate Megan Lloyd George's twentieth anniversary in Parliament, 1949 (standing centre with colleagues including Edith Summerskill, beside her wearing a hat, and Jennie Lee, seated behind her). Parliamentary Archives, PUD 15/2/1

to engage the women's movement in the war effort. It was left to Labour's Edith Summerskill to express her dismay at 'how little interest is displayed in this [woman-power] question' by male colleagues, judged from the sparse attendance in the chamber. She demanded new protections at work for pregnant women, while a colleague from Glasgow, Agnes Hardie, spoke against the practice of requiring munitions workers to leave their young children with untrained minders. She called for state-run nurseries and also argued that young Scottish women should not be forced to quit their homes and families for jobs in English factories.

Unsurprisingly, the Woman Power Committee's influence was strongly resisted by the anti-feminist prime minister, Winston Churchill. Other leading politicians were not much more sympathetic and Ernest Bevin, the Labour minister for labour, sidelined it. A BBC radio programme from 1941 provides a revealing insight into the sexism that pervaded official thinking. The Australian prime minister, Robert Menzies, had been seconded to the war cabinet, and began his talk for the national broadcaster with a morale-boosting tribute to the British women who had joined the war effort. He conjured up what would become a familiar image of 'women conducting vast organisations; women in the uniform of the Royal Navy, the Army and the Royal Air Force; women at fire brigade stations in blue overalls, always ready; . . . women wielding hammers, and riveters in factories'.

But having lauded these heroines in uniform for taking on what had traditionally been men's roles, Menzies then turned to 'that forgotten but splendid woman the housewife . . . who not infrequently goes short herself so that her man and her children may be fed'.[2] Women, in wartime, were caught between competing and contradictory ideas of what their role should be. They could, and did, win praise for stepping up and out into the public world – for issuing orders and handling machinery. But the ideal of the mother and wife who steps back, putting others first (not just her children but also her husband), had not gone away.

After fire-watching was made compulsory for women, Ellen Wilkinson said on the radio that when, in the future, children asked 'What did you do during the war, mummy?' mothers would be able to answer with pride: 'Oh nothing much: I just helped to beat the Luftwaffe.'[3] But Wilkinson, as Labour's most prominent feminist, kept her distance from the Woman Power Committee on the grounds of not wishing to undermine the trade unions. In the event, and just as Eleanor Rathbone and others had feared, a bill was passed in 1942 ensuring that women would be removed from 'male' areas of work after the war. They kept the committee going for long enough to argue, in 1945, that the war nurseries should be kept open to enable

18 Woman carrying onions as part of wartime training at the Women's Horticultural College, Waterperry House, Oxfordshire, 1943

mothers who were not obliged to give way to returning soldiers to hold on to jobs. But in this too, they failed. Of 1,450 council-run nurseries in 1943, offering 65,000 places, by 1947 just 879 remained.[4] That year, thirty-five mothers locked themselves into a Yorkshire children's centre as a protest against its closure.[5]

Women's equal right to employment was not the only issue taken up by feminists in wartime. Between 1943 and 1944, a former suffragette called Dorothy Evans was among the leaders of a campaign for an Equal Citizenship (Blanket) Bill, supported by the Six Point Group. The plan was for a once-and-for-all sweep across legislation that would make all sex-based discrepancies illegal; it also included mandatory income sharing between husband and wife. A demonstration was organized in 1944, but Evans died that same year and momentum drifted away. Also in 1944, Churchill called a confidence motion in the House of Commons to reverse a vote in favour of equal pay for women teachers. The amendment he was determined to overturn, which had passed by one vote, was the wartime coalition's only defeat. Two years later, a Royal Commission offered tentative backing to equal pay claims from women teachers and civil servants – while a minority report argued that the principle should extend to industry as well.

The first family allowances were paid in 1946, and set at five shillings a week for each child from the second one onwards. Even this legacy of pre-war feminism was a victory snatched from the jaws of defeat. Ministers were minded to pay the allowances to fathers instead of mothers, until Eleanor Rathbone led a backbench revolt. For her biographer, Susan Pedersen, this episode formed a fitting finale to Rathbone's extraordinary career (she died soon afterwards). But it took another female parliamentarian, Thelma Cazalet-Keir, to point out to MPs that Rathbone had been the scheme's originator. Labour's Arthur Greenwood preferred to give the credit to 'my friend Seebohm Rowntree' (the York-based social reformer).[6]

This erasure of Rathbone's life's work was an ominous sign of things to come. Even Churchill admitted that the war had altered 'those social and sex balances which years of convention had established', but the post-war years saw many of those balances and conventions re-established.[7] The 1945 Labour landslide swept away the cross-party feminist caucus that had developed out of the suffrage movement. Nancy Astor, always a curious figurehead for the first phase of parliamentary feminism and discredited by her pro-appeasement stance, was persuaded by her husband not to stand for re-election in 1945, as he expected her to lose. Another Conservative who had been an advocate for women's causes, Mavis Tate, lost her seat and took her own life two years later. The number of female MPs climbed to twenty-four – all but three of them Labour. But there was limited interest in feminist policy making in the immediate post-war period. One Labour MP who was active in women's causes, Edith Summerskill, recalled her early impressions of Parliament as being 'a little like a boys' school which had decided to take a few girls'. Summerskill, the first woman doctor elected to Parliament, also took a dim view of the male, public school and arts bias of the civil service.[8]

Having played a crucial role overseeing air-raid shelters, and keeping up morale among bombed-out families, Ellen Wilkinson became education minister and the only woman in Clement Attlee's cabinet. In the official photographs of the new government, she sits at one end of a long front row of men, a position suggestive of peripheral status. Her tenure in education was rocky, with allies on the left angry at her refusal to prioritize comprehensive schools (a grammar school girl herself, she was not entirely supportive of the new anti-selection ethos). Instead, she focused on the school-leaving age which was raised to fifteen. Having been shocked on a trip to Berlin in 1945 by a child who said she had not drunk milk for two years, she also led a drive for free school milk.[9]

Wilkinson died aged 55, of an overdose that was ruled accidental by a coroner. Among the survivors of the pre-war generation of female politicians, Jennie Lee stands out. But although she was re-elected in the 1945 Labour landslide, and remained a powerful figure on the party's left, her most significant achievements came much later. During the Attlee government, and the long period of Tory rule that followed, she placed her own career second to that of her husband, Aneurin 'Nye' Bevan, whose life's ambition was to be a Labour prime minister. Mary Stocks, a former suffragist, was just 149 votes off being elected to Parliament in 1945, as an Independent like her friend Eleanor Rathbone. What difference it could have made to the development of women's politics, had the 1945 Parliament included a feminist Independent, is an interesting counter-factual. Rathbone had shown what could be achieved from such a position. But Stocks fell short, while other prominent suffragists took off in new directions. Sylvia Pankhurst, for example, devoted the latter part of her life to Ethiopia, where she tried to raise awareness of Italian fascism and British attempts to turn the country into a protectorate.

Women and the welfare state

William Beveridge's 1942 report, *Social Insurance and Allied Services*, set out the new social contract between citizens and state. He envisioned a renewed division of labour between men and women as part of this, and expressed plans to counter a falling birth rate in the eugenicist terms that were then in common use. 'In the next thirty years,' the report said, 'housewives as mothers have vital work to do in ensuring the adequate continuance of the British race.'[10] A 1949 Royal Commission on Population referred explicitly to a wife's role 'as a producer of children'.[11]

In the 1931 census, upon which Beveridge relied when making his calculations – the 1941 census having been cancelled – more than seven out of eight married women were recorded as not working outside the home. By the early 1940s, due to the wartime mobilization, this assumption was out of date. But the single-breadwinner family was the model that Beveridge adopted. He saw the married couple as 'a team', and the contributory social insurance arrangements he proposed were aimed at supporting the nuclear family as the base unit of society. While he acknowledged the value of what he called women's 'vital unpaid service', he regarded the male wage as a family's primary resource.[12]

Under the paternalist umbrella of post-war social policy, old ideas about women's inferiority crept back. Arthur Woodburn, secretary of state for Scotland in the Attlee government, said in 1945 that 'nature itself made the first and greatest division of labour and no arguments by super intellectual women can cancel that.'[13] Huge variations in the schooling offered to girls and boys were accepted as a matter of course, and not only by right-wingers. Socialist feminists, including Ellen Wilkinson, were also capable of what the historian Matt Perry calls 'gender-fixing' policies.[14] In 1946, when she was education secretary, she mandated an hour of home craft for secondary schoolgirls each week.

Wilkinson had links to the Electrical Association of Women, whose slogan was 'Emancipation from Drudgery'. She and others hoped that new technologies would soon release working-class women from the relentless grind of keeping homes clean and families fed. In the meanwhile, the question of who was to do the nation's housework and childcare cut across lines of class as well as sex. Reliance on domestic help had been widespread before the war, not only among the wealthy but also the middle classes. But service was in long-term decline, due to terrible pay and conditions, and after the war the number of working-class girls and women obliged to spend their lives lighting other people's fires, cleaning their toilets and washing their floors continued to fall.

For the sociologist Ferdynand Zweig, the chance to work in male-dominated areas that the war gave to working-class women had opened their eyes to new possibilities, and liberated them from a deeply inculcated subservience. 'You can feel the regret that they were not born men, who have the best of everything and the first choice in practically all things,' he wrote of the interviews with war workers that were his fieldwork. Factory jobs had shown them that they were not second-class people. 'So they do as much as they can to prove equal to men, to prove that they are not drones . . .

Paid work, especially work in industry, relieves that sense of inferiority.'[15]

Housework still needed doing, though, and this was vastly more time-consuming then than now. Even in 1955, only 8 per cent of British households had fridges. Food shopping was generally done every day, and shoppers expected to wait in queues (food rationing did not completely end until 1954). In the 82 per cent of homes that lacked washing machines, laundry was a major undertaking. Jarring as it might be for twenty-first-century readers to find left-wing women such as Margaret Bondfield, as well as her male peers, arguing that 'domestic work in a modern home will be a career for educated women,' this view was partly borne of the acceptance that working-class women could no longer be expected to do middle-class people's cleaning for them (the idea that couples could share housework, or that employment could be made more flexible to assist such arrangements, lay some way off).[16]

Another factor in any discussion of post-war family life is the influence of new ideas about child development. This was an international phenomenon, with the first baby-care book by the American paediatrician Dr Benjamin Spock becoming an instant bestseller. But the debate in the United Kingdom played out in distinctive ways. One key figure is the psychiatrist and psychoanalyst John Bowlby who, in his first major work, *Forty-four Juvenile Thieves* (1944), set out to investigate the effects of what he called 'maternal deprivation'. Over the decade that followed, Bowlby developed his theory of attachment, arguing that a strong, reciprocal bond with a primary caregiver, whom he assumed would be a mother, was the fundamental basis of psychic and social health.

Bowlby's ambitions went beyond clinical practice. The historian David Kynaston calls him a 'propagandist' for his ideas, and certainly he saw a role for his discoveries in public policy. He was active in Labour circles and influenced the MP Evan Durbin, who was close to the party's future leader Hugh

Gaitskell (Durbin's career and influence were cut short when he died in a drowning accident). Unsurprisingly, feminists were more dubious about Bowlby's valorization of ultra-attentive motherhood. For Mary Stott, the journalist who would become editor of the *Guardian*'s women's page, 'the name Bowlby became synonymous . . . with guilt'.[17]

Around 800,000 more babies were born in Britain over the three years 1946–8 than in the three years 1939–41, meaning that many more women were engaged in looking after young children than during the war. After six years of conflict, during which almost 400,000 British soldiers and 70,000 civilians had been killed, the baby boom was not simply the consequence of a pro-natalist policy. Many thousands of couples (my maternal grandparents included) had put off having children due to wartime scarcity and fear of a German invasion. Given the low availability of contraception, a surge in pregnancies was the obvious consequence of couples being reunited after wartime separations. Having a baby was also a way to move past the horror of war. And in the absence of childcare, which was not part of the new welfare state, the baby boom was another reason for working-age women to stay at home.

But the idea of women's independence did not simply fade away in the 1940s and 1950s, as the nuclear family conquered all. Marriages ended in unprecedented numbers. From an average of 6,000 a year between 1936 and 1940, the number of divorces rose to 33,922 in 1952, leading the government to establish a Royal Commission to investigate. Such statistics complicate the traditional view of the post-war years as a period of social and marital retrenchment (although divorces subsequently fell back). New civil society organizations pushed for further liberalization of the laws that structured family life. The Abortion Law Reform Association formed in 1936 continued to advocate for liberalization, while a Married Women's Association campaigned for improvements in the economic and legal position of wives. With leading members including the MP Edith

Summerskill and the barrister Helena Normanton (one of the first two female King's Counsel), it pressed throughout the 1940s for reforms including a wife's right to information about her husband's earnings, and a fairer share of joint resources in the event of marriage breakdown. The Association kept an eye on the courts as well as lobbying politicians, and funded an appeal brought by a woman whose savings from her housekeeping allowance had been handed to her husband by a judge after they separated, leaving her penniless.

Some campaigners challenged the sexism of the new welfare state. As a leading figure in the pre-war maternal and child health movement, Juliet Rhys-Williams was appointed to Beveridge's committee, where she tried without success to argue for a basic income policy, instead of contributory social insurance, in the belief that the former would be more favourable to women. She advocated a contract to be signed by all working-age adults, committing them to pay a flat tax which would qualify them for the new state benefit.[18] Housewives would be exempt but would still receive the income, thus freeing them from dependence on husbands. Another pamphlet, from the Women's Freedom League (which was originally a suffragist organization but continued to campaign on women's issues), made its objections more explicit: the Beveridge scheme, wrote Elizabeth Abbott and Katherine Bompas, was 'a man's plan for men'.[19] But such objections and alternatives were limited to the feminist fringe of politics: in the debate on the Beveridge Report in the House of Commons held in February 1943, its impact on women was barely discussed, and only a handful of women spoke at all.

Labour's Eirene White, who was elected to the women's section of the party's National Executive Committee in 1947 (and later became an MP), was another critic of what she regarded as the male bias of post-war social policy. At a conference in 1947, she issued an angry warning that Labour could follow the Liberal Party in destroying itself 'because of the humbug and hypocrisy' with which it treated women. She saw the Attlee government's refusal to get behind a policy of equal pay as an echo of the Liberals' failure, a generation earlier, to deliver votes for women. But the conference ignored her, as did the TUC, which argued that 'it would be doing a grave injury to the life of the nation if women were persuaded or forced to neglect their domestic duties.'[20]

The Attlee government did introduce some explicitly feminist measures. Before the war, women had been forced to resign from some jobs when they married. The bar on married female teachers was one of the first to be lifted, in 1944, followed by the one on civil servants, although women continued to suffer from discrimination, including a presumption of lower pay. In 1948, the British Nationality Act granted women citizenship in their own right, where formerly they had been forced to give it up if they married a non-British husband.

As a junior minister who was also a doctor, Edith Summerskill became a crucial advocate for women's and children's health. In her autobiography, she recalled a story told by her father when she was a child about a birth whose horrifying final stages he had attended when an untrained midwife had accidentally ripped off a baby's arm while trying to deliver it. Unsurprisingly, both mother and baby died. In Parliament, Summerskill drew on her medical background to make the case for increased use of anaesthesia in labour. She argued that opposition from GPs was motivated by professional self-interest since it would force them to rely on other doctors with specialist training. Maternity care, including obstetrics, was one of the pre-war health system's most dangerous weaknesses. By 1950, the maternal mortality rate had dramatically reduced, due to improved anti-infection medicines and processes. Infant and young child mortality also fell steeply between 1945 and 1950, while children's nutrition received a boost from free milk and school dinners.

Since women who did not work outside the home had been excluded from the health insurance scheme that existed before the war, they were among the biggest gainers from the creation in 1948 of the National Health Service. One survey in 1954 found that middle-aged women in particular had benefited, with female cancers among diseases that had previously been chronically under-treated.[21] Michael Young, who was among the authors of Labour's 1945 manifesto, believed that post-war tax and spending decisions (including new taxes on beer and tobacco) saw an overall transfer of income from men to women and children. Even when improving women's position relative to men was not a policy's main purpose, it could still be the result.

A woman's realm

The launch issue of *Woman's Realm* magazine, published in February 1958, carried the following message from its editor:

> Our country today *is* literally a woman's realm – ruled over by our young and beautiful sovereign and containing in itself those other realms in which women are supreme. In the home and in the heart of her husband and her family, every woman finds happiness and fulfilment, as well as duty. This need never be a narrow domain, bounded though it often is by kitchen, nursery and household chores. Indeed, if she chooses to make it so, it can be the widest and most rewarding realm in the whole world.[22]

There could hardly be a more complacent statement of the conservative sexual values often taken to sum up 1950s Britain. Queen Elizabeth II already had two small children when she acceded to the throne, aged 25, in 1952. The arrival at the apex of the British state of a young mother, whose family was the source of her power, was a key ingredient in the cocktail of British domestic ideology in this period. The Labour MP

19 Barbara Castle, 1965

Barbara Castle recognized and regretted the popular appeal of the royal spectacle. Of the televised coronation, watched by 20 million people, she wrote in her diary that she 'hoped this would be the last Coronation of its kind we should see, it was so unrepresentative of ordinary people . . . as I write this the Queen's correct & piping girlish voice is enunciating the formulae of dedication; Winston [Churchill] has just introduced her on the radio, exploiting the romantic mood of the moment to its fruitiest uttermost.'[23]

Socialist women like Castle hoped that, in time, new technology and an expanding economy would release more wives from their homes. But the new advertising businesses and their clients had different ideas. In the 1950s, under a succession of Tory prime ministers (Churchill followed by Anthony Eden and Harold Macmillan), the promotion of starkly differentiated sex roles became a key technique of the burgeoning propaganda arm of the manufacturing industries. Male and female tasks and behaviours were codified in new ways by advertisers, and politicians joined in the celebration of the housewife as the proud custodian of consumer goods. 'We want in modern Britain to have an understanding between the producer and the housewife,' said the Conservative chancellor, Rab Butler, in a speech in 1954. 'We want her to be as "choosey" and independent as she likes . . . We want the consumer to decide and not the man in Whitehall.'[24]

With the winding down of rationing came the wider availability of personal items such as nylon stockings, and some feminists blamed the rapidly advancing fashion and beauty industries for the pitfalls they saw being laid in women's paths. Labour MPs Ellen Wilkinson and Bessie Braddock, for example, spoke out against the tiny waists and full skirts of Christian Dior's 'New Look', with Braddock opining that it was a 'stupidly exaggerated waste of material and manpower, foisted on the average woman to the detriment of other, more normal clothing'. The effect, she declared, was altogether 'too reminiscent of a caged bird'.[25] Such imagery was not limited to French fashion houses. Edith Summerskill wrote of a trip to the United States that 'beauty culture seems to have become an obsession with many women. In buses, on hoardings, in newspapers or magazines, there are so many pictures advertising some form of beauty treatment for the female body that they tend to become embarrassing.'[26]

There were striking changes too in the aesthetics of Hollywood stardom during this period, with the voluptuous female leads of the period markedly different from the spikier characters of the pre-war age. Marilyn Monroe was the exemplar of this new sensualism; as a performer she had wit and charm, but was cast in roles (and given costumes and lighting) that often seemed closer to male sexual fantasies than dramatic characters with their own motivations. It is impossible to gauge precisely the impact of such cinematic iconography in the United Kingdom; this was a period of resistance to American cultural influence as well as enjoyment of it. Cinema attendances fell as the new medium of television tightened its grip on the nation's attention. But in British cultural life, too, the dominant tone of the 1950s was masculinist, with the highbrow effeminacy of the Bloomsbury set cast aside in favour of the upwardly mobile virility of writers such as Kingsley Amis and John Osborne.

A handful of women continued to voice concerns about the pressures on wives and mothers. In their 1956 book *Women's Two Roles*, the social scientists Alva Myrdal and Viola Klein warned against what they called the 'sentimental cult of domestic virtues' that they feared was being fuelled by Bowlby and his allies. In language that prefigured that used by the American author and psychologist Betty Friedan in *The Feminine Mystique* (1963), they warned of the 'vague but pervasive dissatisfaction' of women who had nothing to do but keep house.[27] Drawing on data from several countries, they set out their case for an alternative model, whereby women of all classes would be encouraged to take up paid employment but enabled to opt out while their children were young (their vision did not extend to fathers doing equal childcare).

Like Friedan, Judith Hubback (a daughter-in-law of the suffragist Eva Hubback) honed in on the frustrations of the university-educated wife. Published in 1957 and widely reviewed, her book *Wives Who Went to College* drew on the insights of Simone de Beauvoir, whose seminal study of women's socialization, *The Second Sex*, had its first UK edition in 1953. What women needed, Hubback wrote, was 'the freedom of not having their sex constantly colouring all they do'. Echoing her mother-in-law, an ally of Eleanor Rathbone's, she proposed that a perspective informed by Beauvoir's analysis of the difficulties of combining marriage, motherhood and personal fulfilment should be regarded as 'the new feminism at its best'.[28]

But the story of women's employment in post-war Britain is not a simple tale of women who had been allowed to climb up in wartime being knocked back down. In the first year after the war, the number of employed married women (including part-timers) fell from 7.2 million to 5.8 million. But from 1947, as labour shortages returned, the number of women working outside the home rose steadily, with 710,000 added to the workforce between 1947 and 1951 and another million by 1965 – with the increase in married working women especially marked. Women's hourly earnings also grew more than men's over the period 1938–50 – although full-time female workers in manufacturing still only earned half as much as their male counterparts.[29] After the advances by women into firefighting, engineering and other industries during wartime, the post-war period saw a return to occupational segregation. Nowhere was this clearer than in office work, with the 1961 census recording nearly a quarter of all working women as secretaries. The messages about homemaking from politicians and industry were real enough. But their impact was uneven. Crucially, the situation of women in post-war Britain was very different from the United States, where men earned more money and fewer women worked outside the home. British women's higher rate of employment was also a legacy of their wartime mobilization, which had been more extensive than in any other country – with the possible exception of the USSR.[30]

Equal pay was another policy which feminists continue to push. In a 1952 debate, one MP likened opponents to those who 'believe that the earth is flat'. Irene Ward, a Conservative, said she was seeking not simply pay rises but 'justice for women', and she told the story of a woman who had applied for a job writing an official history of the Second World War. In her application, she had used her initials but when she was appointed, and her sex was revealed, she was told that she would receive a lower salary than had been advertised. In this case, the civil service had backed down and the woman received the full amount, but in future, Ward argued, the discrimination that saw women routinely paid four-fifths of what men earned for the same work must be outlawed. The only way women would get anything would be 'by making a terrible nuisance of themselves', Barbara Castle declared from the Labour benches, for 'women's achievements have never been won by sweet reasonableness.'[31] In 1954, an equal pay protest organized by the Fawcett Society sent female MPs of both parties to Westminster in horse-drawn carriages. The point they sought to make, via this novel protest, was that if horse-drawn carriages were considered outdated, how could it be that the anachronism of sex discrimination by employers was still allowed?

Rattling the chains

From the BBC and the new commercial television companies to the theatre, publishing and music, men continued to dominate cultural life in the 1950s. Even the first presenter of the BBC's *Woman's Hour* was a man – although Janet Quigley and Olive Shapley soon placed their stamp upon it. But talented, creative women found ways to make their mark, despite the pervasive 'anti-female bias' that Doris Lessing blamed for her difficulties in becoming established as a playwright.[32]

One triumphant example of female artistic achievement during this period was the partnership of Joan Littlewood and Shelagh Delaney, which saw the latter's first play, *A Taste of Honey* – written when she was just nineteen – put on by Littlewood's Theatre Workshop first at Stratford East, in 1958, and then in the West End. In her biography of Delaney, the historian Selina Todd argues that the brilliant, working-class teenager from Salford should be seen as a harbinger of feminism's second wave. Other writers, including Rachel Cooke, Clare Mac Cumhaill and Rachael Wiseman, have also sought to reassess the achievements of 1950s women and shown that the decade was not the domestic-goddess backward march that is sometimes portrayed. In their recent book about the philosophers Elizabeth Anscombe, Philippa Foot, Mary Midgley and Iris Murdoch, Cumhaill and Wiseman argue that this remarkable quartet was enabled to tread new ground by men's absence due to war and national service.[33]

Another woman who made a mark on British culture towards the end of the decade was Claudia Jones, the left-wing activist and newspaper editor who came to Britain from the United States in 1955, and initiated the showcase of West Indian performance that became the Notting Hill Carnival. The first event put on by the Caribbean Carnival Committee, which was set up in the aftermath of riots, took place in 1959 and included the crowning of a carnival queen. Three years later, Jones recruited Littlewood to be one of the contest's judges. While Jones's political activities were most strongly focused on anti-racism and the rights of immigrants, the organizations she was involved in also opposed sex discrimination. When she organized a demonstration against the Commonwealth Immigration Act of 1962, it was attended by numerous black nurses in uniform.[34]

Of the 3.5 per cent of school-leavers who went to university in the late 1950s, around three-quarters were boys. But that still left a quarter who were girls, and a degree was not in any case a prerequisite for a woman seeking a career. Muriel Box trained as a dancer and worked as a secretary before becoming a successful playwright and film director. She regarded the 1957 romantic comedy *The Truth about Women* as her proudest achievement, although it was not a commercial success. 'Virginia Woolf's *A Room of One's Own* made such an impression on me in my twenties that I had been possessed ever since with a strong urge to support equality between the sexes,' she wrote of her screenplay. 'Thus my approach to this subject was perhaps more enthusiastic and dedicated than to any other theme previously attempted. Unable to chain myself to the railings, at least I could rattle the film chains.'[35] Box got divorced in 1969 and campaigned for more liberal divorce laws alongside the MP Edith Summerskill. She also co-founded a feminist publishing house. Another woman who cited Woolf's essay as an influence was the civil servant Alix Meynell. Like her friend Evelyn Sharp, who was the United Kingdom's first female permanent secretary (and not to be confused with the suffragist and writer of the same name), Meynell received a damehood. Her obituary in the *Guardian* described her as 'one of the great women of this [twentieth] century', while one of Sharp's contemporaries believed she should have been the head of the civil service.

Obstacles remained in the way of women's achievements. The scientist Rosalind Franklin, for example, may never have received the credit for discoveries that paved the way for the description of the double-helix structure of DNA (the achievement for which two male contemporaries won a Nobel Prize) had it not been for the efforts of her friend Anne Sayers. And in politics, progress towards increased representation was sluggish. In 1958, three women took up seats in the House of Lords, following the Life Peerages Act which brought down the curtain on what had been an all-male chamber. But after the 1959 general election, there were still only 25 female MPs – just one more than there had been in 1945.

Planning and architectural choices in relation to house building were some of the most far-reaching decisions of the post-war period, and this was an area in which Sharp played a key role. With more than a million residential buildings destroyed by bombing, including around a third of all housing stock in Liverpool and half in Coventry, providing people with new homes was understood by all to be an electoral priority. When the sociologist Hannah Gavron interviewed forty-eight working-class women about their lives in 1960, over 60 per cent described them as dominated by 'bad housing'.[36] Bigger, warmer and more convenient homes were arguably of particular value to women, given that they typically spent much more time in them. Sir Frederic Osborn, a leading planner, acknowledged as much when he said that 'the Modernists stand for multi-storey flats and the Mummyfiers for terrace houses.'[37]

His point was that while innovators dreamed of cities in the sky, mothers valued the easy access to the street (for shopping) and private gardens (for children and laundry) that terraced housing offered.

Housing is less often framed as a feminist issue than reproductive health care or equal access to jobs and education. But continued investment in house building, and the domestic ideology of which this formed part, was an important component of Conservative politicians' appeal to women voters in the 1950s. That Attlee, Bevan and company had built not a new Jerusalem but a 'Queuetopia' became a key message, propagated via a Tory women's newsletter, *Home Truths*, among other places. The 'jam today, not jam tomorrow' famously demanded by Barbara Castle at the Labour Party Conference in 1943 had not materialized. Labour was depicted as the party of empty shelves, and more female voters than male ones were won over by Tory promises to fill them up.

Anti-suffragist, left-wing men had always feared that female voters would lean rightwards. In vain, Labour's Eirene White, who had publicly attacked the leadership for its stance on equal pay in 1947, tried to persuade colleagues to pursue a more overtly feminist agenda. But women's voices in the party were marginal and divided; even the two giants of the left, Jennie Lee and Barbara Castle, were only partly allies, while Summerskill belonged to the anti-Bevanite wing. Labour's vote among women lagged twelve and thirteen points behind the Tories in the 1951 and 1955 elections, and the party would not gain an advantage among women until 1966.[38] Thus for fifteen years, the party that had been most reluctant to endorse votes for women disproportionately attracted their votes.

The history of right-wing women's activism is not well known outside academic circles.[39] But in her book *The Iron Ladies*, Beatrix Campbell traced Margaret Thatcher's rise back to the Primrose League, formed by aristocratic women in the 1880s to build up grassroots support for Tory candidates. Like

Labour, the party relied on the work carried out by female activists including MPs' wives. In the 1920s, when the party forsook its old fixation on imperial affairs in favour of a new ideology of common sense, the housewife-manager became a key figure in the Tory revival. In 1945, Conservative central office decreed that every candidate shortlist must have a woman on it.[40] The Tory monthly *Onward* had a women's page during a period when the *Manchester Guardian*'s equivalent had disappeared (it was reinstated in 1957).[41] Right-wing women even briefly considered setting up their own political party after the war, though plans hatched by the anti-socialist, Christian-moralist British Housewives League soon sputtered out and those involved were re-absorbed by the Conservatives.

On the Labour side, Barbara Castle was one who recognized that femininity could be a source of authority, rather than a hindrance, in public life. When she was selected to stand for parliament in Blackburn, her agent advised her to take her future husband Ted Castle's name, even though they were not yet married and legally she was still Barbara Betts. At a selection meeting in 1944, she declared: 'I'm no feminist. Just judge me as a socialist.'[42] Throughout her career, Castle cultivated a homely image, declining to wear her glasses when being photographed, lying about her age, and making sure she was photographed doing wifely things such as darning socks (although the Castles had a housekeeper). 'I have the normal womanly instincts,' she told a journalist in 1959. Her biographer, Anne Perkins, calls her 'a pioneer of the housewife-superstar role picked up by Margaret Thatcher'.[43]

But Castle was a one-off. Generally speaking, the Tory Party was more successful than Labour in channelling aspirations linked to family life. These have generally been viewed as reactionary, and it is true that some men (and women) were only too glad to find, in novel ideas about nurturance, a justification for the traditional division of labour that kept mothers at home (a demand previously supplied by religion, philosophy and evolutionary science). Valorization of the 'maternal instinct' also helped to ensure that single women continued to be stigmatized as frustrated spinsters. In a book on girls' education, the psychologist John Newson argued that teachers should not be 'attempting to iron out their differences from men, to reduce them to neuters, but to teach girls how to grow into women and to relearn the graces which so many have forgotten in the last 30 years'.[44]

But there were also progressive and humanitarian aspects to the new interest in infants and children. London was an important centre for psychoanalysis from its earliest days, and in the 1940s and 1950s Anna Freud and Melanie Klein contributed, along with John Bowlby and Donald Winnicott, to the new science of mental life. Some of their work was abstract and theoretical, but the seriousness with which young people's minds started to be treated also had practical effects, including the provision of child psychotherapy within the National Health Service (NHS). In 1950, the Women's Institute took issue with the widespread practice of not allowing parents to visit their children in hospital. Legislation, including the Clean Milk Act and Clean Air Act, and provision of school meals showed that children too had rights.

The big breakthroughs on access to birth control and abortion came in the 1960s, beginning with contraceptive pill prescriptions for married women on the NHS in 1961. But they were the culmination of a decades-long campaign, which continued throughout the post-war period. There were six attempts to make some abortions legal between 1953 and 1966. And in 1960, an article in the *Guardian* led to the creation of a National Housewives' Register, which worked as a kind of mutual aid network. Its informal, small-group structure has been proposed as a template for the 1970s women's liberation movement.

The women's movement in Britain was unquestionably weaker in the two decades after the war than the two before it

– notwithstanding the fact that millions of women continued to go out to work, including thousands of nurses recruited from the Caribbean to fill posts in the NHS. Economic and technological change, and the accompanying promotion of personal consumption, contributed to a culture in which women's domesticity was celebrated. Progress towards a more equal society stalled in important regards. But women also benefited from post-war policies on health and housing. And the new emphasis on motherhood was not purely a case of patriarchy reasserting itself. Questions about how to reconcile family life with the maximization of individual opportunities for achievement have never had easy answers. And it was into the personal realm of family and sexual life, psychology and relationships that the analytic energy of the women's liberation movement would soon pour.

7

Liberators (1960s–1980s)

The beginning of the women's liberation movement in the United Kingdom is usually dated to around the same time as the 1968 student protests, with the formation of the first women's consciousness-raising groups. The first national conference and a protest against the *Miss World* beauty contest took place in 1970, and an International Women's Day march a year later. But there were important staging posts earlier in the 1960s. 'It is now a conviction that the women's movement began in the sixties. Like sex,' the novelist Doris Lessing wrote in her autobiography. 'The fact is, there were many group discussions, meetings, conversations, about women in the 1940s and 1950s, in and near the Communist parties, and the socialist parties too. Women were on the agenda.'[1]

There were also plenty of books that made feminist arguments of one sort or another before the first edition of Betty Friedan's *The Feminine Mystique* landed in 1963. As discussed in the previous chapter, Virginia Woolf was one reference point, while Doris Lessing's novel *The Golden Notebook* (1962) was felt to be era defining by many who read it. Lessing had left the Communist Party a few years before she wrote it, and her account of two women's intertwined private and political struggles resonated with readers who were themselves trying to forge new ways of living – and to reconcile lofty ideals with human needs and dependencies, including those of children.

Simone de Beauvoir's powerful exploration of the psychic and social dynamics of female subordination in *The Second Sex* was another formative work for many feminists from the 1950s onwards, with the philosopher-novelist Iris Murdoch and the women's and gay rights activist Mary McIntosh among those who cited her influence. In 1961, the satirical magazine *Punch* ran a series called 'The Second Sex?' which included an article on the case for equal pay by the sociologist Barbara Wootton. Wootton had been the first woman to give lectures at Cambridge University and was one of the first four women admitted to the House of Lords in 1958. A few years later, Juliet Mitchell made a point of saying that she had read *The Second Sex* (but not Betty Friedan) when she wrote an essay that was one of the key early texts of British socialist feminism, 'The Longest Revolution'.[2]

Mitchell borrowed her title from Raymond Williams's *The Long Revolution* (1961) and, like Mary Wollstonecraft and Anna Wheeler before her, took an argument made by a prominent male thinker as a provocation. In her case, this was Frantz Fanon's contention that women were a conservative force and 'should be emancipated only after a revolution'.[3] Like Williams, Mitchell sought to extend Marxist analysis beyond its economic base. But rather than Williams's broad sweep of culture and society, she set out to analyse the ideological forces that subordinated women. Along with other New Left thinkers, she and Sheila Rowbotham favoured a more humanistic and less authoritarian form of socialism.

Legal reforms in the 1960s improved the position of women in significant ways, answering some of the demands of pre-war feminists. In 1964, a Married Women's Property Act updated older legislation to give wives increased rights over savings,

20 Women's liberation march in London, 6 March 1971. Photo by Tony McGrath. © Guardian News and Media

and the 1960s saw multiple attempts to widen access to contraception and abortion. In 1961, the pill was made legal for married women, and in 1967 this was extended to unmarried women. In the same year, pregnancy terminations were legalized by the Abortion Act – although criminal penalties were retained for women who did not follow the approved procedure, and the new law did not apply in Northern Ireland. Two years later, the Divorce Reform Act introduced the principle of irretrievable breakdown as grounds for divorce in England and Wales (divorce in Scotland was not liberalized until 1976, while a version of the English and Welsh law was introduced in Northern Ireland in 1978).

In 1968, the issue of equal pay was propelled into headlines by events at the Ford car plant at Dagenham in East London, where female sewing-machinists went on strike in protest at the higher wages paid to male colleagues doing different but similarly skilled work. The strikers attracted the support of the Labour secretary of state for employment, Barbara Castle

– although the compromise she brokered did not fully answer their grievance. But galvanized by their actions, a National Joint Action campaign committee for Women's Equal Rights was formed by trade unionists. With the backing of Harold Wilson, the first Labour prime minister since Clement Attlee, Castle steered the Equal Pay Act through Parliament in 1970.

Small groups, big dreams

With the arrival of consciousness raising in the late 1960s, the women's movement took on a new and different life. This concept and techniques had been developed in the US civil rights movement and arrived in Britain from radical feminists in New York. The idea was for women to come together to share experiences, with a view to developing forms of knowledge grounded in real lives. Infuriated by male dominance of existing political organizations, including radical left and counter-cultural ones, feminists wanted to build their own movement from the grassroots up. The first British groups were in London, which soon had several. They sprang up all over the place: in Shetland in the far north of Scotland, Aberdeen, Yorkshire, and in west Wales.

For Catherine Hall, who in the late 1960s was a recently married mother of one and a budding historian, 'Women's Liberation was absolutely to do with having a baby, and what kind of life I was going to lead. I really had no idea, I didn't know anybody with a child. My friends were students or academics. It was mind-boggling.' Hall was then in her early twenties and living in Birmingham with a husband who was older and further on in his career. In those early months of wheeling her baby around in a pram, and wondering how to carry on studying (at this point she had a bachelor's degree), Catherine met a woman called Val Hart who lived nearby.[4]

> She had a baby several months after I did so we started being together with our babies and that was the beginning of it all. We started a consciousness raising group, and the fact that she was an archivist while I was a historian obviously gave it a particular slant. But the absolute focus of that first group which we started, I think in 1969, was: what did it mean to be a woman? What did it mean to have children? How on earth did you manage to keep going with your work? What did you think about the sexual division of labour? All of that.

The idea of a women's group was itself not new. Women since the nineteenth century had organized themselves into campaigns, study circles and trade unions, which took their place in larger webs of familial, political and religious ties. But this kind of activity expanded from the late 1960s onwards. For some women, whose social lives had previously been based around the interests and preferences of boyfriends or husbands, the experience of consciousness raising was transformative. 'I think it's quite alien for people to understand that now, but women only approached each other through men,' explained one member of a Leeds women's group.

> You couldn't have a direct friendship with a woman, you would only be polite and courteous to her because your husband or partner got on well with her husband or partner, and so you were obliged to be socially nice to one another. So the idea that you would kind of go off and talk to each other alone was just like, no, you don't, you smile at what the blokes are talking about and you show interest in what the blokes are being interested in. So, you know, it was mind-blowing really, that you could actually just say, 'I think you are a fantastic woman and I want to be your friend.'[5]

Another woman described the new emotional opportunities that opened up as a result of her involvement:

> I don't think I'd had as intimate friendships at all before that. I mean, I suppose I thought they probably were, but when I was in the group I realised that actually they hadn't been close . . . it'd be more, I'd invite you round for a cup of coffee, let's talk about, you know, our lives, but nothing intimate, you know, there was that sort of barrier.[6]

Middle-class, university-educated women set up some of the first women's groups, and joined protests, including the women's liberation march held in central London on 6 March 1971. But the new movement's appeal extended beyond that demographic. Beatrix Campbell, whose family were working-class communists, described how consciousness raising left a physical imprint. 'I wasn't connected up with feminist thinking at all. I was a straightforward, rather unthinking communist,' she told me. 'But I had intimations that what was happening was important. For me, something came alive. When I interviewed Sheila Rowbotham's women's group in Hackney for the *Morning Star*, the experience of that roomful of women was a kind of falling in love. I remember it with a kind of ache.'

Some groups planned and carried out actions locally. Sheila Rowbotham and Sally Alexander were part of an early socialist feminist effort to unionize London's low-paid night cleaners. Alexander was also among those who rained flour bombs and leaflets down on the televised 1970 *Miss World* beauty contest from the balcony of the Royal Albert Hall. In Aberdeen, feminists protested against a men-only bar by marching in off the street and asking for pints, and mounted an anti-apartheid protest against the South African rugby team. (When those involved were taken to court, John Lennon paid the fines.) In Bolton, Lancashire, feminists ran a campaign on access to contraception and abortion. An article on the women's page of the *Guardian* in 1976 recorded that: 'Suddenly, Bolton is a great place to have a baby. Nothing special about the facilities or the climate. But a unique little book tells you exactly what you need to know if you are pregnant and living in that area.' A group in Sowerby Bridge, West Yorkshire, produced a booklet about menstruation, following discussions about the silence that surrounded the topic in schools. Their activities led to the establishment of a women's health centre in Halifax.[7]

'The personal is political' became a popular slogan, but women had different priorities. For some, new relationships and the chance to talk about their lives with other women, or about books and ideas, were central. Others regarded consciousness raising as an induction to an activist way of life. To Ellen Galford, who belonged to a women's group in Glasgow, it seemed a continuation of the work done by female luminaries of the radical left-wing past.

> This must have been what it felt like with Rosa Luxemburg [the German socialist] and Emma Goldman [the Russian anarchist] . . . you felt you were a part of a long line of people on the cusp of some kind of revolution, that you were really in the thick of making change. It was very exhilarating and it was really scary . . . there was this huge sense of energy and excitement.[8]

Formed in 1973, the Brixton Black Women's Group was one of a number of black women's groups, with others formed in Liverpool and Manchester. Some of the Brixton group's members were also active in the British Black Power movement, which developed in the late 1960s in response to the revival of racist and fascist politics, and sought to defend the interests of immigrants against abuses by landlords, police and others. By 1975, around 1.5 million people had settled in Britain from Commonwealth countries, and the involvement of black and Asian women in the 1970s women's movement is one of the things that set it apart from feminism up to that point. Olive Morris, Gail Lewis and others were anti-colonial socialists who were committed to anti-racist struggle as well as women's liberation. They drew on traditions of women's organizing

21 Olive Morris, OWAAD co-founder
© Lambeth Archives

outside the United Kingdom, including the Caribbean, India and the United States. (Claudia Jones did not live to see this black women's movement, having died in 1964, but her example inspired later activists.)

Debates about the relative importance of class and sex to women's lives dated back to the early suffrage and trade union movements. Now, black and Asian activists challenged white women's priorities and claims to universal sisterhood.[9] Stella Dadzie, who came to the women's movement in London via radical black politics, regarded the movement's focus on sexuality as a 'luxury',[10] and thought black women's groups should address issues including police brutality and racism in education. At the same time, black feminists sought to persuade anti-racist groups of the importance of women's rights. Ann Phoenix joined a consciousness-raising group as a student at St Andrew's University in Scotland. Later, in Manchester, she was 'the only black woman in my consciousness-raising group, and the only person – or almost the only person – in the Manchester black parents' group who saw feminism as an issue'. Phoenix, who became an academic sociologist, left the Rape Crisis group she was part of in the 1970s because feminist rhetoric about male violence at the time 'cut so close to racism'. But she has remained close to some of those she met through consciousness raising.

A second wave: the 1970s

At the first women's liberation conference, at Ruskin College in Oxford in February 1970, the new movement codified a set of demands. These were equal pay, equal educational and job opportunities, free contraception and abortion on demand, and free twenty-four-hour nurseries (so that women would have access to childcare whatever their working patterns). The first two items on this list were far from new and had been among the aims of the Six Point Group and National Union of Societies for Equal Citizenship in the 1920s. But by adding to them the demands for reproductive freedom and state-funded childcare, the conference struck a more radical note.

Later conferences were held in Skegness (1971), Manchester and London (1972), Bristol (1973), Edinburgh (1974), Manchester (1975), Newcastle (1976), London (1977) and finally Birmingham (1978). In Edinburgh, a new demand for legal and financial independence was added, along with an end to discrimination against lesbians and the right to a self-defined sexuality. But in Birmingham attempts to further amend the movement's programme ended in chaos. The long-winded 'freedom for all women from intimidation by the threat or use of violence or sexual coercion, regardless of marital status, and an end to all laws, assumptions and institutions which perpetuate male dominance and men's aggression towards women' was agreed. While poorly expressed, at least for the purposes of campaigning, the ambition to protect women from rape, 'regardless of marital status', was a bold one. This would finally become law in the 1990s. But the addition of a new preface to each of the demands, asserting every woman's 'right to a self-defined sexuality', pushed to the fore a disagreement within the movement over the political importance of sexuality. The conference broke up amid acrimony, following a physical struggle over microphones in the hall.

This is usually described as the culmination of a conflict between socialist and radical wings of feminism. While socialists sought to integrate their feminism into a Marxian worldview, in which class conflict produced by the capitalist system was the central dynamic, radicals were more concerned with the specific nature of men's domination of women, with a strong focus on violence and a greater inclination towards separatism. But while a division certainly existed, it is questionable whether the majority of activists could be described as belonging to one group or the other. In the words of one women's studies professor, it 'was terribly London centric, because if there were only twenty feminists in your women's group you weren't going to fall out over who was a Marxist and who wasn't'.[11] Recent research has drawn attention to other kinds of divisions that coexisted with the radical-socialist one, for example over issues of inclusion and what kinds of activism should be prioritized. The question of 'how to balance conventional political analysis on the one hand and the creative expression of new forms of female subjectivity on the other . . . did not neatly map on to a clear-cut socialist-radical division,'[12] was one historian's conclusion, after studying the records of local groups in several areas.

While the vast majority of women at the national conferences were white (unsurprisingly in a 97 per cent white population),[13] Gail Lewis was one black feminist who did attend in the mid-1970s. Now an academic and psychotherapist, Lewis was then a London-based activist, and gave this vivid description of her mixed feelings:

> There was a close identification and connection to what was going on, on the one hand, but on the other hand it was like, my God they are posh though . . . listen to how they speak and the words they use – I don't think the Ford women [who went on strike in Dagenham] are like this . . . It was this extraordinary mix of 'yes, I'm completely with you' and 'my God, I'm in a completely foreign world, I don't know who you are, I used to clean for you'. And just a sea of whiteness. Any sense of anti-imperialism here? Or anti-racism? But it was good.[14]

Lewis later travelled to Sri Lanka, where activists caused her to question why black and Asian women in Britain had seemingly allowed white women to take ownership of the term 'feminist' – placing it off-limits to women like herself.

But while other tensions should be recognized along with the socialist–radical split, that does not mean it was not significant.

'Down with Penile Servitude' was among the graffiti daubed on the walls in Oxford at the movement's first conference. The organizers apologized and cleaned it off. But the slogan (funny though it is) pointed to the visceral distrust of men, and of heterosexuality, that was present in the movement – even if liberal feminists later denied or shrugged it off. While most, if not all, feminists believed that women's groups and organizations were important, and had a role to play in politics and culture, there was less agreement when it came to deciding what the terms of engagement with wider society should be. When separatist feminists, some of whom defined themselves as political lesbians, made events women-only, excluded boys as well as men, or attacked heterosexual relationships and family life, some liberal and socialist feminists – who were committed to class as well as sex solidarity – objected strongly.

At the heart of the disagreement lay the question of whether capitalism or patriarchy was the bigger problem for women. For socialists, the workings of capitalism demanded attention, and a great deal of effort was expended by some intellectual feminists in trying to come up with a revision of Marxist theory that included the exploitation of women's labour within the family (the Wages for Housework group's idea that women should be paid for domestic labour was one proposed solution). Radical feminists did not necessarily disagree with this. Many of them were left-wing too. But they were more preoccupied with non-economic forms of coercion, and their immediate concern was trying to reduce the sex-based abuse and discrimination that they saw all around them.

Away from the conferences, activists cooperated on numerous initiatives that were not directly linked to the movement's formal demands. Establishing dedicated women's spaces in the built environment was widely seen to be important as a way of countering the traditional male domination of public space (even if there was disagreement over exactly what admittance policies should be). Women's health had been a theme of feminist campaigners since the nineteenth century, and new women's centres made contraceptive and other health advice easier to access. They became contact points for women seeking information on employment rights, social security and childcare. Women's art collectives sprang up.[15] Feminist trade unionists continued to be active and were an important presence on the picket line at Grunwick. This was the film processing factory in Willesden, north-west London, where Jayaben Desai and other Asian women who worked there led a two-year strike over union recognition from 1976, and where protesters supporting the strikers repeatedly clashed with police.

Increasing the support on offer to victims of domestic abuse was another project. The first women's refuge was opened in Chiswick, west London, by Erin Pizzey in 1971. Two years later, a Women's Aid group persuaded Leeds Council to let them use two adjoining terraced houses to open the first refuge in Yorkshire. In 1975, Women's Aid groups across England decided to form a National Women's Aid Federation, with similar federations soon set up in Scotland, Northern Ireland and Wales. The first Rape Crisis centre was established in London in 1976. The following year, the lenient sentence given to a violent rapist named Tom Holdsworth galvanized anti-rape campaigners to intensify their efforts. By 1984, Rape Crisis had sixty-eight branches.

The horrific series of thirteen murders and seven attempted murders of women between 1975 and 1980, and the failure by the police to catch the killer, Peter Sutcliffe, until 1981, were a formative influence on northern feminists in particular. The unsolved murders were one of the spurs for the Reclaim the Night marches held in English towns and cities on 12 November 1977, with the Revolutionary Feminist Group in Leeds taking a leading role and deciding to march close to where some of the victims' bodies had been found. While feminists were united in their anger over the failed investigation, there were differences in their analysis of violence. While radical feminists emphasized the malign impact of misogynist ideology, and stereotypes linking masculinity with aggression, socialists placed greater emphasis on economic factors and the need to boost women's incomes.[16]

The chaotic finale of the Birmingham conference in 1978 did not signal the end of the women's liberation movement. There were no further national conferences, partly for the reason that no local group offered to organize one, and in the absence of a centralized organization there was no other means to put one on (a Women's National Coordinating Committee, formed in 1970, had quickly fallen apart). But other forms of activity continued. These included lesbian, socialist feminist, radical feminist, National Abortion Campaign and Women's Aid conferences, and several that were organized by the Organisation of Women of African and Asian Descent (OWAAD). This body, formed in 1978, represented a coming together of existing black and Asian women's groups, and an attempt to create a separate space for women of colour to discuss the issues that concerned them. The same year saw the publication of Amrit Wilson's book, *Finding a Voice: Asian Women in Britain*, and Wilson became one of the organizers of protests at Heathrow against the virginity tests that were then carried out on some migrant women when they arrived in the United Kingdom to get married.

Launched in 1972, *Spare Rib* was the best known of the movement's many publications. But there were numerous other newsletters and magazines. These included *Shrew*, from the London Women's Liberation Workshop (a federation of local groups), the socialist feminist *Red Rag*, *Women's Report*, a *Scottish Women's Liberation Journal* (though this only lasted four issues before the editors fell out over how much poetry to include), the internationalist *Outwrite*, and later the radical feminist *Trouble and Strife*. Virago, the best known of the British women's movement publishers, began life as

Spare Rib Books before the founders decided to go it alone. Its first book, *Fenwomen* by Mary Chamberlain, was published in 1975. Smaller, independent presses included Sheba, which focused on marginalized women and published black authors including the poets Jackie Kay and Grace Nichols. The year 1979 saw the launch of an academic journal, *Feminist Review*.

Law reform was never the central aim of 1970s feminists, as it had been for suffragists. Liberation, they thought, required social, cultural and personal change, in addition to legislation. Not everyone endorsed this shift, with the historian Dorothy Thompson among those to argue that the movement should pay less attention to feelings and more to the material conditions of women's lives. And while Labour's Jo Richardson was a parliamentary ally of the movement, some female MPs showed impatience with its introspective emphasis. Barbara Castle thought 1970s 'women should find a cause bigger than themselves', while another Labour MP, Lena Jeger, referred to women's liberation as 'non-politics'.[17]

But there were times when women's liberationists addressed themselves directly to ministers. When Edward Heath proposed to end family allowances paid in cash to mothers, and replace them with tax credits for wage earners – more likely to be fathers – they occupied a Trafalgar Square post office in protest. The Equal Pay Act of 1970 and the Sex Discrimination Act of 1975 (which outlawed discrimination on grounds of marital status as well as sex), and the Equal Opportunities Commission established at the same time, were the most obviously feminist laws of the period, both introduced by Labour under Harold Wilson. Some of the shine was taken off equal pay by the fact that implementation was delayed for five years, and the burden remained on women to bring claims. But the significance of the principle should not be underestimated after decades during which women had routinely been paid less.

Other legislation that specifically benefited women during these years included the 1976 Domestic Violence and Matrimonial Proceedings Act, which made it possible for a court to order a married man out of his family home, whether or not he owned it or the tenancy was in his name (unmarried victims of abuse were not protected). The Housing Act of 1977 made it a priority to rehouse victims of domestic abuse with children. Official recommendations on the provision of refuges were published. Local government was also important, and Southall Black Sisters became one of many groups supported by the Greater London Council. In the words of the historian Sue Bruley, 'by the 1980s most WLM [women's liberation movement] activists had learned that if they wanted to bring practical benefits to women they had to engage with local and national state agencies for funding.'[18] Throughout the 1970s, attempts to roll back the right to abortion that had been gained in 1967 were successfully resisted, and in 1979 a landmark march was jointly coordinated by the National Abortion Campaign and the Trades Union Congress.

Activists were sometimes divided over law reform, just as they were over the movement's wider aims. For example, views on reproductive rights differed, with some black and Asian feminists challenging the emphasis on the 'right to choose' abortion. This, critics argued, was a white, middle-class preoccupation, while a more inclusive agenda would include support for women of colour who wanted to bear children and who faced abuses including virginity testing and forced sterilization. As well as differences in philosophy, there were variations in geography and timing. Racial injustice was obviously of greatest concern in areas of Britain where black and minority-ethnic people lived. In general, black women were less likely to see tougher criminal justice as a solution to violence against women, due to racism in the police and courts. Deborah Cameron, who grew up in a working-class Yorkshire family, says that based on her experience 'the second wave didn't get to places like Hull until the 1980s.'

The election of Margaret Thatcher as the United Kingdom's first female prime minister on 3 May 1979 delivered a nasty shock to all those left-wing women (and men) who had dreamed that this achievement might one day be Barbara Castle's. As far as the hopes of women's liberationists were concerned, Thatcher's victory was a disaster, and as a new decade hove into view, under a fiercely pro-market and socially conservative government, they faced a depressing reckoning with their movement's limitations. Nineteen female Members of Parliament were elected in total that day (eight Conservative and eleven Labour), which was fewer than at any general election since the war, with the exception of 1951. Increased political representation had never been among the women's liberation movement's stated aims – as it had been for feminists in the 1920s. But Thatcher's victory, along with the fractious scenes at the Birmingham conference, created the sense of an ending.

Women disproportionately voted Conservative in 1979, as they would throughout Thatcher's premiership. The attitude of women to the United Kingdom's first female prime minister is a fascinating topic but not one dealt with in this book. Thatcher was not and never claimed to be a feminist (the word 'feminism' does not appear in the index of Charles Moore's three-volume authorized biography). While the women's liberation movement never viewed influence in Westminster as its main objective, there was irony in the fact that a decade of energetic left-wing feminist organizing was capped by the election of a right-wing woman to the highest office (when Thatcher was born, in 1925, women were not yet fully enfranchised). But, on the international stage, 1970s feminism had a dramatic final flourish when the United Nations adopted the Convention on the Elimination of All Forms of Discrimination Against Women (CEDAW) in December 1979. It asserted that 'everyone is entitled to all the rights and freedoms set forth therein, without distinction of any kind, including distinction based on sex,' and was the most important statement to date of the body's commitment to women's human rights.

Keeping going: the 1980s

Like other left-wing movements, feminism in the 1980s came under attack. Inequality increased sharply as the income gap grew. Women have always been over-represented among the poorest households, in Britain and elsewhere, due to their lower earnings and lack of wealth. In the areas of the United Kingdom that were undergoing deindustrialization, particularly where miners were losing their livelihoods, there was intense hardship. Black and Asian women were exposed to racism and lesbians to homophobia, particularly with the introduction of Section 28 in 1988, which banned the 'promotion of homosexuality' by local authorities.

As mentioned above, Margaret Thatcher did not see herself as a feminist. She publicly congratulated Barbara Castle on Labour's equal pay legislation,[19] voted for David Steel's bill to legalize abortion and abstained in subsequent votes aimed at imposing tighter time limits. But her fierce opposition to social democracy placed her sharply at odds with the welfarist tradition of feminist policy making, while her militarism and support for racist regimes in South Africa and elsewhere made her the arch-enemy of the internationalist and anti-authoritarian peace movement. Coined by the Conservative MP Ian Macleod in 1965, the phrase 'nanny state' became a key Thatcherite motif that conveyed nothing but disdain for a feminized government that presumed to act *in loco parentis*, and treated the public as if it were a pack of cosseted or unruly children.

But the 1980s was also, paradoxically, a decade of consolidation for the women's movement, which continued to make inroads into institutions including public services and academia. After falling in the 1970s, the number of female MPs rose in the Thatcher years. Harriet Harman won her place on the Labour benches in 1982, followed by Clare Short in 1983. Short took up the issue of topless models in the *Sun*, making a speech in 1986 in which she complained that the newspaper portrayed women 'as objects of lust to be sniggered over and grabbed at'. In hindsight, this can be seen as the beginning of a renewed focus by campaigners on the commercialization of sex. In 1987, Diane Abbott became the first black woman in Parliament.

Deborah Cameron was among the editors of a radical feminist journal launched in 1982, and she told me that policies such as Section 28 acted as a catalyst for feminist activists like her, who were also committed to lesbian and gay rights. Meanwhile, black and Asian women continued to stress that anti-racism must form part of any liberatory women's movement – especially one with internationalist aspirations. 'What exactly do you mean when you say WE?' was the way that the writer Hazel Carby framed her challenge to white feminists.[20] The conferences organized by the Organisation of Women of African and Asian Descent (OWAAD) stopped in 1982 when a coalition of issues ranging from racist policing to forced marriage proved impossible to hold together. But other initiatives continued, including a landmark special issue of *Feminist Review*, edited by a black and Asian collective.

A tradition of feminist peace activism stretched back to the nineteenth century,[21] and included the Women's International League of Peace and Freedom, as well as women's involvement in the Campaign for Nuclear Disarmament (CND). In the summer of 1981, an anti-nuclear march set off from Cardiff to Berkshire, where the government had agreed to station ninety-six American cruise missiles. The Greenham Common camp started quietly, when some of the demonstrators decided not to go home and pitched tents outside the fence, but it soon

22 Anti-nuclear protesters at the Greenham Common peace camp, 1983

became a cause célèbre. Over Christmas 1982, around 20,000 people answered a call to 'embrace the base' and formed a ring around it. Later, around twice as many turned up to form a 14-mile chain from Greenham, past the Aldermaston atomic research centre – destination of CND marches since the 1950s – to a nearby weapons factory.

At Greenham itself, conflict with the police, local council and Conservative government ramped up as the women adopted direct action tactics in their efforts to close the base down – on one occasion breaking in as a means of highlighting inadequate security. Many women came and went, while others moved in for the long term. High-profile visitors included the actor Julie Christie and artist Yoko Ono. With multiple arrests and trials leading to some women being imprisoned up to twenty times, the echoes of suffragette protests were clear to anyone who knew about them. Earlier feminist arguments over separatism resurfaced and were addressed by the establishment of female-only areas where male visitors were not allowed.

Anti-nuclear activism drew support from the green movement as well as from left-wingers opposed to British involvement in the Cold War. The camp turned political protest into a way of life, and used direct-action and publicity tactics that would be copied by later environmentalists. A French writer, Françoise d'Eaubonne, is usually credited with inventing the term 'ecofeminism'. But, by the early 1980s, feminists in several countries were making efforts to integrate ecological and feminist perspectives, and these ideas influenced the camp. Some women embraced spiritual-mystical beliefs about women's affinity with nature and contrasted this with the destructive power of the phallic warheads. (Mary Mellor, one ecofeminist who was there, remembers a goddess statue surrounded by offerings.) Others rejected what they saw as regressive stereotypes. But for many women, Greenham was a defining political experience.[22]

Much less visible than Greenham, and important in a different way, was the growth of women's studies. This began in adult education but, starting in the late 1970s and following similar developments in the United States, feminists who wanted to study women began to establish a presence for themselves in British universities. A booklet published in 1975, *Women's Studies in the UK*, listed individual courses, and in 1979 the Bristol Women's Study Group produced an introductory text titled *Half the Sky*. The first named Women's Studies degree programme in the United Kingdom was an MA launched in 1980 at the University of Kent. This was followed by courses at the Open University and a handful of others. None of this happened without a struggle, with some universities and individuals strongly resistant to courses or lectureships described as 'women's'. At the London School of Economics, the more neutral 'gender roles' was regarded as more acceptable terminology for such research. In Sheffield, one woman recalled that the reaction to the proposal for an MA programme was 'Women's Studies? Whatever next – Budgerigar Studies?'[23]

Some of those who took or taught these courses have described the way in which divisions in the wider women's movement were replicated in classrooms. One question that inevitably arose was whether and how men should be included, and opposition to separatism is one reason why some academics did not support the new discipline. They thought feminist courses and approaches belonged in broader humanities and social science programmes. Another issue concerned racial bias. One former student on a North London Polytechnic course in the late 1980s recalled a lecture on the representation of women

> where black women really weren't dealt with at all . . . several people pointed this out to the lecturer – that it had to be rewritten, it had to include black women and so forth. And she was basically in a total state afterwards, and was very upset, and we dragged her off to the pub and sort of discussed it with her and from then on she did change the content and the next class was much better.[24]

This pattern of black experience being marginalized was echoed by Gail Lewis, who edited a book of black women's writing in 1988 which received more attention when it was published in the United States than in Britain.[25]

Women's Studies students in Bradford were given what their professor, Jalna Hanmer, described as the equivalent of a health warning: 'this course can change your life.' There was a sense in which the feminist classroom was a continuation of consciousness raising by other means, introducing complicated questions about the difference between peer support and pedagogy, politics and knowledge. One lecturer described this dilemma as follows:

> What do you do when a woman who has been badly hurt starts telling you about how badly she's been hurt in an aca-

> demic seminar? Now that doesn't happen anywhere else in the university and I suspect it no longer happens in women's studies. But there was a time when it did. And it wasn't clear whether that was part of the curriculum or not. Because it was supposed to be the sort of place where that could happen.[26]

Less than one-fifth of all eighteen-year-olds went on to higher education in the 1980s, and seminars involving only a tiny number of students might seem irrelevant. But the feminist move into academia was significant because it was part of a wider process of institutionalization. In time, the research conducted by feminist scholars would come to influence public policy in areas including violence against women and maternal health. And while universities are often characterized as ivory towers, exclusive and disconnected from ordinary life, the feminists working in them during this period were – at least some of the time – linked into a wider network that included bookshops and other workplaces.[27]

The rise of gender

'It takes MEN to carry those banners,' chortled the *Daily Mail* in one news report about an equal pay demonstration. The underground press could be equally condescending in its treatment of women's libbers. A special issue of the magazine *Black Dwarf* headed 'The Year of the Militant Woman' was undermined by a flippant dolly-bird cartoon. In the early days, activists (many of whom were photogenic, idealistic women in their early twenties) were more likely to be laughed at than insulted. Later, stereotypes ranged from the snarling harridan in dungarees to the solipsistic, middle-class wife gathered with her sisters to peer in mirrors at their genitalia. But patronized and demonized as they were, women's liberationists changed Britain. The 20,000 women who are estimated to have played a part in the movement were a far larger number than had been involved in women's rights advocacy at any time since the suffrage movement. In a UK population recorded in the 1971 census as 46 million, the activists were a tiny minority. But their presence marked a huge shift from the 1950s when a women's movement had barely existed.

Through the deliberate practice of consciousness raising, thousands of feminists committed themselves to try to understand the world and their place in it, and to seek the solidarity with other members of their sex known as the sisterhood. This was an intellectual and interpersonal project as well as a political one, which drew on earlier methods but extended them. It raised questions that activist groups of all kinds are familiar with: how to be inclusive and democratic; how to keep dynamics healthy and stop more confident personalities from taking over; how to avoid going back to the beginning every time someone new turns up; how to find enough volunteers to do the things you want to; how to keep going when you cannot. In 1977, following a long journey back to Scotland from a London conference, one woman wrote to a newsletter: 'Would those "high powered" Londoners be so high powered after ten hours in a minibus?'

Academic history of the British women's movement was slow to start, meaning that the memoirs of those who were directly involved were unmediated by any more objective attempt to describe what happened. That has now changed, but much remains inaccessible. Many women's groups did not elect committees or keep minutes. One thing that has been revealed is that some groups were more interested in racism and other inequalities than is sometimes assumed. A series of meetings in Brighton was headed 'How Do We Oppress Each Other?' and aimed to explore the barriers between women in groupings such as mother/non-mother, lesbian/heterosexual, working class/middle class, young/old, black/white, intellectual/non-intellectual and quiet/vocal.[28] Such discussions did not happen everywhere, and did not necessarily have the hoped-for effect where they did. As described above, some black women left women's groups due to racism. Other groups broke down for other reasons.

As for the central question of the significance of sex in politics, it was asked in various ways. Activists since the nineteenth century had recognized the difficulty of reconciling sexual politics with socialism, and the second wave saw various attempts at this by left-wing intellectuals. The British sociologist Diana Leonard worked with a French colleague, Christine Delphy, on an analysis that proposed patriarchy as an economic system that coexisted with capitalism, in which women were the exploited class. This work was extended by another sociologist, Sylvia Walby, and was one of the routes by which the word 'gender' – which Delphy advocated – came to replace 'sex' in much feminist discourse. The word itself was not new in English (or French), as I have already described. But from the 1970s onwards, feminist writers increasingly used it as a way of differentiating social aspects of female experience from biological ones.

This separation of the cultural modes of femininity and masculinity from the natural categories of female and male is part of second-wave feminism's legacy. But such ideas took time to filter out from academia. And despite the new emphasis on gender's malleability, questions about sexual difference did not go away. Scrutiny by women of their bodies was a theme of consciousness raising and feminist artists, as well as of women's health campaigns. Poems about menstruation or childbirth are easily parodied, but this was a period when women actively challenged the myriad ways in which their physical experiences had been marginalized and their liberties curtailed. Violence against women was widely discussed and protested against. Radical feminists and ecofeminists also raised objections to the development of reproductive technologies, fearing that these would lead to exploitation and alienation.[29] For some women, rebellion against patriarchal structures entailed the rejection of heterosexuality.

While some sought to integrate feminist and Marxian analysis, others took the view that such synthesis was a pipe dream. For Sally Alexander:

> [the] political lesson from the women's movement was that you work with many different people. You want to get that refuge going up the road – which we did, and it's still there – so you work with women who do not agree with you . . . I think the relationship between the women's liberation movement, or between any form of feminism when it emerges historically, and socialist parties and movements, is always to be negotiated and very difficult. There is nothing automatic in that relationship at all.

Other negotiations were also attempted, including the beginnings of the reckoning prompted by black and Asian feminists, with the question of whether the British women's movement could, or would, take account of the specific forms of exploitation that women from formerly colonized countries were subject to.

A third set of issues concerned sexuality and the challenge to heterosexual norms and nuclear families that was being mounted by gay liberationists – including radical lesbian feminists – in parallel with the movement for women's liberation. Relationships and psychology more broadly also came under intense scrutiny during these years, partly as a result of consciousness raising and the expansion of psychotherapy, and other practices of self-exploration. The movement did not, and could not, resolve all the conflicts or remove all the obstacles that it identified. But feminist analysis of the injustices and other difficulties still faced by women half a century after their enfranchisement, and collective and creative attempts to overcome these, were remarkable political achievements.

8

Specialists (1990s–2010)

When, as a young feminist activist in west London, Pragna Patel joined the group Southall Black Sisters in 1982, she and the women around her did not know which issues they would prioritize.[1] By the end of the decade, that situation had transformed. As she told me:

> If you were a woman with employment, immigration or housing issues, there were local welfare organizations you could go to. But state and community institutions weren't taking violence against women seriously. So the majority of women who came to us seeking advice and help were women who had experienced violence in the home. At the time that was a revelation.

Patel, who came to the United Kingdom from Kenya as a child, had been politicized partly as a result of her own narrow escape from an arranged marriage that she did not want in India. Soon Southall Black Sisters began to formulate demands based on their casework with women who were being abused within families. They secured public funding for the support services they offered and developed new tactics to draw attention to what was going on. In 1984, after a woman named Krishna Sharma took her own life after years of domestic abuse that was skated over by an inquest, the group organized a march to her abuser's home in Southall. As Patel said:

> We mobilized women from all over the country but particularly our users, some of whom were living in refuges. It was like #MeToo in that it was about naming and shaming in a context where the law was failing women. It was about empowering women and we borrowed from the Indian feminist movement, which was thriving at the time, and where women would surround the homes of perpetrators who had committed dowry-related murders. What we did told the community and the rest of the world that feminism is not a western concept, because that's what we were often accused of by community leaders: 'feminism is not part of our culture, you're just westernized women' – which was nonsense.

In 1989, the case of Kiranjit Ahluwalia came to the group's attention. She had killed her husband, Deepak Ahluwalia, by setting fire to him as he slept at their home in Crawley, West Sussex. Deepak died in hospital several days later, bringing to a horrifically violent end a marriage that over ten years had seen Kiranjit subjected to multiple rapes and beatings. She spoke little English, her parents were dead and her brothers lived abroad. In her first trial for her husband's murder, the defence of provocation failed, partly because her lawyers also argued that she had not intended the burns to be fatal. She was sentenced to life in prison.[2]

Southall Black Sisters heard about Kiranjit's case from a local Women's Aid group and visited her while she was on remand in Holloway Prison. After her conviction, Pragna Patel became involved in preparing an appeal. Kiranjit's supporters believed her life sentence was unjust and failed to take account of the cumulative strain that she had been under. Previously,

Southall Black Sisters and other feminist justice campaigners had focused mainly on women abused or killed by men. Kiranjit Ahluwalia's was one of a handful of cases in the early 1990s that led to a new focus on women who had killed their abusers. This brought with it a range of issues, one of which was the double standard in the way that violence committed by men and women was dealt with. As campaigners worked on the women's cases, they identified problems with the way that provocation was interpreted and a lack of understanding of domestic abuse and of the damage inflicted on children when mothers were imprisoned.

Sara Thornton, like Ahluwalia, was found guilty of murdering a husband who had frequently assaulted her. She was sentenced to life imprisonment in 1990, two months after Kiranjit, after fatally stabbing Malcolm Thornton at their home in Atherstone, Warwickshire. When a government minister, not long afterwards, said that 'brutality in the home' should be treated more seriously, Sara Thornton sent a letter about her case from prison to the *Independent*, which published it. But in 1991 her first appeal was rejected. Two days later, a man, Joseph McGrail, walked free from court in Birmingham with a suspended sentence for killing his female partner. The contrast with her own severe sentence struck Sara as grossly unfair, and she went on hunger strike as a protest. She would eventually be freed in 1995 after Michael Howard, the Conservative home secretary, allowed a second appeal which led to her conviction being reduced to manslaughter.[3]

Southall Black Sisters was not the only feminist group paying attention to domestic violence and the state's response to it. Women's Aid groups were involved, as were various lawyers. And in 1990 another group was formed that would specialize in cases where the law had been applied in a sexist way: Justice for Women. This had roots in the north of England, where feminists had been strongly affected by the 'Yorkshire Ripper' murders and the police's botched investigation of them. They had also run a campaign to reduce the sentences of Charlene and Annette Maw, two sisters who had killed their abusive father in Bradford. But in 1989 an event took place thousands of miles away that led them to raise their ambitions. This was the mass shooting of fourteen women at the École Polytechnique in Montreal, Canada, by Marc Lépine, who claimed to be 'fighting feminism'. In commemoration and solidarity, campaigners held a rally in central London. They aimed to raise awareness about misogyny as an ideology. A few months later, four women launched the new organization, and in the early 1990s they worked with Southall Black Sisters on the Thornton and Ahluwalia cases, holding joint demonstrations outside the Home Office.

In 1992, Justice for Women received a letter from another woman who believed the justice system had failed her. Emma Humphreys was just seventeen when she was convicted of murder and sentenced to life in prison for stabbing to death her boyfriend and pimp, Trevor Armitage, in London. She had already been in prison for seven years when she read about Kiranjit Ahluwalia, who, like Thornton, had finally succeeded in having her conviction reduced to manslaughter. Like Ahluwalia, Humphreys had been beaten and raped many times. She told Justice for Women that on the night she killed Armitage she thought he was about to rape her again. The campaign and appeal mounted on her behalf, which ended with her release in 1995, became a crucial one both for Justice for Women and the wider women's justice movement. Vera Baird, who would later become a Labour MP and government-appointed victims' commissioner, was the junior barrister on the case. Her determination to change the law on provocation was one of her reasons for going into politics. As with Ahluwalia, the crux of Emma Humphreys' appeal was the definition of provocation, as well as the circumstances in which a vulnerable young woman, who had worked as a prostitute from her mid-teens, had signed away her right to appeal. Campaigners were also influenced by new research on domestic violence by academics. Harriet Wistrich, who now leads the specialist legal charity, Centre for Women's Justice, told me that her own encounter with Humphreys had been 'life changing'.[4]

For the writer and campaigner Julie Bindel, who was one of Justice for Women's co-founders, Emma Humphreys stood out because the injustice against her was not limited to her trial. Before she met Trevor Armitage, Emma had been abused by several other men, including a violent stepfather. In prison, she became reliant on prescribed drugs. Three years after her release, she died of an accidental overdose. Bindel and others were troubled by the lack of support for someone so obviously vulnerable. For them, Humphreys' story pointed to issues that went beyond the courts. The underlying issue was the way in which male-dominated crime and justice institutions acted as an enforcement arm of a patriarchal society. They began to gather and publicize statistics such as the fact that between 1982 and 1989, 785 men had killed a female partner or former partner, compared with 177 women who had killed a male one.[5]

Campaigners also saw connections between violence against women and the sale of sex. The arrival of home video in the 1980s meant that pornography could be viewed privately as well as in cinemas, and Bindel and others saw the 'asking for it' tropes of pornography mirrored in the attitudes of violent men. Cases like that of Robert Black, who was convicted of raping and murdering three girls between 1981 and 1986, and who had a collection of child sex-abuse images, heightened the fears of those who saw links between representations of sexual sadism and the real thing. Attitudes to commercialized sex were already a fault line in the women's movement. Opponents of prostitution and pornography had fought fierce arguments, particularly in the United States, with libertarians who opposed censorship and thought the sale of sex should be legal. These arguments continue, and have been lent new urgency by the massive proliferation of online sexual content, much of which is extremely violent – a topic I will return to.

Awareness of what were then called 'battered wives' was also rising across the United Kingdom during this period. In 1992, a pioneering campaign led by women on Edinburgh's Labour council adopted the slogan 'Zero Tolerance', and in 1989 Scottish judges ruled that there was no marital exception in cases of rape. It was following this decision that, in 1991, the House of Lords (in the role it had before the Supreme Court existed) decided that rape in marriage should be criminalized. In the landmark ruling of *R v R*, which followed a lengthy campaign, the right of husbands to insist on sex with their wives was removed across the rest of the United Kingdom. There were further attempts to change laws seen as unfavourable and unjust to women. In 1994, Southall Black Sisters and Justice for Women worked with the Women's Institute and Townswomen's Guilds on a petition calling for the defence of provocation, in cases of murder, to be removed.

A conference on 'Violence, Abuse and Women's Citizenship' held in Brighton in November 1996 hosted speakers from all over the world and saw itself as picking up where the UN Women's Conference held in Beijing the previous year had left off. Speakers in Brighton covered a huge number of topics, including sex trafficking and abortion rights, female genital mutilation, migration and asylum and sexual harassment at work. The steering committee was chaired by Jalna Hanmer, the academic who ran one of the first women's studies courses in Bradford. Kiranjit Ahluwalia, who had been freed from prison four years earlier, gave a speech, and Harriet Wistrich spoke about her work on behalf of Emma Humphreys. Other speakers included Christine Delphy and Andrea Dworkin. While I have sought in this section to describe the development of a highly distinctive women's justice movement

23 Kiranjit Ahluawalia (centre), with supporters including Pragna Patel of Southall Black Sisters (right), on the day her conviction for murder was overturned, 1992

in Britain, the conference's roster of international speakers and range of topics illustrates the links to feminist campaigns elsewhere.

The rise of gender continued

In common with most feminists, campaigners against domestic and sexual violence in the 1990s were committed to a largely sociological account of human behaviour and relationships. They believed boys and men were, to varying extents, schooled to be aggressive and to put their own needs and desires first. Girls and women, by contrast, were inducted into the roles of carers and supporters, first to fathers and brothers, later to boyfriends and husbands. The media and advertising industries, as well as parents and other role models, were understood to play an important part in this conditioning. Many feminists objected as strongly to any notion of an innate male propensity to violence and domination as they did to the stereotype of female submission. It was precisely because they believed human beings were so malleable that feminists were concerned about the influence of pornography and the representation of women in general.

But biological sex differences were not absent from their campaigns or calculations. When it came to domestic violence, average variations in size and strength between men and women were understood to be of central importance. Male socialization was one reason why aggressive men were a threat to women, but another was that they were bigger and stronger. This also explained why women who killed their partners used weapons and tended to act less spontaneously than violent men. And so the changes to UK law that were sought were not based on the equalitarian principle that men and women should be treated exactly the same. Instead, women's justice campaigners drew on an alternative tradition, discussed in previous chapters, of demanding that policy makers recognize circumstances in which women's distinctive physical characteristics must be taken into account.

For a minority of radical and revolutionary feminists, heterosexuality was intrinsically problematic and lesbian separatism the ideal. But the mainstream position was that the domination of women, by men, was a social problem that should be tackled through public policy, including education and criminal justice. By the 1990s, the word 'gender' was in widespread use and understood to signify the *social* experience and effects of being sexed – as distinct from the biological fact of sex itself. This usage (or proposals for this usage) dated back several decades, as discussed in previous chapters, and had been popularized by second-wave feminist sociologists. In her book *Sex, Gender and Society* (1972), Ann Oakley defined sex as 'a biological term' and gender as 'a psychological and cultural one'. Twenty years later, historian Catherine Hall argued that the term's value lay in the fact that it was 'strong enough to counter class without being reducible to sex'.[6]

But by the 1990s the situation had become more complicated, as the validity of the sex/nature versus gender/culture distinction began to be questioned, starting in the humanities and social science departments of universities. In her celebrated books *Gender Trouble* (1990) and *Bodies That Matter* (1993), the philosopher Judith Butler fashioned a critique of sex as a fact of nature into a polemic, drawing on the work of French radical feminists including Monique Wittig, as well as the post-structuralists Jacques Derrida and Michel Foucault. Liberation, she argued, would be achieved not by confronting power and redistributing resources, as left-wing feminists and others had traditionally attempted, but through 'the subversion of identity'.[7]

The ambition of transcending sex on grounds that it imposed undesirable limits had been a dream of women since Mary Wollstonecraft, and Butler was not the first or only scholar to dissent from the sex–gender consensus. Christine Delphy upended the view of sex as prior – being immutable and fixed *in utero* – when she wrote that 'gender in its turn created anatomical sex . . . [which is] devoid of social implications.'[8] Denise Riley, a British writer, wrote a book called *'Am I That Name?'*, which aimed to historicize and thus denaturalize the category of 'women'. But in the 1990s, gender and queer studies became one of the most fashionable sub-genres of critical theory, as the influence of materialist analysis receded.

The significance of this shift should not be overstated. These courses were a minuscule proportion of what was then on offer in British universities. And post-structuralist theories about gender coexisted with other forms of knowledge. Feminist historians and critics continued to dig up new information about female figures from the past in archives, while sociologists gathered sex-specific data in areas such as education and health. In focusing on both race and sex (or gender), black feminist academics, including Gail Lewis and Ann Phoenix, developed what we would now call intersectional research. The view that gender theory offered a more progressive lens for critics of inequality than sexual politics also faced direct challenges. In 1992, Stevi Jackson wrote an article called 'The Amazing Deconstructing Woman', which argued that the logical destination of postmodern feminism – with its rejection of materialist analysis of women's lives in favour of a heavy emphasis on discourse – was 'post-feminism'.[9] Ecofeminists too were moving in a different direction. For them, human embodiment and the relations between social and ecological processes were of fundamental importance. They saw the masculine repudiation of dependence, in favour of a transcendent individuality, as destructive of both women (particularly mothers) and nature.[10]

But these voices were marginal, and they did not attract anything like the same interest. As would soon become clearer, the gender theorists were in the vanguard of a significant shift in public discourse that would extend beyond universities. Most of the women's studies courses that had started in the 1980s either closed down or were renamed 'gender studies' (the sole surviving Women's Studies department in the United Kingdom is at the University of York). The sociologist Sylvia Walby took to using the term 'gender regime' instead of patriarchy because readers thought the latter was essentialist and refused to read her work.

The science of sex

There was something else going on in universities in the 1990s that I want to mention before moving on. While the trend in the humanities was towards critical theory (or just 'theory'), a contrasting shift was to be found in the new field of evolutionary psychology. This was derived from sociobiology, as earlier attempts at applying evolutionary theory to questions previously regarded as sociological had been called. While critical theory was radically anti-universalist, and treated the Enlightenment quest for truth as a veil for western interests, the new biology sought to apply Darwinian ideas to a range of questions that fell outside biology's traditional purview.

Feminists were among this discipline's strongest critics. They knew Darwinism had been used to justify sexism and racism, and this variant appeared to many liberal-left thinkers to be uncomfortably close to social Darwinism – which equated evolution with progress – and eugenics, which saw a role for humans in improving the genetic quality of their own species. In a 1997 piece titled 'Back to Nature', Deborah Cameron dismissed the output of a Darwin seminar, convened by philosopher Helena Cronin at the London School of Economics, as 'wholly ideological claptrap'.[11] Other attacks on what they regarded as a dangerous new determinism came from feminists including Ann Oakley and Lynne Segal. But controversial though all this was, feminists in universities (including me, as a postgraduate English student with an interest in feminism) missed something. Because in the mix of the Darwinian revival was a development, with regard to the theory of sexual selection, that would surely have interested at least some of them.

Whereas the pressure in natural selection is environmental – adaptations that survive are those that give animals an edge in the struggle for life – the pressure in sexual selection is derived from the decisions made by creatures about whom to mate with. Darwin, famously, was prompted to investigate this additional mechanism of evolution by the conundrum of the peacock's tail – an ornament that offers no possible advantage in survival terms, meaning that there must be other forces in play. His conclusion, set out in *The Descent of Man, and Selection in Relation to Sex* (1871), was that female mate-choice and sexual competition between males are two further sources of selective pressure, helping to determine which genes – and the traits associated with them – are carried on into the next generation. In the highly visible battles between males to mate and reproduce, size and strength were clearly important. But on what basis did females make their choices? The existence of the peacock's tail suggested powers of attraction that had nothing to do with the ability to win fights. One debate among Darwin's contemporaries concerned aesthetics. Did female animals choose mates on the basis of appearance, and if so, why?

But while Darwin hypothesized that females might select the 'best performers' among songbirds known for their 'love antics', the emphasis in *The Descent of Man* was on male–male competition.[12] Because he thought females were generally 'coy' and less keen than males on mating, he tended to portray males as active agents – and females as their prizes. Laboratory experiments carried out in the mid-twentieth century on fruit flies appeared to corroborate these assumptions and provide an evolutionary basis for female sexual reserve. Males increased their genetic representation in subsequent generations by mating with multiple partners, while females did not. But starting in the 1970s, and taking time to reach a general audience, field research conducted by a mostly female group of primatologists and anthropologists told a different story. Alison Jolly, who was American but had an English husband and lived in both countries, and Thelma Rowell, were two of the pioneers. While Jolly made discoveries about female dominance in lemurs, Rowell's research emphasized the importance of female–female coalitions.[13]

But there were not many British women working in this field to rank with the leading men of British evolutionary science, such as W. D. Hamilton and John Maynard Smith. The others in the group mentioned above were also Americans: Sarah Blaffer Hrdy, Jeanne Altmann, Patricia Gowaty and Barbara Smuts. The Welsh writer Elaine Morgan had advanced an astute critique of male bias in evolutionary anthropology in the 1970s – although her hypothesis of an 'aquatic ape' stage in human evolution is not supported by evidence.[14] But in 1999 a British trade edition of Sarah Hrdy's book, *Mother Nature: Natural Selection and the Female of the Species*, came out, making the discoveries of Darwinian feminists accessible to anyone who wanted to read it. Combining data on primates with anthropological evidence about a range of human societies, Hrdy argued that the sex bias of male researchers had distorted evolutionary science. Female reproductive strategies, featuring both competition and cooperation, played a far greater role in human evolution than had previously been recognized – one that she believed had been anticipated by early female critics of Darwin, including Marian Evans/George Eliot (as discussed in chapter 3) and Clémence Royer, a French translator who challenged some of the inferences in *The Origin of Species* and was sacked.

Far from an unalterable law of nature, the male dominance hierarchies of some primates, and humans, were just one possible outcome of a struggle between the sexes. Hrdy explained this in sociobiological terms, which recognized the role of historical as well as evolutionary forces, particularly the impact of agriculture. Her argument was that other outcomes than the patriarchal control of female sexuality and reproduction that are seen in so many human societies were – and are – possible. To make this case, she drew on examples including the female dominance seen in bonobos, which are our closest genetic relatives along with chimpanzees, and the more egalitarian pair bonds of some other primate species, which she likened to companionate human marriages. She told her readers that she had read feminist authors including Nancy Chodorow, Shere Hite and Valerie Solanas.

Three years later, Anne Campbell, a British evolutionary psychologist, published *A Mind of Her Own* (2002). Like the American primatologists, Campbell challenged the version of evolution that made males (including men) the stars, and cast females (including women) in roles of lesser importance. Drawing on her own research on young women and aggression, she argued that evolved differences between men and women included a greater male propensity for violence. By the early

2000s, sex difference research was one of science's 'hottest topics',[15] in the words of journalist Angela Saini. But although Campbell gave her book an eye-catching title that riffed off Virginia Woolf,[16] and occupied a prestigious position as a professor at Durham, neither she nor Hrdy attracted anything like the same level of interest as male peers such as Richard Dawkins or the other well-known writers on Darwinian topics around this time. These were all white men, and included Matt Ridley and Steven Rose, and the Americans Steven Pinker, E. O. Wilson and Stephen Jay Gould.

Hrdy addressed the disdain towards evolutionary science shown by feminists in the humanities disciplines directly, describing it in 1999 as 'understandable, if shortsighted'.[17] She was highly critical herself of pronouncements along the lines of 'Men are from Mars, women are from Venus' (the title of John Gray's 1992 bestseller), and at odds with evolutionary psychologists' emphasis on pan-human traits. By contrast, her work stressed adaptation, flexibility and variation. But she saw the tension between maternal and male sexual interests as fundamental and in need of being addressed 'if we are to build the current experiment in women's rights on a more secure foundation, based on a deeper understanding of why issues like "women's reproductive rights" are so charged in the first place'.[18]

Campbell was more acerbic. In *A Mind of Her Own*, she suggested that feminists are frequently unable 'to distinguish between feminist science and good science', and described this bias as a threat to academic freedom.[19]

Feminism and New Labour

The next group of feminists in this chapter are politicians. Margaret Thatcher was and is a role model to many right-wing women. But her politics did not include a commitment to women working together to advance their shared interests. Some feminist initiatives attracted support from Conservatives under her leadership. Michael Howard was the home secretary who granted Sara Thornton's appeal against her murder conviction. Teresa Gorman was a strong supporter of abortion throughout the 1980s, and a champion of hormone replacement therapy for menopausal women when this was treated as eccentric. But parliamentary feminism in the 1980s and 1990s was largely confined to the Labour benches. Clare Short led a high-profile if unsuccessful campaign against the topless photographs featured on page three of the *Sun*, and repeated attempts to restrict access to abortion were successfully resisted. Short remembers the parliamentary battle over reproductive rights as 'very, very hard'. Women MPs were in a tiny minority, and the Commons was 'a bit like a men's club, if you mentioned breast cancer they would giggle; it was like that.'

Boosting women's presence in Parliament was never an explicit aim of the women's liberation movement. But in the 1980s it became a project for feminists in the Labour Party, and in 1989 they formed the Labour Women's Network to oversee recruitment and training of candidates. In 1992, Labour specified that there must be at least one woman on each of its parliamentary shortlists. A year later, it went further and adopted all-women shortlists. This was partly a tactical manoeuvre, aimed at attracting female voters who had previously favoured Tories. Three years later, the policy was challenged in court and ruled illegal under the 1975 Sex Discrimination Act. But thirty-four female candidates had already been selected and, after Labour's 1997 general election victory, the sex balance in Parliament was transformed. Sixty women had been elected in 1992, meaning that Parliament was more than 90 per cent male. In 1997, the number of women MPs doubled to 120, of whom 101 were Labour.

Asked to look back at New Labour's record from a feminist perspective, women who had senior roles in government and policy circles acknowledge failures as well as successes. Mistakes started on day one, with the 'Blair's babes' photo taken after the election, placing the grinning prime minister in the middle of what should have been a celebratory group portrait of Labour women. But even if redistribution to women was not the primary motivation, all the work on economic justice that was led by the Treasury can be described as feminist in its effects. Socio-economic inequality had significantly widened in the 1980s, and easing some of the hardship created by deindustrialization and mass unemployment was among the new government's priorities (although the pro-market policies it adopted meant that the weakening of labour relative to capital that had been Thatcher's overriding objective was consolidated). The Sure Start programme of new children's centres was probably the strongest brand associated with New Labour in the domain of what are traditionally viewed as women's issues (because mothers provide the vast majority of care for the under-fives). But since female-led households have always been over-represented among the poorest households, all the anti-poverty measures introduced in this period disproportionately benefited them. Jacqui Smith, the former home secretary, thinks the introduction of the national minimum wage in 1998 was the single most important thing that New Labour did, 'if you're thinking about women's economic empowerment'.

Katherine Rake was seconded from the London School of Economics to the Women's Unit in the Cabinet Office in 1999, where she wrote a report on women's lifetime incomes that became the basis for policies aimed at what she calls 'evening things up'. In 2002, she became director of the Fawcett Society, the campaigning feminist charity with origins in the suffrage movement. While there, she worked with Jacqui Smith and activist groups, including Object!, on an amendment to a police bill that reclassified lap-dancing clubs as sexual entertainment venues, giving councils new powers to refuse licences. In 2008, the government significantly increased funding to Rape Crisis services. Asked to summarize the period of her involvement, Rake said: 'I think there were two things going on – one was a huge drive on anti-poverty and inequality measures, driven by Gordon Brown at the Treasury. And the second thing was that women ministers, some of whom had grown up with second-wave feminism, took those principles with them into government.'

Valerie Amos, Vera Baird, Caroline Flint, Harriet Harman, Patricia Hewitt, Tessa Jowell, Mo Mowlam, Dawn Primarolo, Clare Short and Jacqui Smith were some of those who fit this description. Others, including Diane Abbott and Jo Richardson, were on the backbenches, while Betty Boothroyd was in the Speaker's chair. The Women's Unit created in 1997, the National Women's Conference and the Women's Parliamentary Party were the main formal structures for feminist discussion and policy making, although Jacqui Smith thinks informal links between female ministers were just as important, if not more so (as the mother of a baby when she entered Parliament, she depended a good deal on colleagues' personal support). One issue taken up by MPs was women's participation in sport, and Tessa Jowell captained a parliamentary five-a-side women's football team.[20] Other examples of feminist law making include the incorporation into statute of the House of Lords' decision to criminalize marital rape, work on equalizing pensions and the introduction of a right for working parents to request flexible working in 2003. Pressure from women in government, as well as justice groups, also lay behind the 2006 Corston Report on vulnerable women in prison. This followed six suicides at Styal Prison in Cheshire, and offered the clearest description to date of the ways in which women were failed by a criminal justice system designed by and for men. But most of Baroness Corston's recommendations were not implemented.[21]

Prisons were not the only area where reformers encountered resistance, which was justified on the basis that there were more urgent priorities or that their proposals were not aligned with public opinion. Smith told me she thought the Women's Unit's impact 'was a bit bitty because it was linked to the individual minister [the newly created role of women's minister] and didn't really have a role across government, so there wasn't a coherent approach.' Ayesha Hazarika, who worked as an adviser to Harriet Harman when she became women's minister and leader of the House of Commons under Gordon Brown in 2007, said: 'If you think of the four great offices of state, the people doing equalities were right at the other end, at the bottom of the pecking order. So the officials were quite beleaguered, people slightly laughed at them; we were very much the square losers.'

But, under Harman, who was the elected deputy leader of the Labour Party and the most senior woman in government, the Women's Unit (which in 2007 became the Government Equalities Office) was injected with a new urgency. In particular, she was determined to seize the opportunity presented by Labour's pledge to streamline anti-discrimination legislation. Rather than a tidying-up exercise, she and others saw a chance to push the equalities agenda forward. This provoked resistance from civil servants, ministerial colleagues and even some trade unions. 'They were like "woah, woah, woah, no, no, no, let's not go crazy here, we don't want to be too radical,"' in Hazarika's words.

Harman and colleagues, including Vera Baird, who in 2007 became solicitor general, also wanted to remove the defence of provocation from the criminal law in cases of murder, and to change the law on prostitution by criminalizing buyers – the so-called Nordic model adopted in Sweden in 1999. 'But for quite a lot of men in the Labour Party that was too much. It was a double whammy, like "crazy feminism,"' Baird told me. So they settled for what she thought of as a 'halfway house', according to which it became illegal to pay a prostitute who had been subjected to force 'because what decent man would have sex with a woman if he knew that the money would go elsewhere, or that she was being pushed into it?' Baird looks back on this compromise with regret and is sorry, too, that she was unable to persuade Harman to stand for the party leadership in 2015, following Ed Miliband's resignation.

But she thinks Labour's improvements to women's pensions deserve more attention, while Hazarika says another initiative, on adverts for prostitutes, was inspired by the actions of grassroots feminists. 'You could look in the back of your nice friendly local newspaper, and sandwiched between lost cats and skips for hire would be little adverts saying "sauna: beautiful fresh girls from around the world arriving every day" – literally code for people trafficking,' she remembers. There were heated exchanges with the Society of Newspaper Editors, who feared damage to their business model if such adverts were restricted, as well as continuing internal rows about what would be included in the upcoming Equality Bill.

'Labour started off with some very good feminist policies, things like childcare, putting violence against women on the map, flexible working, women's representation, but we lost our edge towards the end,' in Hazarika's view. Others question whether more might have been achieved had the feminist infrastructure within the party not been dismantled in the run-up to 1997. In the 1980s, more than a thousand constituency parties had women's sections, which had separate conferences and put forward motions to the main party conference. Ann Henderson, a former member of Labour's National Executive Committee (NEC), thinks the replacement of this internal women's organization with the more skills-focused Labour Women's Network served to weaken feminist policy making, which was sacrificed in favour of an organization aimed at supporting individual women and their careers.

These changes formed part of Tony Blair's wider programme of reforming the party along less democratic, more managerialist (or 'modern') lines, and were anti-left rather than anti-feminist in their intention. But the closure of women's sections also fitted in with an agenda of 'mainstreaming' which came in part from feminists themselves. This was the idea that distinct structures and work streams for women in politics had been superseded in the 1990s. What was needed now, it was argued by some (internationally as well as in Britain), was a confident assertion that feminist ideas belonged in the mainstream. This approach was influential during the early years of the devolved Scottish and Welsh Parliaments, although Northern Irish women bucked the assimilationist trend by setting up their own party, the Northern Ireland Women's Coalition, and adopting the suffragette colours of purple, white and green (the Coalition survived until 2006, by which time it had lost its handful of seats).[22]

Radicalism revived

In 1989, the English journalist Joan Smith, who had covered the disastrous police investigation into the Yorkshire Ripper murders and had nightmares about it, wrote a book called *Misogynies*. In it, she argued that misogyny had enabled the killer of thirteen women to escape detection for as long as he did, and presented this argument alongside other essays about the hatred and abuse of women. Smith's book was prescient. The 1990s and 2000s are widely, and rightly I think, viewed as a challenging period for feminism in Britain. Events in the United States, including the rejected testimony of Anita Hill against Supreme Court nominee Clarence Thomas, and Bill Clinton's affair with Monica Lewinsky, cast a shadow that was greatly enlarged by the power of American media. American authors, including Susan Faludi and Naomi Wolf (author of the 1990 bestseller *The Beauty Myth*), warned of a backlash against feminism even as Wolf and another influential writer, Rebecca Walker, declared their intention to build a third wave of feminism.[23] *Spare Rib* expired in 1993; the men's magazine *Loaded* was launched the following year, and its tone of humorous, get-your-kit-off sexism became part of a wider phenomenon (the lads' mags between them had around 1.5 million monthly readers). When a women's studies lecturer in Leicester, Imelda Whelehan, published one of the first critiques of 1990s popular culture, she ended it by describing the low turnout and depressing mood at a feminist rally she had attended.[24]

Amid a general anti-feminist mood, specific projects continued. The year 1994 saw the launch of Apna Haq, a domestic violence organization in West Yorkshire. The Women's Prize for Fiction emerged in 1996, following several years in which female authors were sidelined in existing literary awards. In 2000, Justine Roberts and Carrie Longton created Mumsnet as an online space for user-generated content and peer support. This was followed by the launch of The F-Word website, in 2001, and a lively phase of online community building ensued, aided by new tools with the launch of Facebook (2004) and Twitter (2006, since renamed X).

As previously mentioned, second-wave feminists were divided over the issue of commercial sex, and whether or not pornography and prostitution were inherently exploitative. Social and sexual liberals recoiled from any correspondence between feminists and conservatives who opposed gay and reproductive rights as well as pornography (in the United Kingdom, Mary Whitehouse was seen to personify these prudish, bigoted views and was detested for it). But Mumsnet was one of the places where, from the early 2000s, some feminists began to voice opposition to the growing sex industry and to challenge the pro-prostitution, anti-censorship, 'sex-positive' approach.

By the early 2000s, the resurgence of grassroots feminism on the internet was being hailed as a new feminist wave of activism – or at least a new format.[25] But there were offline developments as well as online ones. The radical feminist group Object! launched in 2003 with a campaign against sex buyers. The following year saw the creation of the London Feminist Network, which ran three 'Feminism in London' conferences, and had an anti-porn 'Bin the Bunny' subgroup. It also led the relaunch of Reclaim the Night, a form of march protesting violence against women based on a model first used by feminists in Italy, Belgium and Germany before being picked up in 1977 in Leeds.[26] Imkaan was formed in 2004, as a specialist charitable organization for black and minoritized women who are victims of abuse. Women for Refugee Women was set up two years later to focus specifically on the injustices faced by women in the asylum system. And in 2008 was the first demonstration organized by the Million Women Rise collective – which was initiated by Sabrina Qureshi, partly in response to a lack of black and Muslim women at Reclaim the Night.[27]

Apna Haq, as mentioned above, was formed in South Yorkshire in 1994. Its founder, Zlakha Ahmed, was inspired both by Southall Black Sisters and by a group of Indian domestic abuse workers whom she encountered at a conference in Leeds. As a child, Ahmed was the victim of a sex-abuse ring in Telford, and as an adult she became a youth worker with an interest in domestic violence. In particular, she was concerned by the dangers faced by migrant women who had no recourse to public funds, and thus no means of leaving violent husbands, because they had entered the United Kingdom on spousal visas. In the early 2000s, Apna Haq became a council-funded organization, and Ahmed gave up her job in the local youth service to work for it full-time. As well as providing a public service, Apna Haq campaigned for changes in the legal status and entitlements of migrant women – and was criticized for doing so by some of its funders. But in 2009 its advocacy, and that of other charities, brought a result. A pilot scheme offering some support to migrant wives fleeing abusive partners was introduced.

'I didn't start Apna Haq because I was a feminist; it was because there was an unmet need and I thought women had the right to self-determination, to live their lives how they want,' Ahmed told me in an interview. But over time she came to see the organization, which relied on voluntary peer support networks as well as paid staff, as belonging to both the women's and the anti-racist movements. Ahmed was not wearing her hijab when we talked but told me that 'in the early years, when people had started to hear about me, a number of times I was invited to speak at events and when I introduced myself the women's jaws would just drop – this was both white and South Asian women – because they didn't expect a hijabi woman with the ethics that I've got.'

Ahmed recognizes that the term 'feminism' has negative as well as positive associations for some black and Asian women. When the teacher and author Lola Okolosie wrote an article in the *Guardian* about 'the difficult work of turning feminism into feminisms' in order to make more room for the range of black and minority-ethnic women's experiences, this made a strong impression on her.[28] As well as her domestic abuse work, Ahmed played a role in pushing back against stereotyping and far-right attacks, following the exposure of the Rotherham sex abuse ring. More recently, pornography has emerged as an issue for the charity, with casework including support for children harmed by online material. Ahmed told me one of the things children look for on social media is for ways to make money – especially if they and their families do not have enough. This means even young teenagers can be tempted by the idea of earning money by stripping off in front of cameras for payment, even though this is illegal.

For other feminist groups, including Object!, campaigning against the sex industry's influence was the main focus. The increasing prevalence of hard-core, violent pornography was plain to see (the novelist Martin Amis wrote an article for the *Guardian* about this in 2001, while the trade magazine *Adult*

Video News ran a cover story in 2003 that asked 'Can porn get any nastier?').[29] Meanwhile, the number of lap-dancing clubs in the United Kingdom doubled to more than 300 between 2004 and 2008.[30] In Birmingham in 2008, feminists protested against the inclusion of vouchers for a lap-dancing club in the pack handed out to delegates at the Conservative Party Conference. Another grassroots group that took a strong, anti-sex industry position was the Bristol Feminist Network. Formed in 2007, its first project was a women's community arts festival known as Ladyfest, modelled on previous events in the United Kingdom and the United States. Sian Norris was one of the founders and, during the six years she was involved, the network organized three Reclaim the Night marches, hosted monthly discussions and a book group, and saw itself as a partner of the local Fawcett Society branch, which lobbied politicians. The anti-female genital mutilation campaigner Nimco Ali lived in Bristol at the time, and the group worked with her to raise awareness of an issue that was then rarely discussed. Members also joined protests against attempts to restrict abortion. But the single biggest issue, according to Norris, was the normalization of sexual objectification, for example in the semi-nude images favoured by men's magazines and the city's new strip clubs:

> We did have older women in our group; there was an age range. But most of us hadn't experienced childbirth or the lack of childcare, and when you're in your twenties the pay gap hasn't necessarily manifested itself. But the issues around lad culture and porn were very visible to us. We really felt them. We did loads of actions – we made a film of ourselves flyering lads' mags in newsagents; we protested against the opening of a Hooters [a chain restaurant where waitresses wear tiny shorts and low-cut vests]; we had a huge row when Dita Von Teese [the burlesque performer] was booked to perform at a council-funded event. The growth of sex entertainment venues was

impacting our ability to walk around the city and to feel equal to men in that space.

As already mentioned, the law governing sexual entertainment licences was changed under Labour in response to feminist pressure. But following Pornhub's launch in 2007, the main motor for what feminists call 'porn culture' moved online. This shift was documented by a number of authors and is a theme I will return to in chapter 9. But outside women's activist circles, the various forms of sex for sale were not seen as a pressing issue. The efforts of a group of feminist Labour MPs to criminalize sex buyers were thwarted, and most cities and towns did not have an activist scene as energetic as Bristol's. Individual women progressed in academia, politics, trade unions and many other areas of professional and commercial life. In 1999, Caroline Lucas was elected as a Green member of the European Parliament (the EU) and soon became her party's most prominent public figure and an important voice in the wider environment movement. But with the rise of postmodernism in the humanities, academic feminism became more detached from everyday life. The links proposed by the second-wave feminists between consciousness raising, activism and scholarship became more attenuated or gave way under pressure from opponents. Women's studies were overshadowed by other disciplines and forms of knowledge.

Financially speaking, women were better off relative to men in 2010 than they had been before Labour took office. In particular, single-parent families (more than 85 per cent of which are headed by women) and single female pensioners benefited from changes to the benefits and tax systems. Access to maternity allowances was also made easier for low-income women who did not qualify for maternity pay due to their employment status. Between 1997 and 2010, the gender pay gap between men's and women's average hourly earnings (for full-time workers) fell from 20.7 per cent to 15.5 per cent (the gap was and is much larger for part-timers).[31] But changes in the economy in the 1990s, including the privatization of public services and outsourcing of jobs in the health and care sectors, weakened the position of workers in significant ways. This included women, particularly black and minority-ethnic women, who were and remain over-represented in low-paid occupations including cleaning and catering.

As the sociologist Sylvia Walby has pointed out, radical feminists as well as socialists and trade unionists were troubled by the implications for vulnerable women of the shifting balance between state and markets. While women's justice campaigners made violence their focus, they were aware that the problems of women such as Emma Humphreys did not start or end with partners who abused them, or with the way that the criminal law dealt with such crimes. Difficulties in accessing housing and benefits, lack of support with addictions, and specific problems faced by migrant women, were all understood as feminist issues.

A third wave

I chose 'Specialists' as a title for this chapter as it offered a way of describing the variety of routes followed by feminists in this period. It shows how woman-focused activism became both more institutionalized, for example in government, and more fragmented. Feminism has always meant different things to different women – as I demonstrated in my discussion of the 'new' and 'old' feminists of the 1920s, and the women's liberation movement. But in the years after 1990, the range of feminist activities and ideas make it difficult to argue that anything that could be described as a women's movement still existed. Liberal and radical attitudes to commercial sex were one dividing line. Another was the gulf between postmodern and materialist thinkers over the extent to which language and personal identity were relevant to attempts to tackle sex-based injustices. Vigorous debates over the relationship between race, sexual politics and gender politics also continued, often under the label of intersectionality, which was the term coined by the US legal scholar Kimberlé Crenshaw in 1989 to describe the combination of anti-sex discrimination initiatives and anti-racist politics.

There were correspondences, for example, between grass-roots campaigns on rape within marriage, domestic abuse and women's poverty, and reforms taken forward by Labour ministers. But the third wave of feminism in Britain – as some but not all of those involved described it – was characterized by conflict both about what should be feminism's priorities and about the political philosophy underpinning it.

9

Feminists (2010–2023)

The way some of the women involved in the Government Equalities Office tell it, pretty much everything they did in the final years of New Labour involved a fight. Ayesha Hazarika is now a well-known broadcaster, but in 2010 she was a special adviser to Harriet Harman, tasked with supporting the then deputy prime minister's plan to strengthen equalities law. Civil servants were cautious, and even lobby groups were initially tongue-tied when encouraged to present their wish lists. But the real pushback came once the law was drafted. 'We were told we were out of control,' Hazarika told me:

> I remember being at a policy forum where we were negotiating with trade union and constituency representatives and I had the riot act read to me. I was taken into a room, there were two male cabinet members and three male advisers all shouting . . . Another time I said in a meeting that gender pay-gap transparency was my ultimate goal, and that if we could do it unilaterally [through the Government Equalities Office] then we would. Someone obviously grassed me up to another adviser, a man, because I got this horrible phone call, saying 'Who do you think you are?' When I look back, it was outrageous. I was in pieces,

> but Harriet [Harman] just said 'We've got to stick together and we'll get there'. We were under attack a lot, from the right-wing press but also from colleagues.

The Equality Act brought together a range of previous laws, including ones against discrimination based on age and sexual orientation that Labour had only recently introduced.[1] In total, the new Act listed nine protected characteristics, four of which relate to sex or sexism. These are sex, pregnancy and maternity, sexual orientation, and gender reassignment (the characteristic that protects transgender people from discrimination, whether or not they have transitioned medically). Though it has never been enacted, the Act also contains a section that would have made 'combined discrimination' based on two characteristics illegal – for example, sex and race.

Vera Baird, who piloted the legislation through Parliament, described it as a 'kind of people's bill; we consulted everybody under the sun'. When Gordon Brown called an election, Harman had to fight for its place in the legislative timetable, and the Act gained royal assent just four days before Parliament was dissolved. Harman held the line on gender pay-gap reporting, which was included. But despite this achievement, and the label 'Mumsnet election' that was used in 2010 because working mothers were identified as a key group of floating voters, the rights of women and minorities were not prominent issues in the campaign. Politics at the time was dominated by the fallout from the 2008–9 financial crisis and the Iraq War – opposition to which had made the Liberal Democrats popular – and continuing divisions over Labour's leadership and direction. After the Conservative–Liberal Democrat coalition was formed, the early signs for women were not good: the government's leading figures were all men. David Cameron did not appoint many women ministers. Although included in the Equality Act, compulsory gender pay-gap reporting by employers required the government to enact it. Cameron decided against it.

In opposition, things did not get easier for Harriet Harman. Her suggestion that the United Kingdom might host a summit of women leaders from around the world (perhaps called a Gender 7 or Gender 20) was shot down when Labour was in government. Now it was hard to persuade colleagues that a women's event should be attached to the 2010 Party Conference. When agreement was finally given, organizers were told that they should avoid 'the f-word'. Ayesha Hazarika recalled party officials saying, 'We could talk about violence against women, we could have stuff about equal pay, but "We're not having feminism, it's too much, too old school."'

Against austerity and abuse

As discussed in the previous chapter, grassroots activists were galvanized by the increasing sexism of popular culture, and anger that the already porous boundary between mainstream media and commercial sex was breaking down. In 2000, the *Daily Express* and *Sunday Express* newspapers had been bought by Northern Shell, the company owned by Richard Desmond that also ran pornographic satellite television channels and published magazines including *Asian Babes* and *Barely Legal*. Now, as a new government whose most senior figures were privately educated white men announced plans for spending cuts and abolished the National Women's Commission as part of its attack on quangos and 'red tape', concerns rose about the effect of austerity on women, particularly those in low-income groups. In 2010, the Fawcett Society failed to convince a court that the government had broken the law by neglecting to take account of gender inequality when drawing up its first budget.

Kat Banyard worked for Fawcett when it lobbied to restrict sex-entertainment licences, and in 2010 she formed a new pressure group, UK Feminista, and published a book. *The Equality Illusion* challenged what she saw as the feel-good tendencies of her third-wave peers – particularly their commitment to 'finding the feminism' in the sex industry. Another book, *Living Dolls*, saw the journalist Natasha Walter, who had founded the charity omen for Refugee Women four years earlier, declare that her former optimism regarding women's progress had been 'entirely wrong'. She now added her voice to those warning that 'creeping pornification' was harming girls, women and relationships. Like the web-based campaign Pink Stinks, and the Mumsnet women who ran Let Girls Be Girls and Let Toys Be Toys campaigns, Walter was dismayed by the trend towards stereotypes in retail. While some items had always been marketed primarily at children of one sex or the other, many others had been aimed at children rather than at boys or girls. Now, increasingly, shoppers were confronted by walls of pink and blue, and Walter was troubled by 'the strange melding of the doll and the real girl'.[2] Along with other feminist writers, she thought academic research on sex differences was also to blame for a resurgence of sexism by persuading people that sex stereotypes were rooted in nature rather than culture.

Anti-sexism campaigners chalked up some successes. A ban on sex-work advertisements in job centres was made more significant by the toughening of sanctions on jobseekers. Without it, women might have faced losing benefits if they refused offers to work as a stripper or phone sex-line operator. In Sheffield, feminists persuaded the council to prevent a branch of the restaurant Hooters from opening after learning that employees were told to expect sexual innuendo from customers.[3] But the rising sexism that feminists detected went beyond the behaviour of a handful of businesses. The polarized sex roles and extreme body shapes of pornography were infiltrating everyday life, along with habits of objectifying and shaming women that derived new force from celebrity and gossip websites, which had even less regard for privacy than their tabloid-press predecessors. Banyard quoted Hugh Hefner, who told an interviewer in 2010: 'I've won. We now live in a Playboy world'.[4]

One of Walter's interviewees, a regular porn user, told her he was shocked by what he was seeing on websites, including 'this unbelievable obsession with anal sex'.[5]

Amid the gloom about austerity, 2012 saw a landmark equal-pay claim brought by 174 women against Birmingham Council. The women, who had worked as cooks, cleaners and care assistants, persuaded judges that their case should be allowed, despite the usual time limit of six months having elapsed.[6] Grassroots activists continued to focus on harassment and the representation of women in the media in the hope of bringing about change. In 2012, Lucy-Anne Holmes, an author and actor, started a new No More Page 3 campaign. Launched in the same year, the Everyday Sexism website created by Laura Bates was a platform for women to share experiences of being sexually harassed and mistreated. A year later, another woman, Frances Scott, was prompted by her personal realization of the scale of present inequality to found a non-partisan campaign called 50:50 Parliament, aimed at securing an equal number of female MPs.

Three 'Feminism in London' conferences had taken place between 2008 and 2010. Lisa-Marie Taylor, then a single mother in her thirties with no background in feminist organizing, bought a ticket for one of them. She told me that the event 'was the most important day of my life. It changed absolutely everything. I came out and went "How did I not see this before?" It made sense of my life and the world outside, and I thought I really need to be involved in this.' The conferences were a project of the London Feminist Network, and after their organizer, Finn Mackay, moved away, Taylor and another woman took over. In 2013, the conferences resumed. Initially, the sale of sex was the most controversial issue: 'The first letters we got were from academics about the sex trade, telling us that [by opposing prostitution] we were doing it all wrong.'

Taylor's impression that prostitution was the thing that feminist activists at this time were most concerned about is backed up by research. When around forty women in Bristol, Glasgow and London were interviewed about third-wave feminism for an academic study, the issues they ranked as being of greatest concern were commercial sex and violence against women (US activists interviewed for the same study prioritized reproductive and LGBT rights).[7] Also in 2013, UK Feminista and Object! launched a campaign against the display of lads' mags in supermarkets, and succeeded in getting them removed from some stores. Two years later, the conference-organizing group that Taylor was part of renamed itself FiLiA and began planning an event in Manchester.

The early 2010s also brought developments in women's justice campaigning. In 2009, John Worboys had been convicted of assaulting twelve women in his London taxi. Worboys was arrested and released before going on to commit further crimes, and following the trial police admitted to serious failings (Worboys was a suspect in eighty-five further attacks). In response to this case, and wider failures, Labour commissioned a review from the crossbench peer Baroness Stern. Her conclusion was that the emphasis placed by campaigners on the figure of 6 per cent – the percentage of rapes reported to police that resulted in a criminal conviction of a rapist – had been a misjudgement and had made the prospects for complainants appear worse than they actually were. Instead, she argued, more emphasis should be placed on the conviction rate once cases reached court (which was then higher for rape than some other crimes) and on increased support for victims.[8]

A year after Worboys's conviction, another shocking story about the police's treatment of women began to emerge. In 2010, the *Observer* published the first piece in what would become a prolonged investigation of 'spycops'. These were undercover police officers embedded in protest groups, many of them focused on climate change and other environmental issues. Several officers had long-term sexual relationships with women, and at least three fathered children without revealing who they were. In 2011, a group of women who had been deceived into such relationships launched a series of legal actions against the Metropolitan Police. The public inquiry into these events ordered by Theresa May in 2014 is ongoing.

David Cameron's government was persuaded to drop a plan to grant anonymity to those accused of sex crimes. Following the Stern Review, the number of specialist police units and prosecutors increased. But the ratio of rape reports to charges did not improve. Instead, both the rate of referrals to the Crown Prosecution Service from the police and the conviction rate went into decline to the point where experts, including Vera Baird, now believe that rape has been effectively decriminalized.[9] Austerity is part of the explanation since cuts to justice budgets cause delays that put off those involved in difficult cases – not least complainants, who may prefer to get on with their lives than spend years waiting for court dates. Other explanations include the handling of digital evidence, including mobile phones, the attitudes of jurors, and the prevalence of 'rape myths' – the most damaging of which is that women routinely lie about sexual encounters.

Cuts to justice budgets were also felt in the civil courts, where the majority of domestic violence cases have always been dealt with. An increasing number of family law cases proceeded with one or both parties having no legal representation, meaning women faced being questioned by their abusers. Feminist politicians, organizations including the Women's Budget Group and grassroots groups continued to raise concerns about austerity's impact on women, which was worsened by their over-representation in low-paid public-sector jobs, and the reliance by lone parents (nearly all mothers) on benefits that were cut and then frozen for four years from 2016, leading to significantly increased hardship. The direct action group UK Uncut turned Starbucks branches into pop-up refuges and crèches in an effort to highlight the way in which women were harmed by policies that favoured businesses, including those that moved their profits offshore, over public services.

It was against this backdrop that a festival at London's South Bank Centre became the venue for a discussion that led to the creation of the Women's Equality Party (WEP) in 2015. There had been another attempt, a couple of years earlier, at setting up a feminist party, and in 2014 a Swedish party, Feminist Initiative, had won a seat in the European Parliament. In Britain, the 2015 general election campaign had seen Labour mount a 'Woman to Woman' campaign, headed by Harriet Harman and featuring a pink bus that travelled around the country with an invitation to female voters to come aboard and share their concerns.

The Conservatives won a majority in that election, and the bus was not widely seen as a success. But the prospect of a new party appeared to some women to hold more promise. The United Kingdom's smaller parties had already proved amenable to female leadership: Caroline Lucas was leader of the Green Party as well as the only Green MP; in 2012, Leanne Wood was elected leader of Plaid Cymru; and in 2014, Nicola Sturgeon took over as leader of the SNP and first minister of Scotland. All three women made a point of taking up feminist causes, which in Lucas's case included wearing a 'No More Page 3' T-shirt in the House of Commons (she was told to take it off).

Sophie Walker, who became WEP's first leader, got involved in the new party as the single mother of an autistic daughter, and she told me that 'WEP was born out of huge frustration and women asking each other "Who are we going to vote for?" We really wanted to present feminism as a political ideology in and of itself that stood alone and was not to be co-opted by other parties in safe little crumbs.' Concerns around violence against women and the sex industry were discussed from the start, but Walker and others were convinced that the route to electoral success lay in establishing themselves as a credible voice on more mainstream aspects of public policy. The aim was to establish WEP as a national political party (Walker is Scottish) that would 'get asked to go on the BBC's *Today* programme to talk about the budget, and could appeal to women who might not call themselves feminists, or might be beginning to call themselves feminists'. In 2016, ten months after the party's launch, Walker came close to winning a seat on the London Assembly.[10]

It did not require electoral success – which has very rarely been achieved by feminist parties anywhere in the world – to convince some feminists that what was going on in the 2010s, especially online, amounted to a fourth wave of feminism. Others were more sceptical, dismissing the phrase as 'media hysteria'.[11] But many feminists saw value in connections forged online. Sophie Walker, WEP's leader, hugely valued the links she made to other mothers of daughters with autism. Claire Heuchan, the black radical feminist author and activist, wrote that:

> Living in small-town Scotland, Twitter was my first real in – a way of connecting with women beyond my immediate geography . . . Whatever else its flaws may be (and they are legion), Twitter is a powerful tool for connecting counter-publics of women; enabling us to refine our politics, grow in understanding, raise awareness of women's oppression, and – most importantly – mobilize in collective action.[12]

Clashes with trans rights activists

Feminists were not the only activists making use of new technology, and from the early 2010s social media users including Jane Clare Jones started to notice changes. Jones, an independent feminist scholar, returned to the United Kingdom after doing a PhD about rape at an American university. She wrote some pieces for the *Guardian*, including one on Anders Breivik, the Norwegian mass murderer, drawing links between racism and misogyny on the far right,[13] and began swapping messages with another feminist blogger-activist, Marina Strinkovsky, in a comment thread. Both became part of an informal online women's network that discussed issues such as the volume of abuse directed at female public figures. This included the episode known as 'Gamergate', which began in 2014 when accusations made against games developer Zoe Quinn by her ex-boyfriend grew into an online frenzy of anti-feminist polemic. Jones and others also started to notice online clashes between trans rights activists and feminists, for example if feminists declined to use terminology such as 'cisgender' or 'cis privilege', or voiced objections to the principle of self-declared gender. Much of this, though not all of it, seemed to emanate from the United States. 'The tropes of cancel culture and oppression hierarchies suddenly started appearing everywhere,' Jones told me. 'The first iterations were "check your privilege", people being called out, and atonement mechanisms to absolve them.'

Arguments between feminists and transgender activists predated the internet. The criteria for admittance to women's spaces and involvement in feminist politics had been fiercely debated since the 1970s, and the question of transgender (or transsexual) inclusion was one aspect of this. The presence of male visitors had been contentious at the Greenham peace camp, while some men's rights groups had argued against single-sex women's groups for years. Many women as well as men were unsympathetic to the aims of radical feminist separatists. But the conflict between lesbians and trans rights activists was particularly fraught, and it had already caused ructions in the United States. Some same-sex attracted women objected strongly to the idea that male self-identification into the category of 'lesbian' was being normalized, to the point where they faced fierce criticism for questioning it.[14] In the United

Kingdom, Julie Bindel was one of the first feminist activists publicly to clash with trans rights campaigners. In 2008, she came top when a poll chose the winner of a Stonewall award for journalists. But trans rights activists, angered by articles she had written, including one arguing that surgery could not turn someone into a man or a woman, arranged a protest. Stonewall gave the award to someone else.[15]

In 2013, the journalist Suzanne Moore published an essay in the *New Statesman* that provoked a similarly hostile response. The piece was mostly about the impact of austerity on women but referred in an aside to the pressure on women to look like 'Brazilian transsexuals'.[16] Moore has since described her choice of phrase as 'careless', given the high levels of violence experienced by transgender people in Brazil and elsewhere.[17] But a torrent of threats led her to involve the police, and a subsequent column by Julie Burchill, defending Moore and Bindel, was removed from the *Observer*'s website on grounds of offence. Also that year, a Women Up North conference run by Manchester Feminist Network faced fierce criticism for trying to hold single-sex sessions as well as trans-inclusive ones.

In the aftermath of these events, some editors sought to identify common ground, and a series commissioned by Helen Lewis for the *New Statesman* in 2014, 'Rereading the Second Wave', saw the transgender writer Juliet Jacques commissioned to write about classic feminist texts alongside Jones, Strinkovsky and others.[18] Elsewhere, Strinkovsky wrote a piece proposing that the disgust provoked by trans-exclusionary radical feminists, or 'terfs',[19] could also be viewed as 'phobic'.[20] The frustrated organizer of a Reclaim the Night march told Finn Mackay that 'All we get is shit, and every time we send out a press release to The F-Word [a feminist website], we just get two lines back saying "Is it open to trans women?"'[21] Mackay commented that 'It is difficult to explain to readers not immersed in feminist activism just how controversial this topic has become.'[22] Victoria Smith (author of *Hags*) wrote a piece for a website, Socialist Resistance, that was later removed at her request because of the amount of abuse she received.[23] In 2015, a letter to the *Guardian* signed by numerous well-known academics objected to a 'worrying pattern of intimidation and silencing of individuals whose views are deemed "transphobic"', and a lecture at Cardiff University given by Germaine Greer was attended by police after a petition accusing her of holding 'hateful', 'trans-exclusionary' views called for it to be cancelled.[24]

With Labour's loss in the 2015 general election, and Jeremy Corbyn's victory in the leadership election, divisions on the left and centre of UK politics got much sharper. As it became clear that there would be a referendum on the United Kingdom's membership of the EU, the political ground shifted. But between 2016 and 2017 the debate about the interaction between women's and transgender rights was transformed by a report from the women and equalities committee, chaired by Conservative MP Maria Miller. This report claimed that the Equality Act was already 'outdated', despite the fact that it contained several clauses, including the one on gender pay gap reporting, which had not yet been enacted. It said that the United Kingdom had fallen behind other countries on transgender rights and recommended that self-ID be introduced from age 16, and that policy makers should also address the needs of 'non-gendered' people. It also called for the law to be changed so that people with gender recognition certificates could no longer be excluded from single-sex spaces, and proposed that assessment times at England's only NHS youth gender clinic should be reduced. Initially, the government's response was cool; Nicky Morgan promised only to tackle 'unnecessary bureaucracy'. But in July 2017 Justine Greening announced that the Conservatives (now led by Theresa May) would accept the report's recommendation – a rare point of agreement with Jeremy Corbyn's Labour, which had pledged to introduce self-ID in its 2017 manifesto, and with Nicola Sturgeon, who aimed to change the law in Scotland – although the SNP's 2016 manifesto had been less explicit.

The defence of sex-based rights

In 2017, Lisa Mackenzie got a call from a journalist. She worked for the Howard League for Penal Reform at the time, and the reporter wanted to know about a violent offender who was being moved from a men's to a women's prison because they were trans. Initially, Mackenzie did not take much notice. But when similar calls followed, she started looking at the policy and became concerned about what would happen if self-ID became law. 'By the end of the year, I was pulling people into cupboards, saying "You have to read about this stuff, it's really troubling,"' she said when I met her in Edinburgh. Two of those she contacted were Lucy Hunter Blackburn, a former civil servant, and Kath Murray, an academic criminologist. The following year, the three women formed the policy collective Murray Blackburn Mackenzie (MBM).

MBM was not the first group formed by feminists worried about the proposed legislation, or ideas around gender and sex more broadly. That had happened three years earlier when Stephanie Davies-Arai, a parenting writer and trainer in East Sussex, launched Transgender Trend. Davies-Arai had been involved in the No More Page Three campaign, but when that group achieved its goal in 2015, and it was announced that the *Sun*'s topless-model feature would cease, she began to focus on children and gender identity. Davies-Arai wanted to present a critical perspective on the transitioning of children to counter the affirmative approach taken by Mermaids, a charity set up to support trans children and their families. This led to estrangement from friends who disapproved, but Davies-Arai has kept going for nine years so far. She sees herself primarily as a children's health campaigner but, because the vast majority of young people diagnosed with gender dysphoria are girls, she also recognizes transgender identification as a feminist issue. 'I'm really concerned about women's and girls' rights, and liberal feminism has fed into the identity politics movement,' she said. 'But there are aspects of radical feminism that I don't think are helpful either, so while I call myself a feminist I don't think I fit the boxes.'

Other feminist authors and activists were also questioning the claims being made about gender identity. Helen Steel, an environmental campaigner who was one of the women tricked into a long-term relationship with an undercover police officer, had tried to write a leaflet on the subject to distribute at an anarchist book fair. But the UK government's announcement in the summer of 2017 that it would legislate so that in future people could apply for new birth certificates without a medical diagnosis prompted a much wider reaction. On 13 September, a sixty-year-old woman, Maria MacLachlan, was punched in the face by a trans rights activist named Tara Wolf at Speakers' Corner in central London. MacLachlan was on her way to a meeting organized by a group of left-wing feminists and trade unionists to discuss what their collective response to the proposed legislation should be. Later that month, a letter to the *Guardian* calling on the wider trans rights movement to distance itself from such thuggery, and insisting on women's 'right to free association and assembly', attracted signatories including Sam Smethers, the chief executive of the Fawcett Society, and Harriet Wistrich of the Centre for Women's Justice. (Wolf was later convicted for the assault and fined by a judge who criticized MacLachlan for referring to Wolf using male pronouns.)

Woman's Place UK was launched shortly after this, with a model resolution that its founders suggested could be taken to union or Labour Party branches. Judith Green, a midwife and child abuse survivor who is one of the group's leading figures, drafted a proposal that identified Schedule 3 of the Equality Act as a base upon which sex-based rights activists could build their campaign. Schedule 3 sets out the permitted single-sex exceptions to anti-discrimination law, when these are 'a proportionate means of achieving a legitimate aim', making it clear that there are circumstances in which the law allows service providers and others to differentiate biological sex from gender identity. The group's overriding concern was to preserve the entitlement for female people to meet (and do things such as sport) separately from men. In 2018, they held seventeen public meetings, most of which attracted protesters and several of which had to change venues at the last minute due to complaints. Among the speakers was Helen Steel, who had by this time been kicked out of several environmental protest camps following accusations of transphobia.

Meanwhile, on Facebook, a woman called Nicola Williams joined a group where a few hundred women – some of them exiles from Mumsnet, whose forum for discussing feminism had existed since 2010 but where moderation was felt to hamper discussion – were swapping views on the same issues. Dismayed to realize that no one knew how many transgender women were in women's prisons, Williams and a few others decided to find out by looking through inspection reports and other documents. A scientist by training, Williams had recently been made redundant and so had time to volunteer from her home in Leicestershire. They published their research online and adopted the name Fair Play for Women.

'In a loose sense of the word, we're all feminists,' Williams said when I asked if she saw the group as part of a movement. But she does not have either an academic-feminist or activist-feminist background, and is more comfortable with the term 'gender critical'. Fair Play is tightly focused on questions around sex and gender and does not see itself as having a role in other feminist advocacy. But sexuality, and the nature of lesbian attraction, is part of what drew Williams in. 'When

I came out as a lesbian, there was no T attached to the LGB,' she explained.

> I suppose I had my own feminist instincts. I worked in a male-dominated profession, I had been the only woman in the room in meetings, I knew what it was like having to prove yourself and I was conscious of myself as a woman in the way I moved about . . . But where it came very close to me was that when I was growing up, I think I could very easily have been persuaded that perhaps I was a trans man. I had some internalized misogyny going on. It took me a long time to get used to being a lesbian and to feel proud of being a woman.

Other sex-based rights groups were also formed, while numerous women began asking questions about self-identification in organizations to which they already belonged. LGB Alliance was founded by two lesbians, Kate Harris and Bev Jackson, who felt that Stonewall, with its focus on gender identity, no longer represented gay, lesbian and bisexual interests. But from late 2017, when the Scottish government announced that it too would consult on reforming the Gender Recognition Act, an issue that had mostly been regarded as relevant only to special-interest groups, burst into the press. Janice Turner, the *Times* columnist, had written in 2016 about a decision by the International Olympic Committee to allow biologically male transgender athletes to compete in the female category if they reduced their testosterone level. This rule change had prompted an outpouring of protest on Mumsnet in a thread headed 'I am Spartacus' that reached 999 posts – the maximum allowed. In the summer of 2017, Turner interviewed Maria Miller who, when challenged about the steep rise in girls diagnosed with gender dysphoria, threatened to walk out. Turner also wrote about the assault on Maria MacLachlan, which she had witnessed, opening her column with the question: 'When is it OK to punch a woman?'[25]

As the English and Scottish governments' public consultations went live, and lobby groups encouraged supporters to submit responses for and against the proposed changes, broadcast as well as print journalists started to pay more attention. At the 2018 Labour Party Conference, in Liverpool, feminist opponents of self-ID handed out leaflets. Describing this to me, Ceri Williams, one of the organizers, said 'It was scary the whole time.' At one point, a steward tried to push her out of a room. Also during this conference, a billboard carrying the word 'woman' and the definition 'adult human female', paid for by the gender-critical activist Kellie-Jay Keen-Minshull (also known as Posie Parker), was removed by the advertising company Primesight following a complaint.[26] Keen-Minshull sells merchandise bearing the suffragette colours of green, white and purple, organizes regular rallies and at the time of writing is in the process of setting up a political party. But she does not regard herself as a feminist.

A month after the Labour Conference, a committee chaired by the SNP's Joan McAlpine became the venue for the first evidence given by feminists critical of self-ID in a UK parliament or assembly. Rosa Freedman, a professor in international human rights law, was among witnesses who raised objections to the Scottish government's plan to stop collecting data on sex, and instead collect data on the basis of self-identified gender.[27] As the debate continued throughout 2019, it became a cliché to describe it as a toxic topic, with social media widely observed to fuel polarization. At a panel discussion about women's rights in Edinburgh, Julie Bindel had to be protected by security guards after a male trans rights activist lunged at her (the attacker was later cautioned by police). That year also saw attention shift towards the courts. In March 2019, Maya Forstater, who was one of a number of women who had built up a following on Twitter by posting her views on this issue, announced that she had lost her job and planned to sue for discrimination. In December, she lost her case against the Centre for Global Development, the non-governmental organization she had worked for. Forstater's belief in biological sex as a salient fact of life was judged 'not worthy of respect in a democratic society', meaning it did not qualify for protection as a philosophical belief under the terms of the Equality Act. Days later J. K. Rowling, the immensely popular and rich *Harry Potter* author, tweeted her support for Forstater to her 14 million followers. The judgement against Forstater was catapulted into global headlines.

While Forstater prepared her appeal and embarked on a new career in sex-based rights advocacy, more legal cases followed. In 2020, Keira Bell (also known as Quincy Bell) became a complainant, alongside the mother of an autistic teenage girl, known as Mrs A, in a case against the Tavistock and Portman NHS Trust. Bell had been a patient at the trust's gender clinic (GIDS) and regretted the treatment she had received there and subsequently, including a double mastectomy. In a judicial review, she and Mrs A aimed to convince judges that children could not consent to treatment with puberty blockers. A ruling in their favour was overturned in 2021 when the Court of Appeal ruled that it was for clinicians and not courts to make such decisions.

Also in 2020, Allison Bailey, who was then a barrister at Garden Court Chambers in London, launched a crowd-funder to raise money to sue both Garden Court and Stonewall for discrimination. Bailey is a black, lesbian woman from a working-class background, and a child sexual-abuse survivor who believes, along with some psychologists and psychotherapists, that homophobia is one of the drivers of trans identification.[28] Their view is that because it is socially difficult to be gay or lesbian, some teenagers opt instead to identify as the other sex, turning same-sex into heterosexual orientation. Bailey's case was that her role as a founding member of the LGB Alliance led to her being victimized by her employer and by Stonewall, which had links with the chambers. In

July 2022, she won her claim against Garden Court, but lost against Stonewall. At the time of writing, she is preparing an appeal.

Further confrontations between sex-based rights and gender-identity activists stopped short of court hearings. The best-known of these is the furore surrounding Kathleen Stock at Sussex University, which came to a head in October 2021 when activists staged a demonstration against her, leading to her resignation. But Stock was not alone in facing protests. Another professor, Selina Todd of Oxford University, lost a speaking role at a conference, organized to mark fifty years since the first women's liberation conference, after allegations of transphobia. A column written in defence of Todd by Suzanne Moore was followed days later by a petition signed by more than three hundred staff at the *Guardian* and *Observer*. Although the petition did not refer to Moore, and objected instead to 'transphobic content' in general, her photograph was used by the news website, *Buzzfeed*, to illustrate its report. Moore quit the *Guardia*n eight months later. Also in 2020, there was a storm of protest after the Labour MP, Rosie Duffield, tweeted that 'only women have a cervix'.

From 2020, a number of publishing ventures joined existing sex-based rights (or gender-critical) initiatives. Jane Clare Jones became the editor of a magazine, *The Radical Notion*, edited by a collective of radical and socialist feminists. She also produced a report, *The Political Erasure of Sex: Sex and the Census*, with Lisa Mackenzie, which argued that official statistics must continue to include data on sex. A few months later, Kathleen Stock published a groundbreaking book on sex and gender identity. *Material Girls: Why Reality Matters for Feminism* became a bestseller, and was followed by *Trans: When Ideology Meets Reality* by Helen Joyce, a journalist at the *Economist* who had also carved out a niche as a gender-critical tweeter. Joyce later quit the *Economist* and went to work with

Maya Forstater at the human rights organization Sex Matters.

By this time, the main political parties also had their own sex-based rights ginger groups. This began in Aberdeen, on the unofficial fringe of the SNP's 2019 conference, where women, including the MSP Joan McAlpine and MP Joanna Cherry, spoke at the launch of an SNP women's pledge, which asserted women's right to the 'sex-based protections in the Equality Act 2010'. A few weeks later, trans rights activists banged on the windows throughout a Woman's Place UK meeting in Brighton, on the unofficial fringe of the Labour Party Conference. Later that autumn, a group of Labour Party activists held a meeting alongside that year's FiLiA conference, in Bradford, and decided to launch a Labour Women's Declaration. Among the organizers was Ceri Williams, the activist who had felt scared when handing out leaflets at her party's conference the year before.

Political rows continued, and they featured in the 2020 Labour leadership election when most candidates for both the leader and deputy leader positions, although not Keir Starmer, signed a pledge describing Woman's Place UK and the LGB Alliance as 'hate groups'. Increasingly, the arguments went beyond the question of whether self-ID would become law and took in other pieces of legislation. The Scottish government, for example, provoked feminist anger by including transgender people, but not women, among the groups protected by a new law against stirring up hatred. That same year, Andy Wightman resigned from the Scottish Green Party with a statement that made it clear he regretted voting against an amendment to enable victims of sexual assault to request to be physically examined by a person of the same sex. The Scottish Greens and Liberal Democrats had wanted the bill to refer to gender instead.

By then, it was increasingly clear that the Scottish and UK governments were headed in different directions. In September 2020, Liz Truss, the women and equalities minister, announced that plans to introduce self-ID had been dropped. By the end of the year, her party had its own internal lobby group, Conservatives for Women, set up to ensure that ministers held this line. Although the government had rejected self-ID, sex-based rights advocates remained concerned about other legislation, and a flashpoint soon emerged. In February 2021, a bill produced in a hurry to enable Suella Braverman to take maternity leave from her cabinet post initially referred to a pregnant 'person' rather than 'woman' or 'mother'. This was objected to by feminists and others who saw the choice of a gender-neutral term as part of a campaign to alter language for the benefit of a tiny minority of people (trans men or non-binary mothers) without adequate consideration or consultation regarding the effects. Labour Women's Declaration sought support from Labour peers who agreed to back an amendment, after which the government agreed to change it, after a legal opinion confirmed that transgender men who had given birth would still be covered by a law referring to 'mothers'.

A month later the government was defeated in a case brought by Fair Play for Women in the High Court, where a judge ruled that guidance attached to the upcoming census should instruct people to fill in the form on the basis of the sex on their birth or gender-recognition certificates, and not on other documents. Also in 2021, Liberal Voice for Women joined the other internal party groups. But, on 10 June 2021, a decision in the employment appeal tribunal changed everything. Maya Forstater had lost her claim against her former employer in a lower court. That ruling was set aside by a ruling which found that her gender-critical belief 'that biological sex is important, immutable and not to be conflated with gender identity' was legally protected. From this point on, anyone advocating for sex-based rights did so in the knowledge that discrimination against them on grounds of their gender-critical belief was illegal.

24 Maya Forstater (right) on the day the employment appeal tribunal ruled in her favour, with Helen Joyce

Not a single issue

In October 2017, the *New York Times* published its exposé of the predatory sexual behaviour of the film producer Harvey Weinstein, and the #MeToo hashtag created by the US activist Tarana Burke spread around the world as a way for women to share experiences of being abused or assaulted. This movement's urgency derived in part from the fact that Donald Trump, who had boasted of his exploits as a sexual harasser, was then in the White House. In the United Kingdom, senior figures in politics, media, sport and other industries who had mistreated women were publicly identified in a process that has continued, albeit with uncertain results and bringing with it questions about due process and the ethics of public shaming. Initially a media phenomenon, #MeToo soon spawned its own activist groups. In 2020, a London student named Soma

Sara started an online project (now a charity) called Everyone's Invited that sought to gather testimonies in order to expose the rape culture that was prevalent in schools and universities.

The 2010s saw the launch of a number of other new campaigns, as well as the continuation of existing ones around issues including pensions, affordable childcare and women's health. In 2015, Karen Ingala Smith, who was then the head of a women's sector charity, launched the Femicide Census. This project collates information on women killed by men and produces a list which is read out in Parliament by the Labour MP Jess Phillips annually, as a way of raising awareness. In the same year, Joeli Brearley set up Pregnant Then Screwed to campaign against pregnancy and maternity discrimination – after she was sacked while expecting her first child – and a group including Liv Little and Charlie Brinkhurst-Cuff founded *gal-dem*, a digital magazine for women and non-binary people of colour. Another new pressure group, We Can't Consent to This, was created in 2018 to highlight cases in which men who had killed their partners (who were mostly, but not all, women) relied on a so-called rough-sex defence, in effect telling courts that the violence that led to death had been consensual. After rape convictions fell to a record low in 2020, the Centre for Women's Justice and the End Violence Against Women coalition brought a judicial review, which sought to demonstrate that a policy shift within the Crown Prosecution Service had raised the bar on charging decisions and was therefore responsible. But the case did not succeed.[29] Throughout this period, FiLiA conferences were held annually in cities around the country.

The activists involved took a range of views on legal self-ID, and the broader principle of transgender inclusion on the basis of self-declaration. Longer-established women's organizations and charities were also divided. In Scotland, the established women's groups – which receive most of their funding from the Scottish government – support self-ID, and it was left to

25 FiLiA in Portsmouth, 2021. These national conferences have been running for longer than the women's liberation conferences of the 1970s. Photo by Jane Clare Jones

grassroots start-ups, including For Women Scotland, to oppose it. In England, some of the bigger charities avoided making public statements, either because their staff and trustees were split or because they were worried about putting off funders and preferred to focus on other issues or services. Following a consultation exercise, the Women's Equality Party voted to support self-ID.

Soon after she became prime minister, Theresa May announced plans for new domestic abuse legislation, which would widen the definition of abuse to facilitate more prosecutions and lead to the appointment of a Domestic Abuse Commissioner. Southall Black Sisters and other groups campaigned to ensure that provision for abused migrant women would also be improved – but did not succeed in exempting them from a rule known as 'no recourse to public funds', restricting benefit claims on the basis of immigration status. May also committed to ratification of the Istanbul Convention, a European treaty that commits governments to tackle violence against women (this was finalized in 2022). And in 2018 employers with more than 250 staff were, for the first time, compelled to collect and publish data showing the difference in the earnings of men and women. The same year saw a high-profile victory by Carrie Gracie, the BBC's former China editor, who resigned from her job after learning that men in equivalent roles had far higher salaries. She donated her £361,000 settlement to the Fawcett Society, which had supported her and used the money to fund a new equal pay service. Two years later, another BBC journalist, Samira Ahmed, took a similar case to an employment tribunal, where she won.

Fears that a Conservative government might, at some point, seek to tighten the law on abortion resurfaced in 2019 when Jeremy Hunt, who was known to back a 12-week limit, was a candidate in the leadership race won by Boris Johnson. But reproductive rights activism was chiefly focused on Northern Ireland, where the 1967 Abortion Act did not apply, and terminations could be carried out only to preserve the life of the mother. Starting in 2017, the Labour MP Stella Creasy tried repeatedly to change the law, and succeeded in 2020 when new regulations were brought in allowing terminations up to twelve weeks with no conditionality, and later depending on circumstances. Creasy also pushed for a law enabling UK councils to impose buffer zones around abortion clinics, a measure first tried in the London borough of Ealing to prevent women from being harassed. Recent years have also seen rising concern among feminists about surrogacy as awareness of its commercial nature in countries including Ukraine, and the risks to surrogate mothers and babies associated with it, have risen partly as a result of the Ukrainian war.

Despite efforts to commandeer social media for feminist ends, the evidence of women's vulnerability to online harms continued to mount. Attitudes to women did not play a prominent part in the trial of Thomas Mair, who was convicted in 2016 of murdering the Labour MP Jo Cox, but 'matricide' was revealed to have been among his internet searches. Laura Bates, creator of the Everyday Sexism project, went on to spend two years researching the proliferation of internet misogyny. In her book *Men Who Hate Women* (2020), she showed that a twisted version of the female mate-choice hypothesis first advanced by Charles Darwin had become a tenet of men's rights blogs. In angry online spaces, supposedly choosy women were blamed for the plight of men who were involuntarily celibate, or 'incels'. Bates argued that demands for 'sex redistribution' were tightly bound into rising anti-feminism, and that murders inspired by misogynist ideology ought to be classified as terrorism.[30]

Male demands for sexual and reproductive rights are part of white supremacist ideology, particularly the paranoid fantasy about immigrants out-competing white populations, known as the 'Great Replacement Theory'. Feminists from non-white and Jewish backgrounds thus have additional threats to reckon with as racism, anti-Semitism and misogyny combine in dangerous ways. But while concerns around online misogyny and attacks on women's reproductive rights are shared by sex-based rights and gender-focused feminists, the conflict over self-ID continues. This reached a crisis point in December

2022, when the Scottish Parliament passed a law that would, if enacted, enable sixteen-year-olds to change their legal sex. Three weeks later, Rishi Sunak's government blocked it on the grounds that it exceeded the devolved government's remit – a view subsequently backed up by Scotland's highest court.

Gender self-identification will not form part of either a Conservative or a Labour Party manifesto in the next UK general election. Labour followed the government in rejecting it in July 2023. Recent research reveals that, while most British people (64 per cent according to the 2023 British Social Attitudes survey) say they are not prejudiced against transgender people, a 70 per cent majority do not support legal self-ID. Views on the importance of single-sex spaces such as toilets and prisons vary, while just 19 per cent support the inclusion of transgender women in female sports.[31]

Meanwhile, sex-based rights campaigners, including the lobby groups Sex Matters and For Women Scotland, believe that the combination of the Gender Recognition Act and the Equality Act has led to ambiguity about the legal definition of sex. They are pushing for a clarification to the effect that the protected characteristic of sex in the Equality Act refers to biological sex and is not altered by the possession of a Gender Recognition Certificate. The Equality and Human Rights Commission, which monitors equality legislation across the United Kingdom, has offered qualified support for this proposal. At the time of writing, it is unclear whether the current government, or any future one, will take this up. Whether they do or not, the conflict of rights is not limited to this point of law and is certain to continue. In February 2024, it was announced that the UK Supreme Court will hear an appeal brought by For Women Scotland against a Scottish court ruling that transgender women with a Gender Recognition Certificate are eligible for places reserved for women on public boards.[32]

Two women: Shereen Benjamin and Raquel Rosario-Sanchez

On 27 April 2023, I visited Shereen Benjamin in her office at the end of a corridor in the University of Edinburgh's education department. The evening before, I had planned to attend a screening of a documentary film, *Adult Human Female*, made by two gender-critical academics, on the nearby campus. It was cancelled due to trans right activists barring the entrance, and I had watched as the organizers explained the situation to ticket-holders on the steps, while a crowd of around 200 protesters sang songs and chanted. (A subsequent attempt to show the film succeeded in November 2023 amid a heavy police and security presence.) Shereen is a member of the group that organized the screening: Edinburgh Academics for Academic Freedom. She had looked distressed when I first glimpsed her. In her office, the next day, she wore a red T-shirt bearing the slogan, 'I won't stand by and let telling the truth become a crime', and a Labour Women's Declaration badge. Behind her, in a bookcase, was a shelf of 1950s girls' stories and a menorah.

Shereen has worked in Edinburgh for eighteen years, and before that she was a teacher in London. Her PhD was on girls with special educational needs and the intersections between gender, class and disability. She is a lifelong left-wing activist, who went to the Greenham Common peace camp when she left school and has been involved in a combination of feminist, anti-nuclear, gay-lesbian and trade union politics ever since. But in 2022 she left the University and College Union (UCU) after complaints were made against her. While these were not upheld, she told me that the last few years have been emotionally draining.

> Being told you're a right-wing bigot is hard to manage, I'm used to it now but it doesn't make it easy. I have colleagues who

> won't be seen with me; that's probably the most hurtful thing. In 2019–20, it felt like the Staff Pride network was monitoring my teaching. They would go to my head of school with slides from my lectures. I don't teach gender very much anymore.

Shereen does not have as high a profile as some other gender-critical academics. She has spoken at public meetings but does not use X (formerly Twitter) or write about the issues in newspapers or on news websites. 'What I've always thought about universities is that they have to be places where ideas can be thoroughly examined,' she said carefully when I asked how she felt about the way she has been treated by colleagues and managers.

> The idea that your internal sense of maleness or femaleness determines whether you're a man or a woman is a very new set of thoughts based on an unfalsifiable belief that people are at liberty to hold. I think the evidence is fairly overwhelming that this ideology is wrong and has some dangerous impacts, but I could be mistaken . . . Here in higher education we should have the skills to explore that.

A few weeks after my visit to Shereen, I met another gender-critical woman in London. Raquel Rosario Sánchez came to the United Kingdom as a PhD student from the Dominican Republic. As well as her academic research, which is about men who pay for sex, she has a job in a women's prison. I had seen her speak in public and wanted to ask her about the case she had brought – and lost – against Bristol University, where she was a student. Her claim was that staff there had colluded with a trans activist group's campaign against her. But while the judge in her case acknowledged she had been the victim of 'violent, threatening, intimidating behaviour', in 2022 he cleared the university of negligence, breach of contract and sex discrimination.

26 Raquel Rosario Sánchez came to the United Kingdom to study and ended up in court

Raquel told me she did not regret what she had done. She had been aware of growing conflict between trans and sex-based rights activists before coming to England but never imagined she would play a part in it. 'Looking back now, I think that because I had written about these issues before I arrived in Bristol, I had a target on my back,' she told me. 'The other option was to shut up, and there was no universe in which it was conceivable that I would do that. The connections I saw between trans rights activism and the normalization of violence against women in public discourse created a sense of urgency.'

Raquel believes that the attacks on her in Bristol gained added force because as a woman of colour, and a migrant from the Caribbean, her support for sex-based rights angered activists who see trans rights as a cause that aligns them with marginalized people around the world. 'Proponents of gender identity say that the intersectional position, the decolonial position, is to argue that everyone has a gender identity,' she explained.

> They think they're doing liberatory, revolutionary work, but there's nothing liberatory or revolutionary about the same old sexist tropes being revamped under the veneer of gender identity. When they say 'anyone who opposes us is a white feminist', or 'You need to listen to women in the Global South', they're using women in the Global South as props. And when those women speak out against gender identity activism, there is a special level of vitriol. I think that's what happened to me, and I've seen it happen to other women, for example Allison Bailey, who is a black lesbian woman. When she spoke up, people wanted to silence her, maybe more so than if she had been a white woman.

Raquel thinks the current emphasis on sex-based rights in the United Kingdom has international significance. 'I feel part of a global upswell of angry women who are saying "This erasure and rollback of women's rights and protections is not going to happen in my lifetime, or at least I'm going to do everything I can to ensure that it doesn't,"' she told me. She believes what has happened in the United Kingdom is underpinned by 'a very solid legal framework of sex-based rights', which is lacking in many other places. 'In a sense, women in the United Kingdom are really fortunate that they had the Sex Discrimination Act, and then the Equality Act with the single-sex exceptions. You can argue from that base. By contrast, in the United States they are still fighting for the Equal Rights Amendment. That battle has not been won.'

As Raquel knows, this view runs directly counter to the view of many trans rights and gender identity activists, and mainstream LGBTQ rights groups such as Stonewall as well. They believe that legal gender self-identification should be understood as a right, akin to same-sex marriage or other reforms fought for by marginalized groups of people. They point to the hostility towards transgender people demonstrated by authoritarian, socially conservative leaders including Vladimir Putin, Donald Trump, Jair Bolsonaro and Viktor Orban, as evidence that sex-based rights activists have a hidden or unwitting right-wing agenda. Judith Butler, who remains a figurehead for the movement, has written that it makes 'no sense' for gender-critical feminists to align themselves with such forces.

But this is to deny the existence of a feminism which is distinct from hers, and long predates it. This is the view that women have distinct political interests, and rights, based not on their gender (however this is understood) but their sex. Britain has one of the strongest such movements currently, but sex-based rights feminism – which Raquel calls simply feminism – is not limited to one country. At the time of writing, there are at least a dozen legal cases working their way through British courts, brought by women and men who allege they have been discriminated against on grounds of their gender-critical beliefs. Whatever the verdicts, the arguments over the broader principle of self-ID will continue for as long as feminists anywhere in the world are convinced that their sex makes a material difference to their lives.

Epilogue

There are many useful definitions of feminism. What they have in common is a recognition that a power imbalance exists between men and women, that women are subject to various forms of injustice and mistreatment, and that it is desirable to change this. The first advocates for women's rights in Britain were explicit that it was as a sex, or 'the sex', that women were subjugated. In the chapters of this book that describe campaigns of the nineteenth century, I have shown that activists thought about sex-based oppression, and how to fight it, in a variety of ways.

Some second-wave feminists in Britain and elsewhere decided that the word 'gender' served their purposes better. They wanted to get as far away as possible from biological essentialism, and to find a way of describing the relations between men and women that was analogous to analysis of the class system. Since then, gender has become ubiquitous in terminology such as 'gender-based violence' and the 'gender pay gap'. Sometimes, gender is synonymous with sex. At other times, its usage signifies a separation between biological aspects of sex and social or cultural ones. At other times, it means something else entirely. This is when it is used as shorthand for gender identity – the feeling of being male or female, regardless of the sexed body. According to this usage, gender or gender identity is not a social role imposed on a person, and taught to them, but an aspect of their inner self. These diametrically opposed definitions of gender, both of which date back decades, are part of the explanation for the current impasse.

Feminists have responded to this conflict in different ways. Many are content to accept the notion that all human beings have a psychological gender, as well as a biological sex. Others resist it fiercely on grounds that such identifications are derived from stereotypes and risk reinforcing them. They ask, 'What does it mean to feel like a man, or a woman?' Currently, and as described in chapter 9, British feminists are at the heart of the movement to resist the philosophy or ideology that says every human being has an inner gender. I started researching this book because I wanted to understand why. Over the course of writing it, I have become convinced that one reason is the depth and range of the political tradition British feminists have drawn on – with or without knowing it.

The relationship of sex to politics has always been a vexed question. Ever since Mary Wollstonecraft's denunciation of the Enlightenment sexism personified by Rousseau, women have fought to establish their equal humanity, while also advocating for themselves *as women*, who are different in some ways from men. From the late nineteenth century, when the women's suffrage movement took off, campaigners struggled to reconcile their demands for rights and freedoms with rival claims. Initially, such negotiations were mainly between sex and class. Later, inequalities linked to race and colonization were addressed as well.

Often, feminists have sought to downplay the importance of sex. They saw how women's bodies, and their role in reproduction, were used to diminish and inhibit them. They also perceived the potential of sexual politics to divide society – the 'sex antagonism' that early-twentieth-century progressives worried about. When Virginia Woolf imagined setting the word 'feminist' on fire and watching it shrivel, she did so in the hope that the air would clear to reveal 'men and women working together for the same cause'.[1] This was not a position that Woolf held consistently. At other times she asserted her place in a female genealogy ('we think back through our mothers if we are women,' she wrote in *A Room of One's Own*).[2] But the idea that the divisions between men and women would one day be transcended, in a better world, was popular with feminists including Winifred Holtby long before it was taken up by critical theorists in universities.

This utopian spirit lives on in twenty-first-century activist movements, in which calls for climate justice are sometimes joined by calls for gender justice. I think such demands are especially attractive to idealistic young people, who remember the imaginative freedom of childhood and do not want their futures to be hemmed in by biological constraints. But while I can see the appeal of a liberation from sex, as a political demand I believe it carries risks. Sexuality and reproduction are highly contested aspects of human experience. Along with material resources (food, housing, money), opportunities to be physically intimate with other people and have children are among the things that people want and value most. For this reason, unlike utopians who envision a future free from sexual conflict, I think the sexual and reproductive interests of human beings will always need to be negotiated. Even were womb transplants and other body modifications to become possible, sex differences would still matter in public policy.

Another reason why I think sex-based rights activism in the United Kingdom took off in the way that it did is our close connection to the United States. English speakers had easier access than speakers of other languages to the debate about trans and women's rights as it unfolded in the United States and so were quicker to grasp its significance. It was gender-critical women's insistence on certain fundamental words, above all 'woman/women' and 'mother', which led them to resist attempts to change their meanings and usages. As for why sex-based rights have found so few defenders in the other Anglophone countries, I think the Equality Act 2010, with its explicit language about both sex and gender reassignment, has been a crucial support that feminists elsewhere have lacked. The legislation shows that it is possible to craft legislation that protects both groups without eliding them or their interests. It is far harder to advocate for women as a sex, with entitlements that are distinct from trans people's, where trans people do not also have robust protections in law.

It is difficult to feel optimistic about the prospects for women and girls at the moment. Because women globally are poorer and less mobile than men, with more responsibility for children and other dependants, the climate crisis will inflict disproportionate harm on them as it escalates. Closer to home, black and ethnic-minority women, those who are single parents or have large families, are particularly exposed to the hardships caused by low pay, meagre benefits and high prices. The situation regarding violence against women has also deteriorated. A record 193,566 sexual offences were recorded by the police in England and Wales in the year ending March 2022, while the Crime Survey of England and Wales estimates that a further 600,000 female victims did not report crimes.[3] As discussed in the previous chapter, these women struggle to access justice. The disastrous failure to regulate digital platforms has led to the proliferation of online misogyny and contributed to a growing sense that women and girls can be abused with impunity. A survey by Girlguiding in 2022 found that almost one in five girls aged 11–16 do not feel safe at school. In London, where I live, a series of appalling incidents, including the sharing by police officers of images of Bibaa Henry and Nicole Smallman's corpses in June 2020 after they had been murdered, and the rape and murder of Sarah Everard by a police officer a year later, have drastically undermined confidence in those responsible for upholding the law.

Despite all this, the resurgence of grassroots feminism in Britain makes me hopeful. Should it be regarded as a new wave of feminism? The metaphor presents a conundrum in this case. It has always signified forward motion, whereas the renewed support for sex-based rights has been more about defence than advance – at least so far. For this reason, the movement is more of a bulwark than a wave. Or perhaps a 'terf island'.

I still do not understand why subjective claims about identity have been allowed to trump facts about sex to the extent that they have. Other writers have traced the history of gender identity belief – which at its simplest is the conviction that all humans have a psychological gender as well as a sex. In Britain, this idea has an influential, well-connected backer in the charity Stonewall, which helps explain the purchase it gained in politics and civil society before gender-critical activists began to push back. But I think academic feminism, as it developed in the social sciences and humanities at the end of the twentieth century, also facilitated this shift. Scholars discarded sex and the opaque, biological baggage that went with it in favour of a sociolinguistic concept – gender – over which they had more control.

In its most extreme form, I think gender identity ideology is a form of sex (and therefore biology) denial that I find alarming. But I am certain there is an accommodation to be found between feminists (and gay men and lesbian women), who want their sex-based rights to be upheld, and transgender people, who want their gender identities to be respected. How exactly this is to be achieved is something that a historical book cannot tell us.

The previous pages reveal the colossal efforts that have been required to win new rights and protections for girls and women, at every stage, and the fierce resistance that campaigners have had to overcome. Mary Wollstonecraft backed a revolution that overthrew a king, but anticipated laughter when she sheepishly 'dropped a hint' that perhaps, one day, women might have their own representatives. Barbara Bodichon launched a petition before she was forty, but correctly predicted that she would be dead by the time a woman cast a vote. Writers, lecturers and lobbyists worked alongside vandals and arsonists in the suffrage movement. Child benefit was resisted by Labour and the trade unions, as well as on the right. 'Women's achievements have never been won by sweet reasonableness,' Barbara Castle told the House of Commons in an equal pay debate. Two decades later, black and Asian feminists confronted racist as well as sexist prejudice in the women's liberation movement.

Internal conflict was often just as difficult as battles with opponents, or more so. Divergent views about the relationship of sex and politics were only one source of this. Tactics, personalities, religion, socialism, war, sexuality, racism, violence, prostitution, motherhood, men: feminists have disagreed about most things, as they still do. But I think we can learn from the struggles of earlier activists with wildly conflicting ideas about sexual difference – ideas drawn from religion, science, politics and philosophy – and the political commitments they derived from these. These have always been, and still are, among the hardest of all the questions for feminists. The British feminist revival that is now underway does not have easy answers. But continuing to think about the meanings of sex, while holding on to our knowledge about all the ways in which girls' and women's lives are shaped by the material reality of our sexed bodies – as boys' and men's lives also are – is feminist work that needs to be done.

Notes

Introduction: The Return of Sexual Politics

1 'Research Shines Light on Why Women more Likely to Develop Alzheimer's', *Guardian*, 16 July 2019. Caroline Criado Perez's book *Invisible Women* (Chatto & Windus, 2019) sets out many more examples of sex differences and their relevance to public policy.

2 'The Female Face of Poverty: Examining the Cause and Consequences of Economic Deprivation for Women', Women's Budget Group, July 2018.

3 See https://www.gov.uk/government/publications/dit-gender-pay-gap-report-and-data-2021-to-2022

4 See https://www.gov.uk/government/statistics/gender-pensions-gap-in-private-pensions/the-gender-pensions-gap-in-private-pensions. The figure of 35 per cent is based on data from 2018 to 2020.

5 'The Motherhood Pay Penalty', key findings from TUC/IPPR Research, March 2016. This piece of research showed that the penalty applied only to women who had their first child before age 33. See also 'UK Gender Pay Gap for Higher-Educated Parents Has Grown since 1970s', *Guardian*, 7 March 2023.

6 Helen Joyce in her book *Trans: From Ideology to Reality*

(Oneworld, 2021), Kathleen Stock in her book *Material Girls: Why Reality Matters to Feminism* (Fleet, 2021) and Jane Clare Jones in an appendix to *The Political Erasure of Sex* (2020) also provide valuable accounts of the development of the concepts of gender and gender identity, as do several of the essays included in Alice Sullivan and Selina Todd (eds), *Sex and Gender: A Contemporary Reader* (Routledge, 2023).

7 Martina Navratilova is among the best-known gender-critical feminists in the United States and has taken a strong position with regard to women's sports. For an example of gender-critical feminism in Spain, see 'New Trans Law will Destroy Women's Rights in Spain, says Deputy PM', *Times*, 27 September 2022.

8 See 'A Liberalisation in Attitudes?', British Social Attitudes, National Centre for Social Research, September 2023.

9 See, for example, 'The Gender War is Over in Britain', *Atlantic*, 8 August 2023; 'How British Feminism Became Anti-trans', *New York Times*, 7 February 2019, and 'Irish Feminists Must Avoid British Trap of Transphobia', *Irish Times*, 12 March 2021.

10 'Transgender Activist Tara Wolf Fined £150 for Assaulting "Exclusionary" Radical Feminist in Hyde Park', *Evening Standard*, 1 April 2018.

11 The complainants in these cases were Denise Fahmy and Allison Bailey. See 'Sex-change Tribunal Winner says Illogical Views Widespread in Arts', *Times*, 3 July 2023; and 'Law Chambers Discriminated against Gender-critical Barrister, Tribunal Rules', *Guardian*, 27 July 2022.

12 Maya Forstater vs CGD Europe, Center for Global Development and Masood Ahmed. Employment appeal tribunal judgement, 10 June 2021.

13 Jeremy Gavron, her son, wrote a book about his mother's life, *A Woman on the Edge of Time* (Scribe, 2015).

14 Two more books that make this link are Judith Hubback's *Wives Who Went to College* (Heinemann, 1957) and Viola Klein and Alva Myrdal's *Women's Two Roles: Home and* Work (Routledge and Kegan Paul, 1970 [1956]).

15 For example, Ros Coward wrote of Faludi in 1999 that 'Without her first book, *Backlash*, feminism might not have survived the 1980s.' Ros Coward, 'Men on the Verge of Feminist Debate', *Guardian*, 9 September 1999.

16 Doris Lessing, *Walking in the Shade: Volume II of My Autobiography* (Fourth Estate, 1998), p. 206.

17 The hostility of some contemporary feminists towards their second-wave elders is a theme of Victoria Smith's book *Hags: The Demonisation of Middle-Aged Women* (Fleet, 2023).

18 An example is Rafia Zakaria, who in her recent book *Against White Feminism* (2021) rejected the wave metaphor on the grounds that it centres the West at the expense of the rest of the world. In another book published in the same year, *Feminisms: A Global History*, Lucy Delap proposed an alternative metaphor: that of a mosaic. In 2012, Nancy Hewitt wrote an essay which proposed radio waves as an alternative to ocean ones. See Nancy A. Hewitt, 'Feminist Frequencies: Regenerating the Wave Metaphor', *Feminist Studies* 38(3) (2012): 658–80.

19 Differences of sex development (DSD) are a complicated subject. As I understand it, some people with these differences align themselves with the aims of the trans rights movement while others do not. In sport, the classification of DSD athletes is a controversial and difficult subject. Carole Hooven's book *Testosterone* (Cassell, 2021) provides a clear account of the various conditions and their causes.

20 Mary Wollstonecraft, *A Vindication of the Rights of Woman* (Penguin, 1992 [1792]), p. 297.

21 I found a blog by Deborah Cameron, who is a professor of language and communication at Oxford University, extremely helpful in writing this section. See 'A Brief History of "Gender"', 15 December 2016, https://debuk.wordpress.com/2016/12/15/a-brief-history-of-gender/

22 This was Jacob Bright in 1870. See June Purvis, *Emmeline Pankhurst: A Biography* (Routledge, 2002), p. 32.

23 Amia Srinivasan, *The Right to Sex* (Bloomsbury, 2021), p. xiv.

24 See Anne Fausto-Sterling, @Fausto_Sterling, X/Twitter thread, 18 February 2020.

25 'Gender Equality Still "300 Years Away", says UN Secretary General', *Guardian*, 6 March 2023.

26 Cited in *Young People in the Time of Covid: A Fear and Hope Study of 16–24 Year-Olds* (Hope Not Hate Charitable Trust, 2020).

Chapter 1 Rebels (1790s–1840s)

1 Mary Wollstonecraft, *A Vindication of the Rights of Woman* (Penguin, 1992 [1792]), p. 79.

2 Ibid., pp. 82 and 297.

3 Ibid., p. 157.

4 Ibid., pp. 202, 210, 234.

5 Ibid., p. 149.

6 Ibid., p. 265.

7 Mary Wollstonecraft, *Maria*, in *Mary and Maria, and Matilda* (by Mary Shelley) (Penguin, 2004 [1991]), p. 114.

8 Ibid., p. 126.

9 William Godwin, 'Memoirs of the Author of "The Rights of Woman"', in *A Short Residence in Sweden and Memoirs of the Author of 'The Rights of Woman'*, by Mary Wollstonecraft and William Godwin (Penguin, 1987 [1796, 1798]), p. 272.

10 Millicent Fawcett's Introduction to *A Vindication of the Rights of Woman* by Mary Wollstonecraft (T. Fisher Unwin, 1891), pp. 2 and 23.

11 This was Janet Todd in *Mary Wollstonecraft: A Revolutionary Life* (Weidenfeld & Nicolson, 2000).

12 Italics in original. This letter is quoted by Barbara Taylor in *Mary Wollstonecraft and the Feminist Imagination* (Cambridge, 2003), p. 234.

13 William Thompson (and Anna Doyle Wheeler), *Appeal of One-Half of the Human Race, Women, Against the Pretensions of Other Half, Men, To Retain Them in Political and Thence in Civil*

and Domestic Slavery, introduced by Richard Pankhurst (Virago, 1983 [1825]), p. vii.

14 Ibid., p. xxiii.

15 Ibid., p. xxi.

16 See Dolores Dooley, *Equality in Community: Sexual Equality in the Writings of William Thompson and Anna Doyle Wheeler* (Cork University Press, 1996), p. 59.

17 Leslie F. Goldstein, 'Early Feminist Themes in French Utopian Socialism: The St.-Simonians and Fourier', *Journal of the History of Ideas* 43(1) (1982): 100.

18 These details come from Clare Midgley, *Women Against Slavery: The British Campaigns 1780–1870* (Routledge, 1992).

19 Ibid., p. 164.

20 Barbara Taylor, *Eve and the New Jerusalem: Socialism and Feminism in the Nineteenth Century* (Virago, 2016 [1983]), p. 96. This book was invaluable in my research on the Owenite women and their contemporaries.

21 Ibid., p. 75.

22 Dolores Dooley, *Equality in Community*, p. 92.

23 More details about this document, and Anna Wheeler's collaborations with French women, are included in Bonnie S. Anderson, *Joyous Greetings: The First International Women's Movement, 1830–1860* (Oxford University Press, 2000). This is a wonderful book for illuminating connections between women's movements in different countries.

24 Barbara Taylor, *Eve and the New Jerusalem*, p. 73.

25 Ibid., pp. 146, 157, 164.

26 Jean Hatton's *Betsy: The Dramatic Biography of Prison Reformer Elizabeth Fry* (Monarch Books, 2005) is a vivid account of Fry's life.

27 Ibid., p. 245.

28 I have drawn on Antonia Fraser's biography *The Case of the Married Woman: Caroline Norton, a 19th-Century Heroine who Wanted Justice for Women* (Weidenfeld & Nicolson, 2021) in my account of Norton's campaigning.

29 The 1839 Act did not give mothers the same rights as fathers. It stipulated that adulterous women – but not men – should be deprived of parental rights. The Guardianship of Infants Act 1925 equalized the rights of mothers, but only at the point that a dispute reached court. Harold L. Smith, the historian, says that full equality was not achieved until 1973. See his *British Feminism in the Twentieth Century* (Edward Elgar, 1990), p. 55.

30 Anderson, *Joyous Greetings*, p. 13.

Chapter 2 Organizers (1850s–1860s)

1 Letter to Helen Taylor, cited in Pam Hirsch, *Barbara Leigh Smith Bodichon: Feminist, Artist and Rebel* (Chatto & Windus, 1998), p. 31.

2 Hester Burton, *Barbara Bodichon, 1827–1891* (John Murray, 1949), p. 17.

3 Hirsch, *Barbara Leigh Smith Bodichon*, p. 142.

4 Ibid., p. 32.

5 Ibid., p. 31.

6 Bonnie S. Anderson, *Joyous Greetings: The First International Women's Movement, 1830–1860* (Oxford University Press, 2000), p. 124.

7 Hirsch, *Barbara Leigh Smith Bodichon*, p. 99.

8 Ibid., p. 164.

9 Ibid., pp. 101–2.

10 Ibid., pp. 67–9.

11 Ibid., p. 102.

12 Ibid., p. 53.

13 This story comes from Ray Strachey, who described Buss as having been 'almost speechless with nerves', with tears in her eyes, when giving her evidence. See Strachey, *The Cause: A Short History of the Women's Movement in Great Britain* (G. Bell & Sons, 1928), p. 137. Millicent Fawcett also experienced extreme nervousness about public speaking, and described herself as suffering from 'cold spasms'. See Jane Robinson, *Hearts and Minds:*

The Untold Story of the Great Pilgrimage and How Women Won the Vote (Doubleday, 2018), p. 42.

14 This connection is demonstrated by the fact that around half of all students at Newnham College in the 1870s and 1880s went on to become schoolteachers. Pam Hirsch's book about Barbara Leigh Smith Bodichon includes vivid details about contemporaries including Bessie Parkes and Emily Davies.

15 This row took place in March 1871. For more details, see Hirsch, *Barbara Leigh Smith Bodichon*, p. 261.

16 Florence Nightingale, *Cassandra*, pp. 401 and 408. Written in 1852, *Cassandra* was only published privately in Nightingale's lifetime. It appeared as an Appendix in Ray Strachey's *The Cause: A Short History of the Women's Movement in Great Britain* (G. Bell & Sons, 1928).

17 Mark Bostridge, *Florence Nightingale: The Woman and her Legend* (Viking, 2008), p. 502. Bostridge also cites Elizabeth Barrett Browning's view of Nightingale's secular sainthood as retrograde, p. 263.

18 Clare Midgley, *Women Against Slavery: The British Campaigns 1780–1870* (Routledge, 1992), pp. 143–4.

19 Hirsch, *Barbara Leigh Smith Bodichon*, p. 218.

20 The number of signatures on this petition is often given as 1,499, but recent research has shown that some more names were added later. See Robinson, *Hearts and Minds*.

21 Harriet Taylor Mill, 'Enfranchisement of Women', *Westminster Review*, 1851, https://utilitarianism.net/books/enfranchisement-of-women-harriet-taylor-mill/

22 'Woman in France: Madame de Sablé', *Westminster Review*, 1854, https://georgeeliotarchive.org/items/show/84

23 Burton, *Barbara Bodichon, 1827–1891*, p. 189.

24 See Jenny Uglow, *George Eliot* (Virago, 1987), p. 157.

25 The introduction to Sarah Blaffer Hrdy's *Mother Nature* (Vintage, 2000) includes a marvellous commentary on early critiques of Darwin by female readers, including Marian Evans/George Eliot, which describes her as a 'feminist'. Gillian Beer's

book *Darwin's Plots: Evolutionary Narrative in Darwin, George Eliot and Nineteenth-Century Fiction* (Routledge, 1985) was one of the first to trace Darwin's influence in Eliot's novels.

26 Hirsch, *Barbara Leigh Smith Bodichon*, p. 264.

27 This letter, written in 1869, is cited by Hirsch, *Barbara Leigh Smith Bodichon*, p. 254.

28 Barbara Caine, *English Feminism 1780–1980* (Oxford University Press, 1997), p. 96.

29 'Margaret Fuller and Mary Wollstonecraft', *Westminster Review*, 1855, https://georgeeliotarchive.org/items/show/94

30 Anderson, *Joyous Greetings*, p. 163.

31 Hirsch, *Barbara Leigh Smith Bodichon*, p. 254.

32 Hester Burton's biography is the source of this anecdote; see *Barbara Bodichon, 1827–1891*, p. 153.

Chapter 3 Crusaders (1870s–1880s)

1 I have drawn on Jane Jordan's biography of Josephine Butler (John Murray, 2001) in my sketch of her personal life and career.

2 Pam Hirsch, *Barbara Leigh Smith Bodichon: Feminist, Artist and Rebel* (Chatto & Windus, 1998), p. 187.

3 Barbara Caine, *English Feminism 1780–1980* (Oxford University Press, 1997), p. 101.

4 Ibid., p. 143. I am following Barbara Caine in this attribution.

5 Judith R. Walkowitz, *Prostitution and Victorian Society: Women, Class, and the State* (Cambridge University Press, 1980), pp. 130 and 108.

6 Caine, *English Feminism*, p. 109.

7 When the British Women's Temperance Association was founded in Newcastle in 1876, a supportive letter from Josephine Butler was read out. Interesting parallels between the two movements are explored in Brian Harrison's *Drink and the Victorians: The Temperance Question in England 1815–1872* (Faber, 1971).

8 Jordan, *Josephine Butler*, p. 134.

9 Walkowitz, *Prostitution and Victorian Society*, p. 80.

10 Ibid., p. 133.

11 Lucy Bland, *Banishing the Beast: English Feminism and Sexual Morality, 1885–1914* (Penguin, 1995), p. 104.
12 Jordan, *Josephine Butler*, p. 243.
13 Philippa Levine, *Victorian Feminism, 1850–1900* (University Press of Florida, 1994), p. 116.
14 In her book *Striking a Light: The Bryant and May Matchwomen and their Place in History* (Continuum, 2011), Louise Raw argues that the significance of the match factory strike has been underplayed by historians unwilling to credit working-class women with having initiated the wave of industrial action known as 'New Unionism'. By 1913, the number of women trade unionists had risen to 432,000.
15 Jordan, *Josephine Butler*, pp. 66–7.
16 For a discussion of the demographic data uncovered by researchers, and what it suggests about young prostitutes' lives, see Judith R. Walkowitz's *Prostitution and Victorian Society*, pp. 17–21.
17 Josephine Butler, *Woman's Work and Woman's Culture* (Macmillan, 1869), pp. liv, xii, xiii.
18 Caine, *English Feminism*, p. 120.
19 See Harrison, *Drink and the Victorians*, p. 47.
20 Levine, *Victorian Feminism*, p. 143.
21 Cobbe's article appeared in 1878 and is cited by Philippa Levine, *Victorian Feminism*, p. 132.
22 See Caine, *English Feminism*, p. 119.
23 An intriguing essay on Jane Hume Clapperton's life and work appears in Tanya Cheadle, *Sexual Progressives: Reimagining Intimacy in Scotland, 1880–1914* (Manchester University Press, 2020); see p. 177.
24 Bland, *Banishing the Beast*, p. 154.
25 Butler, *Woman's Work and Woman's Culture*, p. xl.
26 Caine, *English Feminism*, p. 117.
27 See Susan Morgan, *A Passion for Purity: Ellice Hopkins and the Politics of Gender in the Late-Victorian Church*, PhD thesis (University of Bristol, 1997).
28 Cited by Jordan, *Josephine Butler*, p. 81.

Chapter 4 Suffragists (1860s–1920s)

1 See Diane Atkinson, *Rise Up, Women!: The Remarkable Lives of the Suffragettes* (Bloomsbury, 2018).

2 Jill Liddington and Jill Norris, *One Hand Tied Behind Us: The Rise of the Women's Suffrage Movement* (Rivers Oram Press, 2000 [1978]), p. 57.

3 Hirsch, *Barbara Leigh Smith Bodichon*, p. 146.

4 Quoted in Liddington and Norris, *One Hand Tied Behind Us*, p. 62.

5 Hirsch, *Barbara Leigh Smith Bodichon*, p. 168.

6 Judith R. Walkowitz quotes an article in the *Times*, which described the campaign as a 'hysterical crusade'. In *Prostitution and Victorian Society: Women, Class, and the State* (Cambridge University Press, 1980), p. 97.

7 Cited by Philippa Levine, *Victorian Feminism, 1850–1900* (University Press of Florida, 1994), p. 70.

8 Liddington and Norris, *One Hand Tied Behind Us*, p. 27.

9 See Tony Judge's book *Margaret Bondfield: First Woman in the Cabinet* (Alpha House, 2018) for a discussion of this interesting politician's life and ideas.

10 Liddington and Norris, *One Hand Tied Behind Us*, p. 71.

11 Ibid., p. 28.

12 Ibid., p. 172.

13 This comment was Enid Stacy's and is quoted in Liddington and Norris, *One Hand Tied Behind Us*, p. 122. Stacy was a teacher turned trade union organizer and Independent Labour Party activist.

14 Ibid., p. 176.

15 June Purvis, *Emmeline Pankhurst: A Biography* (Routledge, 2002), p. 67.

16 Ibid., p. 73.

17 Atkinson, *Rise Up, Women!* p. 39.

18 Ibid., p. 75.

19 Evidence volunteered by eyewitnesses is cited by June Purvis, *Emmeline Pankhurst*, p. 150.

20 Jane Robinson, *Hearts and Minds: The Untold Story of the Great Pilgrimage and How Women Won the Vote* (Doubleday, 2018), p. 65.
21 Purvis, *Emmeline Pankhurst*, p. 238.
22 Leah Leneman, *The Scottish Suffragettes* (NMS Publishing, 2000).
23 Atkinson, *Rise Up, Women!* p. 330.
24 Lucy Bland, *Banishing the Beast: English Feminism and Sexual Morality, 1885–1914* (Penguin, 1995), p. 254.
25 Purvis, *Emmeline Pankhurst*, p. 237.
26 A discussion of Frances Swiney's book, *The Awakening of Woman* (1899), appears in Antoinette Burton's book *Burdens of History: British Feminists, Indian Women, and Imperial Culture 1865–1915* (University of North Carolina Press, 1994), pp. 85–6. Burton suggests that Swiney's is 'the most unabashed elaboration of racial feminism in the late Victorian period'.
27 See Barbara Caine, *English Feminism 1780–1980* (Oxford University Press, 1997), p. 153.
28 Christine Bolt, 'The Ideas of British Suffragism', in June Purvis and Sandra Stanley Holton (eds), *Votes for Women* (Routledge, 2000), p. 44.
29 Liddington and Norris, *One Hand Tied Behind Us*, p. 225.
30 Tania Shew, 'Militancy in the Marital Sphere: Sex Strikes, Marriage Strikes and Birth Strikes as Militant Suffrage Tactics 1911–14', p. 250, in Alexandra Hughes-Johnson and Lyndsey Jenkins (eds), *The Politics of Women's Suffrage: Local, National and International Dimensions* (University of London Press, 2021).
31 Virginia Woolf, *Diary, Volume 1 1915–1919* (Hogarth Press, 1977), p. 104.
32 David Mitchell, *Queen Christabel: Biography of Christabel Pankhurst* (Macdonald and Jane's, 1977), p. 267.
33 Women aged more than thirty were enfranchised in 1918 on the basis of a marriage or a property qualification, with wives qualifying through their husbands. All men over twenty-one were enfranchised at the same time. Older, single women who did not

meet the property threshold were excluded along with women in their twenties.

34 Harold L Smith, 'Sex vs. Class: British Feminists and the Labour Movement, 1919–1929', *The Historian* 47(1) (1984): 19.

35 Purvis, *Emmeline Pankhurst*, pp. 301–2.

36 This slogan is cited by Patricia Hollis in *Jennie Lee: A Life* (Oxford University Press, 1997), p. 37.

37 Cited in John Grigg, *Nancy Astor: Portrait of a Pioneer* (Sidgwick and Jackson, 1980), p. 85.

38 Cited in Mari Takayanagi, 'Parliament and Women, *c.* 1900–1945', PhD thesis, King's College London (2012), p. 125.

39 Ibid., pp. 132 and 138.

40 'To the Victors – the Laurels', *Time and Tide* centenary souvenir edition, pp. 5–6. https://www.timeandtidemagazine.org/read-souvenir-edition

41 Eleanor Rathbone, essay in Ray Strachey (ed.), *Our Freedom and Its Results* (Hogarth Press, 1936), p. 24.

42 Cited in Hirsch, *Barbara Leigh Smith Bodichon*, p. 216.

43 This argument features in a book review. Susan Pedersen, 'A Knife to the Heart', *London Review of Books*, 30 August 2018.

44 Purvis, *Emmeline Pankhurst*, p. 254.

Chapter 5 Legislators (1920s–1930s)

1 I am grateful to Anneliese Davidsen, director of Two Temple Place, and Benjamin Alsop, the curator at Cliveden (now owned by the National Trust), for taking me on a tour of the building.

2 Cited in Tony Judge, *Margaret Bondfield: First Woman in the Cabinet* (Alpha House, 2018), p. 42.

3 Virginia Woolf, *Three Guineas* (Hogarth Press, 1991 [1938]), p. 26.

4 Eleanor Rathbone, *The Disinherited Family* (Falling Wall Press, 1986 [1924]), p. 383.

5 Cited by Pat Thane in Harold L Smith (ed.), *British Feminism in in the Twentieth Century* (Edward Elgar, 1990), p. 135.

6 Erna Reiss's discussion of this issue is in her essay in Ray Strachey (ed.), *Our Freedom and Its Results* (Hogarth Press, 1936).
7 Susan Pedersen's biography *Eleanor Rathbone and the Politics of Conscience* (Yale University Press, 2004) is full of insights into this remarkable politician's life and career.
8 For more details, see Sally Alexander, *Becoming a Woman and Other Essays in Nineteenth- and Twentieth-Century Feminist History* (Virago, 1994), p. 165.
9 It remains the case today that families with three or more children are over-represented among the poorest households, a situation which has been exacerbated by the 'two-child limit' for benefit claims. See, for example, 'The Living Standards Outlook 2023', a report by the Resolution Foundation in January 2023. Two differences a century ago were the lack of reliable contraception and the legal right of husbands to insist on sexual intercourse with their wives.
10 Rathbone, *The Disinherited Family*, pp. 121 and 136.
11 Olive Schreiner was the author of a pioneering examination of the status of women under capitalism, *Woman and Labour* (1911), among other works.
12 I am indebted to Susan Pedersen's biography, *Eleanor Rathbone and the Politics of Conscience*, for its thoughtful discussion of Rathbone's personality and relationships.
13 Pedersen, *Eleanor Rathbone*, p. 222.
14 Harold L. Smith, 'British Feminism in the 1920s', in Harold L Smith (ed.), *British Feminism in the Twentieth Century* (Edward Elgar, 1990), p. 62.
15 Eleanor Rathbone, in Ray Strachey (ed.), *Our Freedom and Its Results* (Hogarth Press, 1936), p. 37.
16 Pedersen, *Eleanor Rathbone*, p. 108.
17 Some other countries had their own versions of this maternalist versus anti-maternalist split. In Japan, for example, Hiratsuka Raicho advocated motherhood allowances, while other feminists thought these kinds of payments could reinforce

women's subordination. See Kumari Jayawardena, *Feminism and Nationalism in the Third World* (Verso, 2016 [1986]), p. 248.

18 Cited in Angela V. John, *Turning the Tide: The Life of Lady Rhondda* (Parthian, 2013), p. 394. See Pedersen, *Eleanor Rathbone*, pp. 244–54, for a longer discussion of this episode.

19 See Susan Pedersen's biography of Rathbone for more details of this episode, pp. 246–58. Amrit Kaur would go on to become Gandhi's secretary and, later, the health minister in Nehru's government.

20 Ray Strachey's view is cited by Martin Pugh in 'Domesticity and the Decline of Feminism, 1930–1950' in Harold L. Smith (ed.), *British Feminism in the Twentieth Century* (Edward Elgar, 1990), p. 144.

21 John, *Turning the Tide*, p. 322.

22 Ibid., p. 488.

23 Rachel Reeves, *Women of Westminster, The MPs Who Changed Politics* (Bloomsbury, 2019), p. 55.

24 This volcano metaphor was used by Harold L Smith. See chapter 4, note 34.

25 Patricia Hollis, *Jennie Lee: A Life* (Oxford University Press, 1997), pp. 150 and 392.

26 See Harold L. Smith, 'Sex vs. Class: British Feminists and the Labour Movement, 1919–1929', *The Historian* 47(1) (1984): 24.

27 See Antoinette Burton's book, *Burdens of History*. Also essays by Barbara Ramusack and Mrinalini Sinha (details in Sources and Further Reading).

28 Laura Beers, *Red Ellen: The Life of Ellen Wilkinson – Socialist, Feminist, Internationalist* (Harvard, 2016), p. 259.

29 Woolf, *Three Guineas*, p. 187.

30 Mary Agnes Hamilton, essay in Ray Strachey (ed.), *Our Freedom and Its Results* (Hogarth Press, 1936), pp. 260 and 283.

31 The article appeared in *Good Housekeeping* in May 1929 and is cited in Beers, *Red Ellen*, p. 215.

32 Winifred Holtby, *Virginia Woolf: A Critical Memoir* (Wishart & Co, 1932), p. 178.

Chapter 6 Housewives (1940s–1950s)

1 See Hansard, the official report of all parliamentary debates. https://hansard.parliament.uk/

2 Details of this broadcast were included by the feminist Labour MP Edith Summerskill in her memoir, *A Woman's World* (Heinemann, 1967), p. 78.

3 Matt Perry, *'Red Ellen' Wilkinson: Her Ideas, Movements and World* (Manchester University Press, 2014), p. 360.

4 See Harold L. Smith, 'The Womanpower Problem in Britain during the Second World War', *Historical Journal* 27(4) (1984): 925–45.

5 Beatrix Campbell, *The Iron Ladies: Why Do Women Vote Tory?* (Virago, 1987), p. 71.

6 See Hansard, https://hansard.parliament.uk/

7 Cited in Harold L. Smith, 'The Womanpower Problem', p. 925.

8 Summerskill, *A Woman's World*, p. 61.

9 Perry, *'Red Ellen'*, p. 370.

10 Nicholas Timmins, *The Five Giants: A Biography of the Welfare State* (William Collins, 2017 [1995]), p. 54.

11 David Kynaston, *Austerity Britain 1945–51* (Bloomsbury, 2007), p. 567.

12 Timmins, *The Five Giants*, pp. 54–6.

13 Cited in Alva Myrdal and Viola Klein, *Women's Two Roles: Home and Work* (Routledge and Kegan Paul, 1970 [1956]), p. 444.

14 Perry, *'Red Ellen'*, p. 76.

15 These observations, made by Ferdynand Zweig in his 1952 book, *Woman's Life and Labour*, are cited in Kynaston, *Austerity Britain*, p. 420.

16 Kynaston, *Austerity Britain*, p. 670. I am much indebted to Kynaston's research for the facts and figures about housework cited here.

17 Cited by Virginia Nicholson in *Perfect Wives in Ideal Homes* (Viking, 2015).

18 Juliet Rhys-Williams first set out her ideas in a privately circulated pamphlet in 1942, and subsequently in a book, *Something*

to Look Forward To (1943). See Peter Sloman's essay, 'Beveridge's Rival: Juliet Rhys-Williams and the Campaign for Basic Income 1942–55', *Contemporary British History* 30(2) (2016).

19 Elizabeth Abbot and Katherine Bompas's pamphlet, privately printed in 1943, was titled 'The Woman Citizen and Social Security: A Criticism of the Proposals Made in the Beveridge Report as They Affect Women'.

20 Campbell, *The Iron Ladies*, pp. 72–3.

21 Kynaston, *Austerity Britain*, p. 630.

22 David Kynaston, *Modernity Britain 1957–62* (Bloomsbury, 2014), p. 113.

23 Anne Perkins, *Red Queen: The Authorised Biography of Barbara Castle* (Macmillan, 2003), p. 119.

24 David Kynaston, *Family Britain 1951–57* (Bloomsbury, 2009), p. 398.

25 Kynaston, *Austerity Britain*, p. 257.

26 Edith Summerskill, *Letters to my Daughter* (Heinemann, 1957), p. 94.

27 Myrdal and Klein, *Women's Two Roles*, p. 188.

28 Judith Hubback, *Wives Who Went to College* (Heinemann, 1957), p. 85.

29 Figures from Myrdal and Klein, *Women's Two Roles*, p. 79; and Kynaston, *Austerity Britain*, p. 415.

30 By 1943, it is estimated that 90 per cent of all able-bodied single women and 46 per cent of working-age women had been directly employed in the war effort. See Harold L. Smith's essay, 'The Womanpower Problem', p. 937.

31 See Hansard, 16 May 1952 https://hansard.parliament.uk/

32 Doris Lessing's *Walking in the Shade: Volume Two of My Autobiography, 1949–62* (Fourth Estate, 1998) includes an account of these difficulties and analysis of them. See p. 232.

33 Clare Mac Cumhaill and Rachael Wiseman, *Metaphysical Animals: How Four Women Brought Philosophy Back to Life* (Chatto & Windus, 2022).

34 Jones was a speaker at an Africa Women's Day event in London,

while the Inter-Racial Friendship Co-ordinating Council, formed in 1959 after the racist murder of Kelso Cochrane, opposed sex as well as race discrimination. See Marika Sherwood, *Claudia Jones: A Life in Exile* (Lawrence & Wishart, 1999), pp. 95, 98, 106, 151.

35 Rachel Cooke, *Her Brilliant Career: Ten Extraordinary Women of the Fifties* (Virago, 2013), p. 202.

36 Hannah Gavron, *The Captive Wife: Conflicts of Housebound Mothers* (Routledge and Kegal Paul, 1966), p. 52.

37 Kynaston, *Austerity Britain*, p. 614.

38 See Amy Black and Stephen Brooke, 'The Labour Party, Women, and the Problem of Gender 1951–66', *Journal of British Studies* 36(4) (1997): 419–52.

39 A more recent book which does explore this history is Clarisse Berthezène and Julie Gottlieb, *Rethinking Right-wing Women: Gender and the Conservative Party, 1880s to the Present* (Manchester University Press, 2017).

40 Katie Haessly, 'British Conservative Women MPs and "Women's Issues", 1950–1979', PhD thesis, University of Nottingham (2010).

41 For more detail, see Campbell, *The Iron Ladies*, pp. 90–3.

42 Perkins, *Red Queen*, p. 78.

43 Ibid., p. 168.

44 John Newson, *The Education of Girls* (1948), cited in Kynaston, *Austerity Britain*, p. 574.

Chapter 7 Liberators (1960s–1980s)

1 Doris Lessing, *Walking in the Shade: Volume Two of My Autobiography, 1949–62* (Fourth Estate, 1998), p. 306.

2 Originally published in *New Left Review* in 1966, Juliet Mitchell's essay was later reprinted in her book, *The Longest Revolution: Essays in Feminism, Literature and Psychoanalysis* (Virago, 1984).

3 Ibid., p. 17.

4 In this chapter, and the next two, I draw on material from inter-

views with feminists carried out by me in 2022 and 2023, as well as on written sources. Books and articles are credited in endnotes as usual. For a list of my interviewees, see Sources and Further Reading. Catherine Hall is my mother's younger sister and therefore my maternal aunt.

5 'Lee', interviewed by and quoted in Anna E. Rogers, 'Feminist Consciousness-raising in the 1970s and 1980s: West Yorkshire Women's Groups and their Impact on Women's Lives', PhD thesis, University of Leeds (2010). First names only used for reasons of privacy.

6 'Joanna', interviewed by Anna E. Rogers, as above.

7 Ibid., p. 226.

8 Ibid., p. 157.

9 As the historian Natalie Thomlinson has explained, the terminology of intersectionality introduced by the US legal scholar Kimberlé Crenshaw in 1989 'put a name to an understanding of the way in which racial, gender and class oppression interacted that had been current in feminist circles, and particularly in Black feminist circles, since the 1970s'. See Natalie Thomlinson, *Race, Ethnicity and the Women's Movement in England, 1968–1993* (Palgrave Macmillan, 2016), p. 18.

10 Beverley Bryan, Stella Dadzie and Suzanne Scafe, *Heart of the Race: Black Women's Lives in Britain* (Virago, 1985), p. 58.

11 Interview with Stevi Jackson; see Sources and Further Reading.

12 See Emily Grace Flaherty, 'The Women's Liberation Movement in Britain 1968–1984: Locality and Organisation in Feminist Politics', PhD thesis, University of Glasgow (2017), p. 185.

13 Alice Sullivan and Selina Todd (eds), *Sex and Gender: A Contemporary Reader* (Routledge, 2023), p. 88.

14 Gail Lewis, interviewed by Rachel Cohen, 2011, for *Sisterhood and After* (see Sources and Further Reading).

15 This book was mostly complete when the exhibition *Women in Revolt! Art and Activism in the UK 1970–1990*, opened at Tate Britain in November 2023. But I think the pluralistic nature of the exhibition reinforces the argument made in this chapter about

the range of activities and people associated with the women's movement.

16 The route of the march in Leeds was controversial as it went through a predominantly ethnic-minority neighbourhood, which was seen by some as proof of racial prejudice. For further details, see Finn Mackay, *Radical Feminism: Feminist Activism in Movement* (Palgrave Macmillan, 2015), pp. 83–9.

17 Rachel Reeves, *Women of Westminster: The MPs Who Changed Politics* (Bloomsbury, 2019), p. 128.

18 Sue Bruley, 'Women's Liberation at the Grass Roots', *Women's History Review* 25(5) (2016): 736.

19 When presenting the legislation in Parliament, Barbara Castle paid tribute to its Conservative backers, naming Irene Ward and Thelma Cazalet-Keir. Cited in Reeves, *Women of Westminster*, p. 124.

20 Cited in Thomlinson, *Race, Ethnicity and the Women's Movement*, p. 53.

21 See Jill Liddington, *The Long Road to Greenham* (Virago, 1989).

22 Mary Mellor's memory of Greenham is mentioned in her book, *Feminism and Ecology* (Polity, 1997), p. 41.

23 Kelly Coate, 'The History of Women's Studies as an Academic Subject Area in Higher Education in the UK: 1970–1995', PhD thesis, Institute of Education, University of London, 1999, pp. 152 and 184. An unnamed informant told Coate, of the debate over the new course at the LSE, that 'they kind of did allow it to go ahead provided it wasn't called women's studies but had to be called the Sociology of Sex and Gender Roles'.

24 Ibid., p. 172.

25 The book is S. Grewal, Jackie Kay, Liliane Landor, Gail Lewis and Pratibha Parmar, *Charting the Journey: Writings by Black and Third World Women* (Sheba Press, 1988). Lewis was speaking to Rachel Cohen for an interview for *Sisterhood and After*, 2011 (see Sources and Further Reading).

26 Coate, 'The History of Women's Studies', p. 188.

27 Emily Grace Flaherty uncovered records of a conference held in

Edinburgh in 1983, which aimed to bring together the various branches of feminist literature. Workshops were held on topics including feminist science fiction, feminists in journalism, and academic, lesbian and working-class writing. See Flaherty, 'The Women's Liberation Movement in Britain' (2017).

28 This and other records of this Brighton group are discussed by Flaherty, 'The Women's Liberation Movement in Britain'.

29 FINRRAGE (Feminist International Network of Resistance to Reproductive and Genetic Engineering) was launched in 1985 in Sweden. Feminists in India launched another group to campaign against sex-selective abortion. See Mellor, *Feminism and Ecology*, p. 37.

Chapter 8 Specialists (1990s–2010)

1 Southall Black Sisters was set up in 1979 as part of the community response to clashes between anti-racists and fascists in Southall (this is where the teacher Blair Peach, who was part of an anti-fascist demonstration, was killed). Three years later, when Pragna Patel joined, its focus was less clear, and she described herself in an interview as having 're-founded' it.

2 For a full account of Kiranjit Ahluwahlia's case, and Southall Black Sisters' part in it, see Kiranjit Ahluwahlia and Rahila Gupta, *Circle of Light: The Autobiography of Kiranjit Ahluawalia* (HarperCollins, 1997).

3 One of the first journalists to report on Sara Thornton's case, Jennifer Nadel (then home affairs editor at ITN), wrote a book about it. Jennifer Nadel, *Sara Thornton: The Story of a Woman Who Killed* (Gollancz, 1993).

4 After her death, Julie Bindel and Harriet Wistrich put together a book to commemorate Emma Humphreys' life, including some of her own writings. See *The Map of My Life – The Story of Emma Humphreys* (Astraia Press, 2003).

5 Ahluwahlia and Gupta, *Circle of Light*, p. 367.

6 See Catherine Hall, *White, Male and Middle Class: Explorations in Feminism and History* (Polity Press, 1992), p. 13.

7 Judith Butler's sources can be scrutinized in her own references. The first endnote in *Gender Trouble* (1990) cites works by Michel Foucault, the second cites Jacques Derrida, and the third cites Denise Riley's book, *'Am I That Name?'* (Palgrave Macmillan, 1988). Butler discusses Monique Wittig at some length in her text, along with Luce Irigaray and others, but not Christine Delphy, whose name does not appear in the index to *Gender Trouble* or its sequel, *Bodies That Matter* (1993).

8 Cited in Stevi Jackson, *Christine Delphy* (Sage, 1996), p. 121.

9 Stevi Jackson, 'The Amazing Deconstructing Woman' (1992), in Deborah Cameron and Joan Scanlon (eds), *The Trouble and Strife Reader* (Bloomsbury Academic, 2010), p. 148.

10 Mary Mellor, *Feminism and Ecology* (Polity, 1997) and Maria Mies and Vandana Shiva, *Ecofeminism* (Bloomsbury Academic, 1993) offer two accounts of ecofeminism in the 1990s.

11 Deborah Cameron, 'Back to Nature' (1997), in Cameron and Scanlon, *The Trouble and Strife Reader*, p. 156.

12 Charles Darwin, *The Descent of Man, and Selection in Relation to Sex* (Princeton, 1981 [1882]), pp. 67–8.

13 Cited in Sarah Blaffer Hrdy, *The Woman That Never Evolved* (Harvard, 1999), p. 201.

14 Alison Jolly's books include *The Evolution of Primate Behaviour* (1972) and *Lucy's Legacy: Sex and Intelligence in Human Evolution* (1999). Elaine Morgan's *The Descent of Woman*, in which she advanced her aquatic ape hypothesis, was published in 1972.

15 Angela Saini, *Inferior: How Science Got Women Wrong and the New Research That's Rewriting the Story* (Beacon Press, 2017), p. 9.

16 Virginia Woolf said 'never let anybody guess that you have a mind of your own' in a speech on women's professions given in 1931. Cited in Bonnie S. Anderson, *Joyous Greetings: The First International Women's Movement, 1830–1860* (Oxford University Press, 2000), p. 45.

17 Hrdy, *The Woman That Never Evolved*, p. xvii.

18 Ibid., p. xxvii.
19 See Anne Campbell, *A Mind of Her Own: The Evolutionary Psychology of Women* (Oxford University Press, 2002).
20 The Women's Unit, which was created by the Labour government in 1997, became the Women's and Equality Unit in 2001, and the Government Equalities Office in 2007.
21 'The Corston Report: A Review of Women with Particular Vulnerabilities in the Criminal Justice System' (Home Office, 2007).
22 Monica McWilliams co-founded the Northern Ireland Women's Coalition and later became a member of the Northern Ireland Assembly. An interview with her by Liz Kelly, titled 'Taking on the Dinosaurs' (1997), appears in Cameron and Scanlon (eds), *The Trouble and Strife Reader*, pp. 182–9.
23 See Rebecca Walker's essay 'Becoming the Third Wave', published in the US magazine *Ms* in 1992.
24 Imelda Whelehan, *Overloaded: Popular Culture and the Future of Feminism* (Women's Press, 2000). For lads' mag readership figures, see p. 66.
25 Finn Mackay described feminism as 'sweeping our shores' in the early 2000s in her book *Radical Feminism: Feminism Activism in Movement* (Palgrave Macmillan, 2015); see p. 7.
26 Mackay's account of the origins of Reclaim the Night is informative and excellent.
27 This is not a comprehensive list of feminist activities and organizations in this period, but a sample chosen to illustrate an increased presence in the early 2000s, relative to the decade before.
28 Lola Okolosie, 'As a black feminist, I see how the wider movement fails women like my mother,' *Guardian*, 9 December 2013.
29 Martin Amis, 'A Rough Trade', *Guardian*, 17 March 2001. The 2003 *Adult Video News* piece is referenced in Kat Banyard, *Pimp State: Sex, Money and the Future of Equality* (Faber, 2016), p. 46.
30 Banyard, *Pimp State*, p. 32.
31 David Perfect, 'Gender Pay Gaps, Equality and Human Rights

Commission', briefing paper, 2011 https://www.equalityhumanrights.com/sites/default/files/briefing-paper-2-gender-pay-gap_0.pdf

Chapter 9 Feminists (2010–2023)

1 Four years earlier, in 2006, the Equality and Human Rights Commission (EHRC) replaced the three separate bodies that had monitored compliance with the Sex Discrimination Act 1975, Race Relations Act 1976, and Disability Discrimination Act 1995.

2 Natasha Walter, *Living Dolls: The Return of Sexism* (Virago, 2010), p. 2.

3 Kat Banyard, *The Equality Illusion: The Truth about Women and Men Today* (Faber, 2010), p. 120.

4 Kat Banyard, *Pimp State: Sex, Money and the Future of Equality* (Faber, 2016), p. 3.

5 Walter, *Living Dolls*, p. 114.

6 With more than £750 million in liabilities remaining, the ramifications of this decision are still unfolding.

7 See Elizabeth Evans, *The Politics of Third Wave Feminisms: Neoliberalism, Intersectionality and the State in Britain and the US* (Palgrave Macmillan, 2015), p. 165.

8 *The Stern Review: A Report by Baroness Vivien Stern CBE of an Independent Review into How Rape Complaints are Handled by Public Authorities in England and Wales* (Government Equalities Office, 2010).

9 Melanie Newman, 'Are CPS Performance Measures to Blame for Fall in Rape Convictions?', Bureau of Investigative Journalism, 6 May 2014.

10 The party, which is now led by Mandu Reid, has not matched this result since and does not have any councillors above parish/town council level.

11 See, for example, Finn Mackay, *Feminism Activism in Movement* (Palgrave Macmillan, 2015), p. 139.

12 Claire Heuchan. See @ClaireShrugged, Twitter thread, 25 September 2022.

13 Jane Clare Jones, 'Anders Breivik's Chilling Anti-Feminism', *Guardian*, 27 July 2011.

14 Germaine Greer had written about these disputes in her bestselling book *The Whole Woman* (Black Swan, 2007), and was not the first feminist author to do so. On BBC *Newsnight* in October 2015, Greer reiterated her view that trans women are 'not women', but said she would use people's chosen pronouns as a courtesy.

15 See, for example, Julie Bindel, 'Gender Benders, Beware', *Guardian*, 31 January 2004, and 'My Trans Mission', *Guardian*, 1 August 2007. For Julie Bindel's account of the award blocked by Stonewall, see 'Triumph of the Trans Lobbyists', *The Critic*, January 2020.

16 Suzanne Moore, 'Seeing Red: The Power of Female Anger', *New Statesman*, 8 January 2013.

17 Suzanne Moore's account of these events is included in her essay, 'Why I Had to Leave the Guardian', UnHerd, 25 November 2020. https://unherd.com/2020/11/why-i-had-to-leave-the-guardian/

18 Helen Lewis, 'Rereading the Second Wave: Why Feminism Needs to Respect its Elders', *New Statesman*, 12 May 2014.

19 The term 'terf', which is an acronym for trans-exclusionary radical feminist, was coined in or around 2008 and has been attributed to the Australian journalist Viv Smythe. See Viv Smythe, 'I'm Credited with Having Coined the Word "Terf". Here's How It Happened', *Guardian*, 28 November 2018. In her article, Smythe suggested that others may have used the term before her in blogs that have not survived, noted that it had since been 'weaponized' and pointed out that she had no control over this.

20 Marina Strinkovsky, 'It's Not a Zero Sum Game', 16 September 2014. https://notazerosumgame.blogspot.com/2014/09/radfem-panic-when-demands-for.html?m=1

21 Mackay, *Radical Feminism*, p. 234.

22 Ibid., p. 226.

23 Rebecca Reilly-Cooper and Sarah Ditum are two more feminist writers who wrote articles about gender identity and feminism in 2016. See Sarah Ditum, 'What is Gender Anyway?', *New*

Statesman, May 2016, and Rebecca Reilly-Cooper, 'Sex is Not a Spectrum', *Aeon*, June 2016.

24 'We Cannot Allow Censorship and Silencing of Individuals', *Guardian*, 15 February 2015; 'Germaine Greer Gives University Lecture Despite Campaign to Silence Her', *Guardian*, 18 November 2015.

25 Janice Turner, 'Transgender Athletes are Unfair to Women' *Times*, 28 January 2016; 'How Do You Solve a Problem like Men in Changing Rooms, Maria?', *Times*, 29 July 2017; 'The Battle Over Gender Has Turned Bloody', *Times*, 16 September 2017.

26 'Woman Billboard Removed after Transphobia Row', BBC News, 26 September 2018. https://www.bbc.co.uk/news/uk-45650462.

27 See Census (Amendment) (Scotland) Bill: MBM evidence to the CTEEA Committee, 4 December 2018. https://murrayblackburnmackationenzie.org/2018/12/04/census-amendment-scotland-bill/

28 Matt Bristow, Anna Hutchinson and Anastassis Spiliadis are three UK clinicians who hold this view. See Hannah Barnes, *Time to Think: The Inside Story of the Collapse of the Tavistock's Gender Service for Children* (Swift Press, 2023), pp. 159–64. Stella O'Malley is another psychotherapist and author with similar concerns.

29 Caelainn Barr, 'Legal Challenge Over CPS Policy on Prosecuting Rape Cases Dismissed', *Guardian*, 15 March 2021.

30 Laura Bates, *Men Who Hate Women: The Extremism Nobody is Talking About* (Simon & Schuster, 2020), p. 49.

31 See 'A Liberalisation in Attitudes?' British Social Attitudes, National Centre for Social Research, September 2023. The figure of 19 per cent who support the inclusion of transgender women in female sports comes from research by the More in Common think tank. See 'Britons and Gender Identity: Navigating Common Ground and Division', 16 June 2022. https://www.moreincommon.org.uk/our-work/research/britons-and-gender-identity/

32 'Clarifying the Definition of "Sex" in the Equality Act', Equality and Human Rights Commission, 3 April 2023.

Epilogue

1 Virginia Woolf, *Three Guineas* (Hogarth Press, 1991 [1938]), p. 117.

2 This tension in Virginia Woolf's philosophy was brought out in a discussion of *A Room of One's Own* between Michèle Barrett, Alexandra Harris and Hermione Lee, hosted by Melvyn Bragg, on BBC Radio 4's *In Our Time* (March 2023), https://www.bbc.co.uk/programmes/m001kh32

3 Office for National Statistics: Sexual Offences in England and Wales Overview, year ending March 1922 (23 March 2023).

Sources and Further Reading

This book is mostly based on written sources. As part of my research for the last three chapters, I conducted a number of interviews in 2022 and 2023 and am very grateful to the following people for agreeing to talk to me by telephone, video or in person: Zlakha Ahmed, Sally Alexander, Vera Baird, Shereen Benjamin, Julie Bindel, Beatrix Campbell, Jane Clare Jones, Stephanie Davies-Arai, Sarah Ditum, Cátia Freitas, Judith Green, Catherine Hall, Vivienne Hayes, Ayesha Hazarika, Ann Henderson, Zoe Hollowood, Stevi Jackson, Lisa Mackenzie, Suzanne Moore, Sian Norris, Pragna Patel, Ann Phoenix, Katherine Rake, Raquel Rosario Sánchez, Clare Short, Jacqui Smith, Helen Steel, Mary-Ann Stephenson, Marina Strinkovsky, Lisa-Marie Taylor, Sylvia Walby, Sophie Walker, Ceri Williams, Nicola Williams and Harriet Wistrich. I have also been greatly helped by numerous informal conversations.

I also spent hours in the British Library, listening to interviews with Gail Lewis, Amrit Wilson and others carried out for *Sisterhood and After: The Women's Liberation Oral History Project*, produced in partnership with The Women's Library (at the London School of Economics) and directed by Margaretta Jolly at the University of Sussex, 2010–13. These recordings are an invaluable resource; I'm so glad they are publicly accessible. I also made use of the *Sisters Doing*

It for Themselves oral history archive, produced by the Women's Resource Centre, 2019–2021 (LSE Digital Library). Hansard, the official record of parliamentary debates, is invaluable. Some references to newspaper articles and weblinks which are included in endnotes are not repeated here.

Books, articles and theses

Ahluwalia, Kiranjit and Gupta, Rahila, *Circle of Light: The Autobiography of Kiranjit Ahluawalia* (HarperCollins, 1997).

Alexander, Sally, *Becoming a Woman and Other Essays in 19th and 20th Century Feminist History* (Virago, 1994).

Alison, Belinda, Helen Steel, Lisa and Naomi with Veronica Clark, *Deep Deception: The Story of the Spycops Network and the Women Who Uncovered the Shocking Truth* (Ebury Spotlight, 2022).

Amos, Valerie, Lewis, Gail, Mama, Amina and Parmar, Pratibha, 'Many Voices, One Chant – Black Feminist Perspectives', *Feminist Review* 17(1) (1984).

Anderson, Bonnie S, *Joyous Greetings: The First International Women's Movement, 1830–1860* (Oxford University Press, 2000).

Ashton, Rosemary *George Eliot: A Life* (Hamish Hamilton, 1996).

Atkinson, Diane, *Rise Up, Women! The Remarkable Lives of the Suffragettes* (Bloomsbury, 2018).

Banyard, Kat, *The Equality Illusion: The Truth about Women and Men Today* (Faber, 2010).

Banyard, Kat, *Pimp State: Sex, Money and the Future of Equality* (Faber, 2016).

Bates, Laura, *Men Who Hate Women: The Extremism Nobody is Talking About* (Simon & Schuster, 2020).

de Beauvoir, Simone, *The Second Sex*, trans. H. M. Parshley (Vintage, 1997 [translation first published in 1953; first French edn 1949]).

Beer, Gillian, *Darwin's Plots: Evolutionary Narrative in Darwin, George Eliot and Nineteenth-Century Fiction* (Cambridge University Press, 2000 [1983]).

Beers, Laura, *Red Ellen: The Life of Ellen Wilkinson – Socialist, Feminist, Internationalist* (Harvard, 2016).

Berthezène, Clarisse and Gottlieb, Julie, *Rethinking Right-Wing Women: Gender and the Conservative Party, 1880s to the Present* (Manchester University Press, 2017).

Bindel, Julie, *Feminism for Women* (Constable, 2021).

Bindel, Julie and Wistrich, Harriet, *The Map of My Life – The Story of Emma Humphreys* (Astraia Press, 2003).

Black, Amy and Brooke, Stephen, 'The Labour Party, Women, and the Problem of Gender 1951–66', *Journal of British Studies* 36(4) (1997): 419–52.

Blackburn, Sheila, 'How Useful are Feminist Theories of the Welfare State?', *Women's History's Review* 4(3) (1995): 369–94.

Bland, Lucy, *Banishing the Beast: English Feminism and Sexual Morality, 1885–1914* (Penguin, 1995).

Bostridge, Mark, *Florence Nightingale: The Woman and her Legend* (Viking, 2008).

Brown, Adrienne Maree, *Pleasure Activism: The Politics of Feeling Good* (AK Press, 2019).

Brown, Andrew, *The Darwin Wars* (Simon and Schuster, 1999).

Bruley, Sue, 'Women's Liberation at the Grass Roots, A View from Some English Towns, c.1968–1990', *Women's History Review* 25(5) (2016): 723–40.

Bryan, Beverley, Dadzie, Stella and Scafe, Suzanne, *The Heart of the Race: Black Women's Lives in Britain* (Virago, 1985).

Bunce, Robin and Linton, Samara, *Diane Abbott: The Authorised Biography* (Biteback, 2020).

Burton, Antoinette, *Burdens of History: British Feminists, Indian Women, and Imperial Culture, 1865–1915* (University of North Carolina Press, 1994).

Burton, Hester, *Barbara Bodichon, 1827–1891* (John Murray, 1949).

Butler, Josephine (ed.), *Woman's Work and Woman's Culture* (Macmillan, 1869).

Butler, Judith, *Gender Trouble: Feminism and the Subversion of Identity* (Routledge, 1990).

Butler, Judith, *Bodies That Matter* (Routledge, 2011 [1993]).

Byrne, Alex, *Trouble with Gender* (Polity, 2023).

Caine, Barbara, *English Feminism 1780–1980* (Oxford University Press, 1997).

Cameron, Deborah, *The Myth of Mars and Venus: Do Men and Women Really Speak Different Languages?* (Oxford University Press, 2008).

Cameron, Deborah and Scanlon, Joan (eds), *The Trouble & Strife Reader* (Bloomsbury Academic, 2010).

Campbell, Anne, *A Mind of Her Own: The Evolutionary Psychology of Women* (Oxford University Press, 2002).

Campbell, Beatrix, *The Iron Ladies: Who do Women Vote Tory?* (Virago, 1987).

Campbell, Beatrix and Coote, Anna, *Sweet Freedom: The Struggle for Women's Liberation* (Picador, 1982).

Chamberlain, Geoffrey, 'British Maternal Mortality in the 19th and Early 20th Centuries', *Journal of the Royal Society of Medicine* 99(11) (2006): 559–63.

Cheadle, Tanya, *Sexual Progressives: Reimagining Intimacy in Scotland, 1880–1914* (Manchester University Press, 2020).

Clay, Catherine, *Time and Tide: the Feminist and Cultural Politics of a Modern Magazine* (Edinburgh University Press, 2018).

Coate, Kelly, 'The History of Women's Studies as an Academic Subject Area in Higher Education in the UK: 1970–1995', PhD thesis, Institute of Education, University of London, 1999.

Cobbe, Frances Power, *Essays on the Pursuits of Women* (Cambridge University Press, 2010 [1863]).

Cobbe, Frances Power, 'Darwinism in Morals', *Theological Review*, 1871, darwin-online.org.uk

Cooke, Lucy, *Bitch: A Revolutionary Guide to Sex, Evolution and the Female Animal* (Doubleday, 2022).

Cooke, Rachel, *Her Brilliant Career: Ten Extraordinary Women of the Fifties* (Virago, 2013).

Cronin, Helena, *The Ant and the Peacock: Altruism and Sexual Selection from Darwin to Today* (Cambridge University Press, 1991).

Darley, Gillian, *Octavia Hill: A Life* (Constable, 1990).

Delap, Lucy, *Feminisms: A Global History* (Pelican Books, 2020).

Dooley, Dolores, *Equality in Community: Sexual Equality in the Writings of William Thompson and Anna Doyle Wheeler* (Cork University Press, 1996).

Emecheta, Buchi, *The Joys of Motherhood* (Allison & Busby, 1979).

Evans, Elizabeth, *The Politics of Third Wave Feminisms: Neoliberalism, Intersectionality and the State in Britain and the US* (Palgrave Macmillan, 2015).

Faludi, Susan, *Backlash: The Undeclared War Against Women* (Vintage, 1993 [1992]).

Fine, Cordelia, *Delusions of Gender: The Real Science Behind Sex Differences* (Icon, 2010).

Flaherty, Emily Grace, 'The Women's Liberation Movement in Britain, 1968–1984: Locality and Organisation in Feminist Politics', PhD thesis, University of Glasgow (2017).

Fraser, Antonia, *The Case of the Married Woman: Caroline Norton, a 19th-century Heroine who Wanted Justice for Women* (Weidenfeld & Nicolson 2021).

Friedan, Betty, *The Feminine Mystique* (Penguin, 2010 [1963]).

Gavron, Hannah, *The Captive Wife: Conflicts of Housebound Mothers* (Routledge and Kegan Paul, 1966).

Gavron, Jeremy, *Woman on the Edge of Time* (Scribe, 2015).

Gleadle, Kathryn, *The Early Feminists: Radical Unitarians and the Emergence of the Women's Rights Movement, 1831–51* (New York: St Martin's Press, 1995).

Goldstein, Leslie F, 'Early Feminist Themes in French Utopian Socialism: The St.-Simonians and Fourier', *Journal of the History of Ideas* 43(1) (1982): 91–108.

Grigg, John, *Nancy Astor: Portrait of a Pioneer* (Sidgwick and Jackson, 1980).

Haessly, Katie, 'British Conservative Women MPs and "Women's Issues", 1950–1979', PhD thesis, University of Nottingham (2010).

Hall, Catherine, *White, Male and Middle Class: Explorations in Feminism and History* (Polity Press, 1992).

Harrington, Mary, *Feminism Against Progress* (Forum, 2023).

Harrison, Brian, *Drink and the Victorians: The Temperance Question in England, 1815–1872* (Faber, 1971).

Hatton, Jean, *Betsy: The Dramatic Biography of Prison Reformer Elizabeth Fry* (Monarch Books, 2005).

Hays, Mary, 'Appeal to the Men of Great Britain in behalf of Women', in Edith Kuiper (ed.), *Women's Thought in the Eighteenth Century, Volume I, The Economy of the Household* (Routledge, 2014), pp. 393–410.

Hewitt, Nancy A., 'Feminist Frequencies: Regenerating the Wave Metaphor', *Feminist Studies* 38(3) (2012): 658–80.

Higonnet, Margaret Randolph, Jenson, Jane, Michel, Sonya and Collins Weitz, Margaret (eds), *Behind the Lines: Gender and the Two World Wars* (Yale University Press, 1987).

Hinton, James, 'Militant Housewives: the British Housewives' League and the Attlee Government', *History Workshop Journal* 38(1) (1994): 129–56.

Hirsch, Pam, *Barbara Leigh Smith Bodichon: Feminist, Artist and Rebel* (Chatto & Windus, 1998).

Hollis, Patricia, *Jennie Lee: A Life* (Oxford University Press, 1997).

Holmes, Rachel, *Sylvia Pankhurst: Natural Born Rebel* (Bloomsbury, 2020).

Holtby, Winifred, *Virginia Woolf: A Critical Memoir* (Wishart & Co, 1932).

Hooven, Carole, *Testosterone: The Story of the Hormone that Dominates and Divides Us* (Cassell, 2021).

Hrdy, Sarah Blaffer, *The Woman That Never Evolved* (Harvard, 1999).

Hrdy, Sarah Blaffer, *Mother Nature: Maternal Instincts and the Shaping of the Species* (Vintage, 2000 [1999], originally published with the subtitle *Natural Selection and the Female of the Species*]).

Hubback, Judith, *Wives Who Went to College* (Heinemann, 1957).

Hughes-Johnson, Alexandra and Jenkins, Lyndsey, *The Politics of Women's Suffrage: Local, National and International Dimensions* (University of London Press, 2021).

Iglesias, Marta, 'Why Feminists Must Understand Evolution', *Quillette*, 29 October 2017.

Jackson, Stevi, *Christine Delphy* (Sage, 1996).

Jacques, Juliet, *Trans: A Memoir* (Verso, 2015).

Jayawardena, Kumari, *Feminism and Nationalism in the Third World* (Verso, 2016 [1986]).

John, Angela V., *Turning the Tide: The Life of Lady Rhondda* (Parthian, 2013).

Jolly, Margaretta, *Sisterhood and After* (Oxford University Press, 2021 [2019]).

Jones, Jane Clare, with Lisa Mackenzie, *The Political Erasure of Sex: Sex and the Census* (Woman's Place UK/ University of Oxford, 2020).

Jones, Jane Clare, *The Annals of the Terf Wars and Other Writing* (The Radical Notion, 2022).

Jordan, Jane, *Josephine Butler* (John Murray, 2001).

Joyce, Helen, *Trans: When Ideology Meets Reality* (Oneworld, 2021).

Judge, Tony, *Margaret Bondfield: First Woman in the Cabinet* (Alpha House, 2018).

Kiss, Charlie, *A New Man: Lesbian, Protest, Mania, Trans Man* (Matador, 2017).

Kynaston, David, *Austerity Britain 1945–51* (Bloomsbury, 2007).

Kynaston, David, *Family Britain 1951–57* (Bloomsbury, 2009).

Kynaston, David, *Modernity Britain 1957–62* (Bloomsbury, 2014).

Langhamer, Claire, 'Feelings, Women and Work in the Long 1950s', *Women's History Review* 26(1) (2017): 77–92.

Lawford-Smith, Holly, *Gender-Critical Feminism* (Oxford University Press, 2022).

Leneman, Leah, *The Scottish Suffragettes* (NMS Publishing, 2000).

Lessing, Doris, *Walking in the Shade: Volume Two of My Autobiography, 1949–62* (Fourth Estate, 1998).

Levine, Philippa, *Victorian Feminism, 1850–1900* (University Press of Florida, 1994).

Levy, Ariel, *Female Chauvinist Pigs: Women and the Rise of Raunch Culture* (Pocket Books, 2006).

Lewis, Gail, *Race, Gender, Social Welfare: Encounters in a Postcolonial Society* (Polity, 2000).

Lewis, Helen, *Difficult Women: A History of Feminism in Eleven Fights* (Jonathan Cape, 2020).

Liddington, Jill, *The Long Road to Greenham* (Virago, 1989).

Liddington, Jill and Norris, Jill, *One Hand Tied Behind Us: The Rise of the Women's Suffrage Movement* (Rivers Oram Press, 2000 [1978]).

Littler, Jo, *Left Feminisms: Conversations on the Personal and Political* (Lawrence and Wishart, 2023).

Lorde, Audrey, *Sister Outsider* (Penguin, 2007 [1984]).

Mackay, Finn, *Radical Feminism: Feminist Activism in Movement* (Palgrave Macmillan, 2015).

Maitland, Sara (ed.), *Very Heaven: Looking Back at the 1960s* (Virago, 1988).

McCarthy, Helen, 'Social Science and Married Women's Employment in Post-War Britain', in *Past and Present* 233(1): 269–305 (2016).

Midgley, Clare, *Women Against Slavery: The British Campaigns 1780–1870* (Routledge, 1992).

Midgley, Clare, *Feminism and Empire: Women Activists in Imperial Britain, 1790–1865* (Routledge, 2007).

Mill, Harriet Taylor, 'The Enfranchisement of Women' (1851), https://utilitarianism.net/books/enfranchisement-of-women-harriet-taylor-mill/

Miller, Milo (ed.), *Speak Out! The Brixton Black Women's Group* (Verso, 2023).

Mirza, Heidi Safia, *Black British Feminism: A Reader* (Routledge, 1997).

Mitchell, David, *Queen Christabel: Biography of Christabel Pankhurst* (Macdonald and Jane's, 1977).

Mitchell, Juliet, *The Longest Revolution: Essays in Feminism, Literature and Psychoanalysis* (Virago, 1984).

Morgan, Susan, 'A Passion for Purity: Ellice Hopkins and the Politics of Gender in the Late-Victorian Church', PhD thesis (University of Bristol, 1997).

Myrdal, Alva and Klein, Viola, *Women's Two Roles: Home and Work* (Routledge and Kegan Paul, 1970 [1956]).

Nadel, Jennifer, *Sara Thornton: The Story of a Woman Who Killed* (Gollancz, 1993).

Nicholson, Virginia, *Perfect Wives in Ideal Homes* (Viking, 2015).

Oakley, Ann, *Sex, Gender and Society* (Temple Smith, 1972).

Pedersen, Sarah, *The Politicization of Mumsnet* (Emerald Publishing, 2020).

Pedersen, Susan, *Eleanor Rathbone and the Politics of Conscience* (Yale University Press, 2004).

Perkins, Anne, *Red Queen: The Authorised Biography of Barbara Castle* (Macmillan, 2003).

Perry, Louise, *The Case Against the Sexual Revolution: A New Guide to Sex in the Twenty-first Century* (Polity Press, 2022).

Perry, Matt, *'Red Ellen' Wilkinson: Her Ideas, Movements and World* (Manchester University Press, 2014).

Phoenix, Ann, *Young Mothers?* (Polity Press, 1990).

Phoenix, Ann and Tizard, Barbara, *Black, White or Mixed Race?* (Routledge, 2001).

Purvis, June, *Emmeline Pankhurst: A Biography* (Routledge, 2002).

Purvis, June and Stanley Holton, Sandra (eds), *Votes for Women* (Routledge, 2000).

Ramusack, Barbara, 'Cultural Missionaries, Maternal Imperialists, Feminist Allies: British Women Activists in India, 1865–1945', *Women's Studies International Forum* 13(4): 309–21 (1990).

Rathbone, Eleanor, *The Disinherited Family* (Falling Wall Press, 1986 [1924]).

Raw, Louise, *Striking a Light: The Bryant and May Matchwomen and their Place in History* (Continuum, 2011).

Reeves, Rachel, *Women of Westminster: The MPs Who Changed Politics* (Bloomsbury, 2019).

Reid, Marion, *A Plea for Woman: Being a Vindication of the Importance and Extent of Her Natural Sphere of Action* (Cambridge University Press, 2018 [1843]).

Rendall, Jane, *Equal or Different: Women's Politics, 1800–1914* (Blackwell, 1987).

Riley, Denise, *War in the Nursery: Theories of the Child and Mother* (Virago, 1983).

Riley, Denise, *'Am I That Name?': Feminism and the Category of 'Women' in History* (Palgrave Macmillan, 1988).

Robinson, Jane, *Hearts and Minds: The Untold Story of the Great Pilgrimage and How Women Won the Vote* (Doubleday, 2018).

Rogaly, Joe, *Grunwick* (Penguin, 1977).

Rogers, Anna E., 'Feminist Consciousness-raising in the 1970s and 1980s: West Yorkshire Women's Groups and their Impact on Women's Lives', PhD thesis, University of Leeds (2010).

Rowbotham, Sheila, *Daring to Hope: My Life in the 1970s* (Verso, 2021).

Rowbotham, Sheila, Segal, Lynne and Wainwright, Hilary, *Beyond the Fragments: Feminism and the Making of Socialism* (Merlin Press, 1979).

Rubenhold, Hallie, *The Five: The Untold Lives of the Women Killed by Jack the Ripper* (Doubleday, 2019).

Saini, Angela, *Inferior: How Science Got Women Wrong and the New Research That's Rewriting the Story* (Beacon Press, 2017).

Scott, Joan, 'Gender: A Useful Category of Historical Analysis', *American Historical Review* 91(5) (1986): 1053–75.

Setch, Eve, 'The Women's Liberation Movement in Britain, 1969–79: Organisation, Creativity and Debate', PhD thesis, Royal Holloway, University of London (2001).

Shaw, Marion, *The Clear Stream: A Life of Winifred Holtby* (Virago, 1999).

Sherwood, Marika, *Claudia Jones: A Life in Exile* (Lawrence & Wishart, 1999).

Sinha, Mrinalini, 'Suffragism and Internationalism: The Enfranchisement of British and Indian Women under an Imperial State', in Ian Christopher Fletcher, Laura E. Nym Mayhall and Philippa Levine (eds), *Women's Suffrage in the British Empire: Citizenship, Nation and Race* (Routledge, 2012).

Sloman, Peter, 'Beveridge's Rival: Juliet Rhys-Williams and the Campaign for Basic Income 1942–55', *Contemporary British History* 30(2) (2016).

Smith, Joan, *Misogynies* (Westbourne Press, 2013 [1989]).

Smith, Harold L. 'The Womanpower Problem in Britain during the Second World War', *Historical Journal* 27(4) (1984): 925–45.

Smith, Harold L. 'Sex vs. Class: British Feminists and the Labour Movement, 1919–1929', *Historian* 47(1) (1984): 19–37.

Smith, Harold L. (ed.), *British Feminism in the Twentieth Century* (Edward Elgar, 1990).

Smith, Karen Ingala, *Defending Women's Spaces* (Polity Press, 2022).

Smith, Victoria, *Hags: The Demonisation of Middle-Aged women* (Fleet, 2023).

Snyder-Hall, R. Claire, 'Third-wave Feminism and the Defence of Choice', *Perspectives on Politics* 8(1) (2010): 255–61.

Srinivasan, Amia, *The Right to Sex* (Bloomsbury, 2021).

Stock, Kathleen, *Material Girls: Why Reality Matters for Feminism* (Fleet, 2021).

Stocks, Mary, *Eleanor Rathbone* (Gollancz, 1949).

Strachey, Ray, *The Cause: A Short History of the Women's Movement in Great Britain* (G. Bell & Sons, 1928).

Strachey, Ray (ed.), *Our Freedom and Its Results* (Hogarth Press, 1936).

Sullivan, Alice and Todd, Selina (eds), *Sex and Gender: A Contemporary Reader* (Routledge, 2023).

Summerskill, Edith, *Letters to my Daughter* (Heinemann, 1957).

Summerskill, Edith, *A Woman's World: Memoirs* (Heinemann, 1967).

Takayanagi, Mari, 'Parliament and Women, c. 1900–1945', PhD thesis, King's College London (2012).

Takayanagi, Mari, Unwin, Melanie and Seaward, Paul, *Voice and Vote: Celebrating 100 Years of Votes for Women* (Regal Press, 2018).

Taylor, Barbara, *Mary Wollstonecraft and the Feminist Imagination* (Cambridge, 2003).

Taylor, Barbara, *Eve and the New Jerusalem: Socialism and Feminism in the Nineteenth Century* (Virago, 2016 [1983]).

Theakston, Kevin, 'Evelyn Sharp 1903–85', *Contemporary Record* (now known as *Contemporary British History*) 7(1) (1993): 132–48.

Thomlinson, Natalie, *Race, Ethnicity and the Women's Movement in England, 1968–1993* (Palgrave Macmillan, 2016).

Thompson, William with Anna Wheeler, *Appeal of One Half the Human Race, Women, Against the Pretensions of the Other Half, Men, To Retain Them in Political, and Thence in Civil and Domestic, Slavery*, intro. Richard Pankhurst (Virago, 1983 [1825]).

Timmins, Nicholas, *The Five Giants: A Biography of the Welfare State* (William Collins, 2017 [1995]).

Tomalin, Claire, *The Life and Death of Mary Wollstonecraft* (Penguin, 1992 [1974]).

Uglow, Jenny, *George Eliot* (Virago, 1987).

Vandermassen, Griet, *Who's Afraid of Charles Darwin? Debating Feminism and Evolutionary Theory* (Rowman and Littlefield, 2005).

Walby, Sylvia, *The Future of Feminism* (Polity Press, 2011).

Walker, Sophie, *Five Rules for Rebellion* (London: Icon Books, 2020).

Walkowitz, Judith R., *Prostitution and Victorian Society: Women, class, and the state* (Cambridge University Press, 1980).

Walkowitz, Judith R., *City of Dreadful Delight: Narratives of Sexual Danger in Late-Victorian London* (Virago, 1992).

Walter, Natasha, *Living Dolls: The Return of Sexism* (Virago, 2010).

Wandor, Michelene, *Once a Feminist: Stories of a Generation* (Virago, 1990).

Whelehan, Imelda, *Overloaded: Popular Culture and the Future of Feminism* (Women's Press, 2000).

Wilson, Amrit, *Finding a Voice: Asian Women in Britain* (Daraja Press, 2018 [1978]).

Wilson, Elizabeth, *Only Halfway to Paradise: Women in Postwar Britain, 1945–1968* (Tavistock Publications, 1980).

Wolf, Naomi, *The Beauty Myth* (Chatto & Windus, 1990).

Wollstonecraft, Mary, *A Vindication of the Rights of Woman* (Penguin, 1992 [1792]).

Wollstonecraft, Mary and Godwin, William, *A Short Residence in Sweden and Memoirs of the Author of 'The Rights of Woman'* (Penguin, 1987 [1796, 1798]).

Wollstonecraft, Mary and Godwin, William, *Mary and Maria, and Matilda* by Mary Shelley (Penguin, 2004 [1991]).

Woolf, Virginia, *The Diary of Virginia Woolf: Volume I, 1915–19*, ed. Anne Olivier Bell (Hogarth Press, 1983 [1977]).

Woolf, Virginia, *Three Guineas* (Hogarth Press, 1991 [1938]).

Woolf, Virginia, *A Room of One's Own* (Penguin, 2004 [1928]).

Zakaria, Rafia, *Against White Feminism* (Hamish Hamilton, 2021).

Index